After theory

POSTMODERN THEORY

Series editor:

THOMAS DOCHERTY

School of English, University of Kent at Canterbury

This series openly and vigorously confronts the central questions and issues in postmodern culture, and proposes a series of refigurations of the modern in all its forms: aesthetic and political, cultural and social, material and popular. Books in the series are all major contributions to the re-writing of the intellectual and material histories of socio-cultural life from the sixteenth century to the present day. They articulate or facilitate the exploration of those new 'post-theoretical' positions, developed both inside and outside the anglophone world – inside and outside 'western' theory – which are pertinent to a contemporary world order.

Other titles in the series include:

Justice Miscarried: Ethics, Aesthetics and the Law
Costas Douzinas and Ronnie Warrington

Postmodern Wetlands: Culture, History, Ecology
Rodney James Giblett

Towards a Postmodern Theory of Narrative
Andrew Gibson

Jarring Witnesses: Modern Fiction and the Representation of History
Robert Holton

POSTMODERN THEORY

After theory

Thomas Docherty

Edinburgh University Press

For Bridie May Sullivan

© Thomas Docherty, 1996

Transferred to Digital Print 2009

Edinburgh University Press
22 George Square, Edinburgh

Typeset in $9\frac{1}{2}$/12 point Melior by
Photoprint, Torquay, Devon and
printed and bound in Great Britain by
CPI Antony Rowe, Chippenham and Eastbourne

A CIP record for this book is available
from the British Library

ISBN 0 7486 0840 0

Contents

List of Illustrations

Introduction

After theory is not 'in the wake of theory': this book purports to write that wake in the first place. Its arguments can be situated within the problematic of the postmodern debate and in terms of a *differend* or dispute with Marxism. It is an attempt to work not within the tradition of critique, nor 'within' the more traditional dissent, nor even 'within' the more radical theoretical criticisms which have been articulated in recent times. Rather, it aims to work at the limits of critique and to accept the implications of an impossibility of consensus. The point is to leave a certain 'modernist' project of theory in its wake. Yet it will not stop in this negative critique. This study delineates and explicates a more positively radical position for the intellectual working within the institution of cultural practices in the academy. While writing the book, my abiding concern was the apparent inefficacy of the theoretical intellectual in terms of social and political practice. The successful institutionalisation of theory, of Modernism and Marxism has stymied the radical pretensions of their movements and philosophies. What is worse, theory and Marxism have become, doubtless despite themselves, complicit with the institutional imposition of limits upon their revolutionary credentials. Here, I am proposing that postmodernism and postmarxism are called on to 'wake' theory and Marxism to a proper vigilance against their own inherent tendency to conservatism.

There have been various moments of 'modernism' in history, including a medieval theology which questions magic, a European Renaissance which promotes individualism, an Enlightenment philosophy of the triumph of reason, and an artistically self-conscious experimentation at the turn of the twentieth century. Not every moment is 'modern' as it arises: to be 'modern' implies a particular self-consciousness and a consciousness of one's difference from the immediate historical locale along with an alignment elsewhere or with another time than the present, be it a revitalised ancient world or a hypothetical 'futurist' world. The instant of modernism which is of most interest here is that which overlaps between the eighteenth and twentieth centuries. This is the Habermasian 'project of modernity', called into question either explicitly or implicitly by Lyotard, Baudrillard, Vattimo and others.

Habermas advances a succinct description of what is at stake in the project of modernity:

The project of modernity formulated in the 18th century by the philosophers of the Enlightenment consisted in their efforts to develop objective science, universal morality and law, and autonomous art according to their inner logic. At the same time, this project intended to release the cognitive potentials of each of these domains from their esoteric forms. The Enlightenment philosophers wanted to utilize this accumulation of specialized culture for the enrichment of everyday life — that is to say, for the rational organization of everyday social life.[1]

The project of enlightened modernity, as thus described, leads inexorably to the validation of Theory as it came to be practised in the twentieth century. In the earlier half of that century, there is a drive towards the possibility of what has been termed 'Grand Theory', that is to say, towards a rational and abstract theorisation of social and cultural practices under the rubric of a generalised semiotics. This comes to one seeming culmination in the failure of structuralism. The impetus towards totalisation which was inscribed in structuralism was exploded by the unsettling manoeuvres of some poststructuralist thinkers, and was most obviously displaced by deconstruction. Structuralism's desire to rest critical analysis on the sure foundation of a scientific linguistics was frustrated by deconstruction's constant displacing of that ground, and the concomitant drive towards sceptical undecideability.

For thinkers such as Habermas, however, this is not at all the logical terminus of the 'incomplete' project of modernity. Rather than leading to deconstruction, Habermas sees the project of modernity leading to the validation of Marxism, in a specifically linguistic and then communicative turn, as a guarantor of a reasonable or rational epistemological ground (in some cases, the very ground which deconstruction shows to be always already displaced) for a social formation. In this, enlightenment rationality goes hand in hand with universal history and with the drive towards emancipation from despotism and towards the democratic rights of historical self-determination: its fundamental purpose is the establishment of autonomy for the subject.

When Habermas attacks those he calls the 'young', 'old' and 'neo-'conservatives, he misses an important point; for they do not question the enlightenment *tout court*, and would indeed share some of the marxisant desire for a generalised emancipation from despotism. It is the case, however, that they will complicate the issues of rationality, emancipation and history which Derridean deconstruction disrupts and which enable Habermasian Marxism. At this point, it is important to bear in mind the relation of the intellectual to the social formation, a relation which is the practical realisation of the relation between knowledge and power. In modernity, the position of the intellectual was relatively uncontentious. Intellectuals were 'a motley collection of novelists, poets, artists, journalists, scientists and other public figures who felt it their moral responsibility, and their collective right, to interfere directly with the political process through influencing the minds of the nation and moulding the actions of its political leaders'.[2] Such a group of people would have, as it were, a point to their intellection; they had some purpose, direction or programme in the service of which their intellectual activity operated. In its crudest formulation, this programme concerned enlightenment under the rubric of education and knowledge-formation, which would lead in turn to the emancipation of human subjects through the development of the possibility of a willed direction to their own independent history and to that of the social formation in and through which they had their existence. Knowledge thus became the basis for the exercise of a democratically willed rationality, which transformed itself in practice into the elaboration of the emancipation of the subject from despotism. In this, the intellectuals figure as an avantgarde in the project of enlightened modernity.

That position for the intellectual, as avant-garde legislator, has become less easily maintained, and less easily justified. As Vattimo indicates, the postmodern attitude questions the firmness of the will and of the self which the enlightenment project of modernity, thus understood, assumes. He prefers, for political as well as ethical reasons, a form of *il pensiero debole*, a weak thinking, a feebleness of self which counters the rigours of a particular kind or mode of rationality, This is more fully explained by Lyotard:

When the German philosophers today, or the Americans, speak of the neo-irrationalism of French thought, when Habermas gives lessons in progressivism to Derrida and to Foucault in the name of the project of modernity, they are making a serious mistake about what is at issue in modernity. It was not, and it is not (for modernity is not finished), simply the Enlightenment, what was and is at issue is the introduction of the will into reason.[3]

It is for this reason, among others, that Lyotard, insofar as he is postmodernist, refuses the function of the traditional intellectual. Bauman argues that the postmodern situation demands a different kind of function for its intellectuals: no longer is the intellectual a legislator, acknowledged or not; she or he is now, in the postmodern condition, an interpreter. Lyotard would not yet concur with this. He condemns the intellectual to a tomb, writes its wake so to speak, and considers instead the place of the philosopher who, in postmodernism, is akin to the writer and artist. The passage cited above continues with a reference to Kant, who 'spoke of a thrust in reason to take it beyond experience', and he understood philosophy anthropologically as a *Drang*, as an impulse to fight, or to generate disputes (*Streiten*). Insofar as there is some truth in Bauman's description of the situation of the intellectual, it would be accurate to suggest that there arises in postmodernism a *differend* between the intellectual and legitimation as such, including its most direct form of legislation. In short, the 'intellectual' has gone 'critical'. Governments are well apprised of this situation, which explains in some measure the current mistrust of the intellectual, and her or his simplistic politicisation. Lyotard's paper, 'Le tombeau de l'intellectuel', was itself written in response to a Government request for support, and it is support, rather than criticism or avant-garde legislation, which governments require from intellectuals today. In contradistinction to this, Lyotard prefers the position of the artist or philosopher, who has no special political responsibilities, and whose only responsibility is to questions such as 'What is painting?', 'What is music?' or 'What is thought?'.[4] To respond to them demands, as I shall argue below, a postmodern rather than a modern disposition. To be a philosophical thinker at all in these terms demands a rejection of the modernist impetus towards theory; to be a radical philosopher, a thinker, demands the rejection of the modernist critique inscribed in Marxism. This situation demands some fuller explication.

Althusser rearticulates a Gramscian distinction between political and civil society in terms of the Repressive State Apparatus — RSA — which functions primarily by force and violence — and the Ideological State Apparatuses — ISAs — which function in the first instance by ideology. The ISAs are, for the most part, institutions (such as family, religion, education, etc.) which are experienced as private in the first instance, and political only through the unveiling of their ideological formation. I'll suggest here that this distinction might be re-thought in terms of an opposition between the political and the social. According to Althusser, the dominant class can lay down the law at the level of the RSA (the political) more immediately than at the level of the ISA (or social). Hence, the ISAs become a prime site for the advancing of the class struggle. Here is the nexus of the question: how efficacious is theory, which exists primarily in the educational ISA (the dominant ISA of the capitalist moment, according to Althusser)? The response to this rests on the rejection of the category of the free willed agency of the subject, the very subject so necessary to enlightenment modernity. In existentialist thinking, being is doing: the subject is located in her or his actions. But for Althusser, actions and subjects can only be constituted as such through *practices*, those into which actions are inserted and according to which subjects delineate themselves as such. These practices are themselves governed according to the problematic of their determinant category as an ISA. Hence 'there is no practice except by and in an ideology';[5] but hence also 'philosophy is, in the last instance, class struggle in the field of theory'.[6]

It is at this moment that Althusser has effectively re-inserted theory, strictly appropriate to the ISA, into the RSA: he has collapsed the social into the political in such a way that the social in the social, the sociality of the social, has been erased. I am not arguing here that this is entirely wrong, but simply that it is premature, and that it leads to a banal politicisation of theory, and an effective erasure of the question of the place of philosophy in postmodernity. While acknowledging that the social is thoroughly imbricated in the political, it remains important also to acknowledge that the Althusserian near-identification of the two leads to a simplification of philosophical and political issues. Feminism would be only one of the political positions which, in one form, returns to a concern with a complicated empiricism at the social level. But the most fundamental danger in this collapsing of the social into the political is the loss of radical credentials suffered by any Marxist theory, since Althusser. For when inserted into the RSA, the radicalism of Marxism is assigned a proper place, one of 'opposition' or 'critique'. Politics, the RSA, requires that philosophers become 'mere' intellectuals; and, further, that intellectuals support them by functioning in complicity with the demands of the primacy of the political. More complex issues of the other, often heterogeneous, functions of the intellectual are elided, erased under the rubric of the political: this is, in fact, what the dominant political ideology requires, for class-struggle in the ISAs has now become impossible since the ISA's specificity is lost in its crude homogenisation with the RSA. Philosophers must refuse this modernist categorisation of the intellectual, if they wish to avoid complicity with the functioning by violence and force ('discipline' and 'punishment' in Foucauldian terms) by which the RSA operates. The philosopher who wishes to avoid this complicity is responsible first and foremost to the question, 'What is thought?' But this responsibility is already a social, though not yet a political, responsibility. This is not a denial of the political implications of philosophy; rather, it is an attempt to complicate that issue through the saving of the social.

It is insofar as they remain in theory, and in the remains of Grand Theory or Enlightenment projects of modernity that deconstruction and Marxism become potentially complicit with this banalisation of thinking and its reduction to the 'merely' political. Ryan has outlined a critical articulation of Marxism and deconstruction together, but at an early stage in his study he has already inadvertently revealed the root of their material inefficacy, the root of their inability to materialise themselves from their position as theory. Both share what I can call the 'nostalgia of the backward glance'. In his introductory consideration of language and politics in Hobbes, where a fear of sedition is thought in terms of a fear of metaphor, Ryan demonstrates succinctly that:

The final point of a deconstructive analysis would be to say that sovereignty is itself merely a form of displacement, that it cannot define itself other than as the displacement of the ever-open possibility of displacement. Absolute meaning is the displacement of metaphor, is, in other words, the metaphor of metaphor. As the displacement of displacement, absolutely proper meaning becomes a name for metaphor . . . Absolute political sovereignty, in turn, is the displacement of sedition, is, in other words, the sedition of sedition.[7]

The fact that this may be revealing, even correct, is also the fact that disables the radical potential of both deconstruction and Marxism. For Ryan shares with Jameson the distrust of a Whiggish version of historical periodisation. Jameson offers a perfect example of the radical mistrust of this simple historicism when he considers the notion of 'the demise of individualism', which can be considered in two ways. The first of these accepts a bland historical progression in which the individual as bourgeois subject, once dominant, no longer exists. But the more radical position adds to this: 'not only is the bourgeois individual subject a thing of the past, it is also a myth; it *never* really existed in the first place'.[8] In other words, the poststructuralist, especially the deconstructor, is concerned not so much to displace the ground on which the theorist is presently standing, but rather to demonstrate through the backward glance that such a ground is impossible because the past is not where it was. In Ryan's case, it is not that deconstruction has displaced a normative language of absolute meaning; rather, the norm was always already displacement. All that deconstruction adds to this is an epistemological factor:

now we know that the ground was not where we thought it was. In short, deconstruction is exactly akin to an enlightenment demystification. Marxism shares the tendency to demystify, specifically with respect to ideology, in exactly the same way as deconstruction here. This, in fact, is why a critical articulation of them together is possible; but is also why they have no radical credentials left. They are merely epistemological. More than this, they indulge in what can be thought of as a violent epistemology, an epistemology which functions not so much at the level of the 'terroristic reason' which Habermas thinks is at issue but at one which figures in the political terms of the RSA, eliding the social — and with it historical specificity — in the name of a totalising political theory as such.[9]

The postmarxists then, among whom I number myself in this study, accept the formation of postmodernity in which the specificity of the historical political is retained, precisely through its ability to determine its heterogeneity from other aspects of social historical life. It is the evasion of homogeneity which marks the postmarxist and postmodernist off from the marxist and modernist. But here a question of history must properly be addressed.

POSTMODERNITY AND HISTORY

Clearly, this study does not take any simple periodising view of postmodernism. Lyotard argues for a much more complex notion of the term, involving the elaboration of a position in which the postmodern becomes the founding condition of the possibility of the modern, that the 'post-' might be understood in terms of an analogy with the 'ana-' of anamnesis, anagogy, anamorphosis, etc.[10] At one level, of course, this overlaps with Jameson's desire for the 'more radical' re-reading of history described above, a re-reading which loses its radical credentials precisely because of its inherent limitations as the nostalgia of the backward glance. But Lyotard goes further than this, with ramifications for our understanding of postmodernism as a condition rather than as a period or moment.

A primary set of discriminations can be made between history, historiography, and historicity. History I take here as the interiority of past events or of the referent of historiography as such (i.e., 'what happens'). Historiography is the transcription of those events into some kind of narrative, with the concomitant loss of the referent as such (i.e., how we think 'what happens'), a loss explicitly acknowledged by Foucault and integral to American 'New Historicisms' as practised by Greenblatt and others.[11] Historicity is more difficult to describe in any simple formulation, but it involves the interior temporality of any historical referent or element of being, as in Bergson and Heidegger (i.e., an 'it happens' in which the 'it' is not yet determined).

To elaborate this, I can make a further distinction between what I'll call 'punctuality' and 'eventuality'. These two terms relate to questions of time and history, and are at one level a simple re-working of the neo-Aristotelian distinction between 'being' and 'becoming', or of the existentialist distinction of 'essence' from 'existence'. But I aim to make more than the conventional Heideggerian points about historicity from this. The 'punctual' is not only 'to the point', but is also 'on time' or 'timely'; the 'eventual' is, on the contrary, 'untimely', somehow out of its proper instant or moment. But the eventual also therefore refuses to be assigned a simple straightforward or chronological allotment; it enters the realm not of history, nor of historiography, but of historicity. Historicity, thus, involves a seeming contrary of proper history, for it depends not upon a notion of chronological accuracy of placement, but rather upon *anachronism*. Such anachronism is not at the level of the historiographical narrative, but is rather more fundamenally an anachronism interior to the referent of any such historiography. This is the historicity which has made such a difference to French philosophy as practised not only by an expressed postmodernist such as Lyotard but also to thinkers such as Deleuze and Virilio, among others.[12]

In these terms, the eventual eventuates in the punctual ('it happens' becomes 'what happens'). That is to say, historicity takes root, or 'forms an earth', as Baudrillard would have it[13] in the punctualities or timeliness of that which we call history. The historical referent, thus, can be thought of as the punctual, but now a punctual which 'contains' the energetic historicity of the eventual, collapsing its interior duration or difference into a single constitutive instantiation or instant. In aesthetic terms, this 'punctual' is nothing other than the 'work' of art, the reified or

represented object as such which is available for all the epistemological or theoretical work which criticism performs upon it, or
for the production, reproduction and consumption which an
ideology or politics perform upon it.

Jameson's prefatory slogan in *The Political Unconscious*,
'Always historicize!'[14] can be countered with another, more postmodern slogan: 'Be unprepared!'. Marxist historicisation is inextricably caught up in the modernist impetus towards a punctual
demystification: it reveals the 'point', the ideological purposes
inscribed in a work of art, and ascribes the work its proper or
punctual moment in a historiography. Postmodernism and postmarxism counter this with the release of historicity in the form of
an untimeliness or unpreparedness. It is in this sense, of course,
that these positions can be understood as avantgarde: they are
untimely, anachronistic.

Eventuality and unpreparedness as I describe them here can be
easily transposed into a particular set of occurrences on the
interface of aesthetics and politics, broadly known as *les événe-
ments '68*. This is not entirely accidental. What we must call, after
Ferry and Renault, *La pensée '68*, is marked by a dissatisfaction
with punctuality and an increased legitimation of the eventual,
the 'happening'. But the thought which led up to 1968 is not the
same as thinking after 1968. The failure of the students and
intellectuals in leading a political revolution in that year led to a
different manner of locating the 'intellectual' in the social formation, sometimes as Kristevan 'dissident', sometimes as Saidian
'opponent', sometimes, as in Lyotard, as a corpse to be con-
signed to the tomb.[15] In any case, something more new than the
European New Left would be required to effect any serious
change.

It is broadly in the wake of the failures of 1968 that the idea of
abandoning the 'project of Modernity' gains significant ground.
Here, my opposition between the timely punctual and the
untimely eventual assumes greater importance. Habermas indicates that 'Aesthetic modernity is characterized by attitudes
which find a common focus in a changed consciousness of time.
This time consciousness expresses itself through metaphors of the
vanguard and the avant-garde'.[16] His argument against the 'neo-
conservatives' follows from this, but fails to address squarely the

issue of postmodernism. Although he indicates correctly that there have been a number of moments of self-conscious 'modernity', in which intellectuals have established more or less troubled relations with antiquity, the twentieth century is the first moment in which intellectuals have considered themselves to be not merely modern but postmodern, to be in a postmodernist avantgarde rather than merely at the exploratory forefront of serial developments. But the term 'avantgarde' suggests precisely the untimeliness of the contemporary postmodern. She or he is not in the right moment, not in their correct time; they are 'unprepared' for the work which they do, and hence that work is always out of historical step with them. Accordingly, it is typically never realised in essential concrete form. In aesthetic terms, the 'happening' or the historically oriented conceptual art-form is thus the extreme caricature of the postmodern. A more genuine 'happening' transgresses the category of the merely political and becomes something like the events of May 1968, in which there was no real central control. Had the imagination achieved power, had Cohn-Bendit, Krivine, Sauvageot — and, indeed, Lyotard — assumed some kind of directed control, the events would have become merely modern. When de Gaulle in France reassumed precisely such programmatic control, the events were drained of their postmodern energy, and did, in fact, become merely a moment conceptualisable now in terms of a modern pastiche of Dada or of anarchy. Modernity in this instance is the collapsing of eventuality into punctuality, a 'point' which may be realised in terms of a cross on a ballot-paper, or in terms of the crushing of the energy of the Prague Spring, an energy which is in some measure re-released by the contemporary photographs of Koudelka.[17]

The project of modernity is based upon this timely correspondence: action provoking appropriate reaction at the appropriate moment for the construction of a situational nexus in which power is formulated or articulated in terms of oppression or control. In aesthetic terms, the project of modernity leads to the realisation of an essential object (the work of art) which is in timely correspondence with its social formation (and can thus be analysed as historical product). The project of modernity is thus tied to the project of phenomenology: in both, a spatial configuration is produced which enables not only an epistemological proposition concerning the form, structure, status and power inscribed in a subject/object relation, but which also enables the characterisation of a point of perception, of a homogeneous historical moment. It is precisely such a metaphysics of presence which Derrida attempts to deconstruct, of course. But such a deconstruction — and this is the crucial factor here — is a displacement of presence, its deferral, albeit one which necessitates the re-inscription of the constituents of the metaphysics of presence, and not a deferral which opens both subject and object to the kind of eventual historicity which is at issue in postmodernity. As opposed to this, we might explore the modes of thinking advanced by Baudrillard, in his questioning of the very notion of the real as such. When he attacks thinking which makes claims upon reality, he is being, in my terms here, a postmodern philosopher who refuses to collapse eventuality into punctuality, into a point which claims to be grounded in a reality principle. That principle depends upon punctuality, upon the timely correspondence between subject and object available to phenomenology; postmodernism, as in the thinking of Lyotard, Baudrillard, Virilio, Deleuze and others is more interested in the maintenance of eventuality, of the untimely or anachronistic introduced into the power relations produced through phenomenology and its deconstruction.

This move in philosophy counters the theoretical tendency to homogenise historiography; it evades the homogenisation of the past in terms of a single trope of power or oppression. In this respect, it complicates history by refusing the too simplistic or banal collapsing of the social into the political. This enables the movement beyond all forms of merely 'oppositional' critique, in both social and political terms. After 1968, it is clear that critique or opposition is not enough, though it might remain important. As Baudrillard has indicated, opposition is already inscribed into the authoritarian structure of totalitarian practices: capitalism needs Marxism for its successful innoculation against serious dysfunction. By and large, Marxism has obliged in its series of 'timely' interventions against the dominant ideology, serving inadvertently to strengthen rather than weaken it (at least if empirical evidence is anything to go by).[18]

Coincidentally, during the late 1960s, there was a tendency in French philosophy to shift from an obsession with questions stemming from Hegel and the dialectic towards a re-prioritisation of Kantian 'auto-critique', in a re-thinking and revaluation of Kant's *Critique of Judgement*.[19] It is here that Lyotard finds the possibility of saving the honour of thinking, as he often phrases it. An analogy between the aesthetic and the political judgement here becomes available in terms of the prioritisation of 'reflective' over 'determining' judgement. In brief, determining judgement works within the bounds of theory; reflective judgement eschews theory in favour of a necessary judging without criteria, theoretical or otherwise. This enables the evasion of the homogenisation of the historical into the punctual, and produces instead a heterogeneity of the historical which aims to release the historicity of both the past and the present referent: that is, to release the historicity between, in crude terms, the work of art or political phenomenon being considered, and the thinker or subject doing the considering. But since this thinking or judging has no criteria, and since it is always 'anachronistic', it becomes difficult or complex to understand: in fact, it is broadly unamenable to epistemology as such. Lyotard's postmodern 'sublime' is thus thinking at the very limits of thought; hence its difficulty. It is a major contention of the present book that this sublime is only attained by the releasing of the historicity of thinking, by what might be called an unpunctual working which will eventuate not in a thought but in thinking. At that point, it might be possible to rehabilitate the intellectual, this time as philosopher, writer or artist.

After Theory

The concerns of this book are fairly eclectic. After an initial characterisation of postmodernism in aesthetic terms, I discuss the relation between violence and knowledge in terms of hermeneutic, arguing that a postmodern hermeneutic eschews a particular violence which is inherent in enlightenment notions of knowledge-formation. Subsequent chapters explore what could, in broad terms, be thought of as the shift from spatial to historical representation. In this section of the study, the aim is to introduce historicity into our thinking on representation, via considerations of photography, deconstruction and theory, and more specifically exemplary representations of the Self and of America in twentieth-century American poetry. This opens up two related issues. In the first place, with the introduction of historicity into the question of representation, the whole question of sound, noise or 'interference' in twentieth-century culture becomes important. Noise enables a social occupation of space, and the political establishment of forces within a demarcated arena. Secondly, the corollary of this relates to the entire question of how intellectual, theoretical or cultural practices themselves demarcate space, such as national boundaries or identities. At this point, I examine the relation of poetry to the land and to questions of tradition, heritage and history in the specific exemplary case of twentieth-century Irish poetry. As a closing gesture, there is a brief sketch of the basic outlines of a postmarxist theory, the kind of theory which the text in fact has practised throughout. This closing chapter is a 'coming clean', and an attempt to outline some possible proposals for further consequential study in this area.

= I =

Getting Going

1

Postmodernism

Some time ago, the major intellectual controversy in the fields of anthropology, politics, psychoanalysis, literary criticism and related cultural areas of inquiry focussed on structuralism. Indeed, as Culler indicated in his descriptive poetics of structuralism, to lay claim to the title of 'structuralist' used to be tantamount to a kind of call to arms. With the failure of the structuralist project and the more recent supervention of various poststructuralisms in recent years, the focus of debate has clearly shifted, and the most pressing issue now for intellectuals — perhaps *male dictu* — is the question of postmodernism.

As was the case in the structuralist and poststructuralist controversies, however, many of those engaged in the debate have not bothered to acquaint themselves fully with the determining instances of what constitutes the object of their debates and arguments. In this introductory chapter, I will outline some of the more salient features of postmodernism in the arts and cultural practices. Some of the categories under which I shall discuss postmodern works, such as their tendency to attack totality, are already familiar, though they have rarely been systematically treated. As Hutcheon has pointed out in one of the most recent interventions in the debate, most argument around the topic has fallen into one of two camps. Either postmodernism is seen as a counter to — or in opposition to — modernism, or it is seen as its bizarre continuation. In both cases, a binary opposition is set up, which limits examination of postmodernism to tenets already established and known in modernism, and the specifics of postmodernism are lost.[1]

17

In the outline of some of the determining instances of the postmodern offered here, I strive to avoid the fall into binary thinking which, Hutcheon argues, limits and falsifies the description of the postmodern. I shall discuss some works under four basic and recurring figures. Firstly, *postmodernism does not produce*: the postmodern work of art does not actually exist, is not produced as product or object in the representationalist sense of this word, and prefers to organise itself around a trope of *seduction*.[2] Secondly, *postmodernism transgresses*: the postmodern work typically transgresses all sorts of institutional or conventional bounds or boundaries, and works against totality.[3] Thirdly, *postmodernism prioritises the aural*; it is an art which works against the specular, and even against theory or speculation in order to re-install the lost sense of hearing; it shapes itself around the model of the labyrinthine ear.[4] Fourthly, *postmodernism flees 'culture'*: it is concerned to discover or to construct metaphors to replace the guiding modernist and pre-modern metaphor of 'culture' itself.

These four heads, then, might be systematised as *seduction, transgression, aurality, flight*. It is important to note at the outset, however, that these are no more than shorthand descriptions of a series of practices which condition the postmodern, and which, properly speaking, should be extended to include certain aspects which will dominate the discussion which follows. These would encompass such recurring effects as:

— the deterritorialisation of the work of art, its tendency to counter all forms of 'rootedness', be they figured in terms of national cultural roots, traditions or heritages, personal, biographical or self-identifications;
— the immaterialisation of the work, a tendency to erase the age-old aesthetic opposition of appearance and reality, and its replacement with an aesthetics of disappearance;
— the explicit historicity of the work, its awareness of its temporal location and historical mutability;
— the heterogeneity or alterity of the work, its tendency to be constructed on a principle of self-difference rather than as a self-identical whole;
— the eclecticism which allows the work to draw widely upon an extensive range of signifying and cultural practices;
— the tendency to sublimity or ek-stasis in the work's attack on conventional representability;
— the work's plurality, aesthetic and political, and so on.

Ultimately, it is mistaken to conceive of postmodernism as a periodising concept, as Jameson tries to do. The postmodern is not synonymous with the contemporary. As Lyotard has indicated, postmodernism is, in fact, the founding condition of the possibility of modernism:

> What, then, is the postmodern? What place does it or does it not occupy in the vertiginous work of the questions hurled at the rules of image and narration? It is undoubtedly a part of the modern. All that has been received, if only yesterday (*modo, modo*, Petronius used to say), must be suspected. What space does Cézanne challenge? The Impressionists'. What object do Picasso and Braque attack? Cézanne's. What presupposition does Duchamp break with in 1912? That which says one must make a painting, be it cubist. And Buren questions that other presupposition which he believes had survived untouched by the work of Duchamp: the place of presentation of the work. In an amazing acceleration, the generations precipitate themselves. A work can become modern only if it is first postmodern. Post-modernism thus understood is not modernism at its end but in the nascent state, and this state is constant.[5]

Thinking postmodernism in this way has a dramatic effect. It negates the mistaken idea that postmodernism is just that puzzling batch of art which comes after 1945. Rather, it now becomes more important to consider those moments in cultural history which have *explicitly* thought themselves as 'modern'. In terms of western history at least, 'modernism in its nascent state' has not been constant; rather, only three such moments properly advance themselves for consideration. First, there is the moment of the Renaissance; secondly, that of the eighteenth-century Enlightenment; thirdly, that of the artistic experimentations of the early twentieth century. In all three cases, there is an explicit appeal in the tendency to modernity to a tradition of sorts: the Renaissance is a re-birth of some ancient values; the Enlightenment rediscovers and revalues some other classical models; and modernism, of course, was profoundly traditional, at least in Eliot's sense of that term.[6] Each of these moments of modernism or of nascent modernity have within themselves the kernel of a postmodernity, for all are dominated by art which is experimenting in the interests of finding and formulating the rules which will govern subsequent ('modern') art. All are characterised by extreme

formal innovation, and, as with the current wave of postmodernism, the 'presence of the past' is an important guiding concern for
such innovations and experimentations. All that differs here is
that in the twentieth century's postmodernism, there is a coterminous and contemporaneous *rejection* of the impulse to modernity
or to modernism. We are thus left with a postmodernism 'stripped ·
bare', a postmodernism which is not the condition of our modernism, but is rather coming into its own in our rejection of the
modernist project.

The precise location of the 'postmodern debate', of course, lies
here, for not everyone rejects the modernist project. Most
famously, Habermas has called for the completion of the 'project
of Modernity', a project whose roots lie in the Enlightenment
notion of rationality. He has been followed, if often with some
circumspection, by many other Marxists, in the rejection not of
the project of modernity but rather in the outright rejection of
postmodernism. 'Always historicize!' proclaims Jameson at the
beginning of *The Political Unconscious*. Many of his fellow
Marxists have 'historicised' postmodernism by noting the fact that
its current wave (the only one they recognise) is happening
broadly at a moment they identify as that of 'late capitalism'.
Postmodernism is then seen as the more or less direct aesthetic
manifestation of this economic moment. This is clearly an
extremely crude 'historicising', more akin to a Symbolist aesthetic
or a Baudelairean notation of serendipitous 'correspondences',
wherein history cedes place to the merest temporal 'coincidence'.[7]
The postmodern debate thus opens up another pressing concern
of the moment, the demise of some marxisms and the exploration
of various postmarxisms. This is detailed more fully in the final
chapter of this book. Meanwhile I will now attend to some
specific examples of postmodernism in contemporary arts, in an
attempt to articulate more fully the four major figures which I
argue characterise the postmodern: seduction, transgression, aurality and flight.

1.1 SEDUCTION

When Christopher Bruce and Lindsay Kemp made the ballet *Cruel
Garden* in 1977, they named the dance after a drawing by Cocteau

depicting a bullring where the bloodstains on the ground are figured as blossoming flowers. But what seemed of most interest to them — and especially to Bruce whose subsequent work developed similar themes — was not just the ambivalence of this drawing, but also the ambivalence inscribed in the life and work of Federico García Lorca who provided the explicit inspiration for the dance. Lorca had been able to make a fusion between a local, traditional art — the soil of his local culture, as it were — and the international artistic movement of his moment, the Surrealism of Dali and Buñuel. This paradoxical ability to be both of a specific place and yet also unrooted is typical of the postmodern condition, and is akin to the 'Critical Regionalism' which Frampton identifies as a significant aspect of contemporary architecture, or, indeed, to the poetry of a writer such as Paul Durcan who mimes the accents of rural Ireland while locating their poems in 'The Berlin Wall Cafe'.[8] It finds its most obvious paradigmatic space in

Figure 1 Still from the ballet *Cruel Garden*, by Christopher Bruce

the dance, where movement is of the essence, and where, as in the most ancient rituals involving dance, the dancer is both in one precise location while yet transfigured and relocated in a different symbolic space. The dancer's leap, of course, is the locus of exactly the postmodern tension between localisation and deracination.

Cruel Garden is performed in three parts: 'Spain', 'America' and 'Spain, August 19, 1936', and the first and third parts here take place haunted by the spectre of the bull-ring or 'cruel garden' in which the poet both triumphs and suffers, always facing the deadly horns of the bull yet always, until the end, accommodating this danger in the ritualised labyrinthine movement of the dance itself. The two Spanish framing parts of the dance — surrounding 'America' — take place in a mythical rural cafe, *El Cafe de Chinitas*, with all its local colour and the specific inflection of traditional songs. The 'central' part anachronistically introduces silent film into the scenario — 'The afternoon stroll of Buster Keaton' — thereby confounding two historical moments as well as two places. Structurally, therefore, the dance itself mimics the postmodern paradoxical fusion of local and international, of traditional and modern. Its explicit 'Spanishness' in its use of instantly recognisable fluent Spanish dance steps is set in conjunction with an American filmic movement, danced partly under a strobe, which gives a particularly disjunctive effect. In its narrative structure, the poet makes a movement away from 'home' (from Spain to America, from a tradition to novelty) and then returns; but the place he returns to turns out to be different from the place he left. The postmodern dancer knows fully the paradox of Heraclitus who could not step twice into the same river.

In the postmodern tension between the local and the international, between a domestic 'culture' and the flight from that culture, there is a replacement of a principle of identity with a principle of difference or alterity. The place a dancer's feet return to after a leap or movement is never the same place that she or he left; the identity of the ritual space of the dance, the *orchestra* or cruel garden, turns out to be different from itself. Like the site of Bruce's dance here, it is simultaneously two things: the site of blood or of death, cruelty, and the site of a growth or development, Cocteau's flowers. In the Renaissance and its aftermath, the ritual space of the garden was clearly *identifiable*: More's Utopia is a kind of Eden; Milton's ideal garden is the garden of England, modelled on Eden. In the Enlightenment, similarly, Voltaire's garden is identifiable as one's own individual biography, one's own lived-space or *Lebensraum*. In the postmodern condition, the 'identity' of such a garden is no longer available; the postmodern garden or space is typically ambivalent or disjunctive, self-contradictory, like a drawing by Escher. Its 'identity' is founded upon the ways in which it actually 'differs' from itself in its paradoxical ambiguity or ambivalence, as a site of blood or of flowers.

The postmodern tension I describe here is more explicitly articulated in Bruce's 1984 ballet, *Sergeant Early's Dream*, whose theme is the migration from the old world to the new, from Ireland to America. This deracination offers once more a postmodern politics of which a microcosm can be found in the most basic grounds of dance itself. Bruce writes that throughout this ballet 'there is a feeling of sadness at leaving the old home and losing touch with old roots. However, people take with them threads of their own culture which will inevitably develop separately'.[9] It is as if the movement from home is inevitable — as, of course, migration has often been for the people of Ireland — and that, in this movement away from the land there is a kind of nostalgia, but also a vital emancipation or release, permitting the spread of the local culture internationally. However, the postmodern condition more fully arrives when these threads of various different migrant local cultures interweave into an eclectic multiplicity or pluralistic 'culture'. This happens to a limited extent even in this ballet itself, where there is a meshing of Irish and American folksongs, played by musicians on stage. But the kinds of migration choreographed by Bruce here are, precisely, nothing more nor less than the essence of dance itself; for dance involves a movement in which the identity of an individual merges with that of others in the establishment of a significant configuration. Dance involves the loss of contact with one's own earthy roots (or 'culture'), and an ecstatic movement outwards towards difference and alterity — or at least community. This is the postmodern condition in its most basic aspect: the orientation towards alterity. As in the history of the rituals of dance, at least from Salome onwards, it is not any final product which is of major concern but the seduction of the dance itself, its ability to seduce one into the loss of one's own identity or selfhood.

The dissolution of identity here, a kind of immaterialisation of the self, is danced in Bruce's *Ghost Dances* of 1981, another political ballet dedicated to the peoples of Latin America who have suffered oppression since the time of the Spanish conquests. Here, the major part of the dance is danced by 'The Dead', a number of characters who are haunted by the 'Ghost Dancers', figures of violence and power like 'The Inquisitor' in *Cruel Garden*. Dance, with its incipient seductiveness, is everywhere figured as a means of escape from the totalitarian authority of such figures.

Bruce's choreography is political in its postmodernity precisely because it concerns itself less with the production of identity than with the seduction of difference. In this respect, it is properly a counter to the alleged postmodernism of, say, Michael Clark, in whose dance seduction – and all its effects of deterritorialisation, immaterialisation, the tension between local and international — has no proper articulation. Clark's dances, though often making use of similar tropes, seem more fully concerned with the elabora- tion of a particular style; and, through repetition of stylistic manoeuvres, his work produces an identity in the manner out- lined by Leslie Fiedler when he indicates that many abstract artists, such as Motherwell or Rothko, are basically painting their own signature in their repeated canvasses.[10]

Dance, of course, is an art of occasion; it avoids any easy mechanical reproduction and, like ritual, gains its sense or significance from the varying situations of its different occur- rences or performances. However, as with the most extreme forms of reproducible art — photography — it is impossible to identify the 'original' work; there are only enactments of the work without any Benjaminian 'auratic' original. Dance, quite literally, becomes *ungrounded*, and is, almost by definition, an art of deterritorialisa- tion, an art concerned with movements to and from the earth, with the relation of the human body to the space around it.

This has become a pressing interest for some twentieth-century 'sculpture in the expanded field', as Krauss calls it.[11] Ever since Moore, much of whose work was designed to be located outdoors, the relation of sculpture to landscape has become important. Traditionally, and even in Moore's work, sculpture is exhibited upon a plinth which effectively works like a frame in painting, to separate the work from the earth upon which it stands. But in his abstract steel sculptures of the 1960s, Anthony Caro (who had worked as Moore's assistant) abandoned completely this traditional plinth, thereby allowing the art to establish or foreground the search for a new relation between sculpture and the earth or space around it. Caro's *Prairie* of 1967 opens fully the question of this relationship. The work is in painted steel, and its main feature consists of four extremely long steel tubes, painted bright yellow, and all supported at only one end. There is a broad yellow plate, in undulating steel, hovering slightly beneath these rods. The yellow, of course, suggests the colour of the prairie land itself; but the most significant factor in the success of this sculpture is not its new materials or the fact that it is painted, but rather the fact that the long parallel yellow rods appear to hover above the ground. Since the supporting steel is actually a part of the sculpture itself, the work not only appears to be part of the 'natural' world which surrounds it, but also appears to be slightly deterritorialised. As Susan Compton has indicated, the extreme length of the parallel rods and the fact that they are supported at one end only allows them to move, be it ever so slightly.[12] The sculpture is not stable or fixed, but becomes part of the mutable world around it.

Here, clearly, is the beginning of a profound ecological consciousness in sculpture which developed an articulation not only in the work of Beuys, but perhaps even more importantly in that of Richard Long. Long, though quite different from Caro, follows the logic of the abandonment of the sculptural plinth to a fully ecological conclusion. This has remarkable effects, most notable in his 'earth-works'. One example will demonstrate particularly well the specific relation of postmodern art to the land.

In 1967, the same year that Caro made *Prairie*, Long made *A Line Made by Walking, England, 1967*. In this, Long has fully respected the ecological priorities in his sculpture, and has shown the respect that he has for the field within which he works. He entered a field, and walked back and forth in a straight line for sufficiently long to leave a trace of the walking, a line worn in the

Figure 2 *Prairie*, by Antony Caro

grass. He then photographed this, and simply left it. Here, the eradication of the plinth is complete; sculpture has become fully a part of the world and of history. As Long himself suggested, these outdoor works are places: 'The material and the idea are of the place; sculpture and place are one and the same'.[13]

Three things should be noted about the postmodernity of this work. Firstly, there is its pure historicity. The line takes a lengthy period of time to make, and, once made, is fully open to the vagaries of history in which it will, in time, disappear, existing only in the photographed record or document. Unlike most sculpture, whose element is space, this work exists primarily as a *temporal* piece. The sculpture, as object, then, is not produced; rather, it remains fully at the level of *event*, and, like all historical events, it is transient. Secondly, the line suggests the presence of someone walking it; but the walker is absent from the surface of the photographic record itself — and, indeed, from the actual space in the field. There is, then, a rather ghostly effect of immaterialisation here; it is as if in making the sculpture, the sculptor has become less and less material, more and more ghostly, himself. Thirdly, though again like Caro's work in establishing a new relation to the land, the implicit immaterialisation suggests also its deterritorialisation. Long, as it were, hovers above this work, in his explicit refusal to impose anything other than the historical presence of his own body in nature upon the field. Historicity, immaterialisation, deterritorialisation: these are of the essence to this sculptural event. The status of the work as event is itself important. As I stress here, postmodernism fails to produce, but concentrates rather on seduction. Long's lines and circles inscibed upon the land or in art galleries are akin to the magical or ritual standingstones or 'earth-works' of ancient cultures, themselves magical sites of the attempted seduction of the gods; yet

Figure 3 *A Line Made by Walking, England,* by Richard Long

this 'presence of the past' in his work, even of the prehistoric past, is profoundly historical. It is of the greatest importance that the works take a long time to make, and that the temporal duration of this is fully inscribed upon them.

1.2 TRANSGRESSION

The eradication of the sculptural plinth in Caro, which makes the steel rods of *Prairie* appear to be unsupported, is a primary move in postmodern transgression. As I argued above, in Long's work, as in the performance art of Beuys and many others, the (eco)-logical result of this is the establishment of a new relation between art and place. There is, ultimately, a transgression of the bounds of art itself. This changes the relation of art to history. Bounded works allow the easy bracketing-off of art from something called reality; but in the postmodern work, the transgression of bounds makes it difficult to sustain such a categorical distinction between the aesthetic and the historical.

The notion of 'entering the frame', of course, has long since been established as a staple ingredient of much contemporary art,[14] but the effect of this has not been fully understood. At least since the paintings of Seurat, there has been increased attention paid to the framing of art, both in terms of the physical frame itself and also in terms of the institutional frameworks within which we think it. In a whole series of his paintings, Frank Stella allowed the shape of the frame to determine the content of the work itself, painting a set of parallel lines all following the frame's often irregular format. Howard Hodgkin followed Seurat in painting the frame of his works, leaving uncertain the boundary between painting and surrounding context of the exhibition space. The end result of this kind of transgression of the bounds of the art-work itself, the crossing of its frames, comes typically in the work of the Boyle Family. If the frame of the work of art is to be transgressed, then the categorical separation of art from history (like that between sculpture and land) can be questioned. In the work of Mark Boyle and Joan Hills, the historical world makes its way into the arena of art itself. To enter a museum exhibiting their work is not to enter an institution categorically separable from history, for their work fully attempts to incorporate the historical world into the institution itself. Typically, they re-create tiny areas of the world, selected by the aleatory (and magical, voodoo-like) process of sticking pins into a map and recreating exactly whatever is found at the precise coordinates of the pin-prick. After this, to stare at a pavement-kerbstone is itself to witness a ritualising work of art; the effect is akin to that produced by the work of Long or of Beuys in which the space and historical time of the world itself become the art.

But the transgression of the frame can be more fully integrated into the very structural form of the work itself. This is the case in, for example, those extremely heavily textured paintings of Dubuffet or de Kooning or Ayres, where the frame is not transgressed laterally, so to speak, but is rather overcome frontally. These works build layers of paint out towards the spectator in the antithesis of the 'flatness' so despised by Wolfe,[15] invading the space of the spectator in just the same manner as the plinth-less works of Caro.

While a painter such as Pollock 'danced' over his canvas in order to make the painting, an artist such as Rauschenberg, it could be suggested, 'sculpted' the space of the work, inserting books, plates, cutlery and various other 'jutting' elements into its surface. That surface now has a literal depth, allowing the painting to invade the exhibition space and frontally transgress its frame. Such transgression becomes more fully postmodern, however, only when it works in alignment with the seductive techniques of immaterialisation and deterritorialisation. This can be seen in Amey's *Red Dog IV* painting of 1984.

This painting is in four parts, and thus has four 'micro'-frames within its larger 'macro'-frame. But each of these internal frames is itself transgressed by the partial figure of a dog which appears to be running over a yellow and green backdrop. It is as if we have four stages in a narrative, involving a dog 'entering the frame' only to run over an abstract painting in a most irreverent manner. The effect of this is firstly to question what is 'the' painting: is it the dog, or is it not the yellow and green abstract configuration over which it runs; could it not even be the (painted) shadow left by the dog? Once more, postmodernism does not produce an essential object. This is further complicated by Amey's materials. He did not work on canvas at this time, but painted onto cardboard

which is sculpted or built up into several layers. What we find is
that the dog-figure is actually raised above the surface of the
backdrop in an ungrounded or deterritorialising motion, leaving
behind, but on another level, an immaterialising shape in the form
of the shadow cast by it in its motion across the work. Long's 'line
walked in England' becomes the shadow left by Amey's running
dog who has no respect for the conventional institutional frames
of art but who constantly transgresses even its own space, never
fitting properly into any of the micro- or macro-frames in which it
appears and disappears.

The narrativity of this painting opens it to its version of Longian
postmodern historicity; it is as if the dog is trying, always

Figure 4　*Red Dog IV*, by Paul Amey

belatedly, to catch up with itself, as if it is anachronistic with respect to itself. That temporality of the painting raises the fundamental issue of the frame and its transgression: is the dog in or out of the frame; is the painting one of a dog, or an abstraction over which a dog runs leaving a shadowy immaterial trace? This transgressing of the frame and its function opens the possibility of thinking the work's trangression in terms of *sublimity*. The work approximates to the condition of the postmodern sublime as sketched by Lyotard, though it does so in a most unLyotardian comic fashion.

For Lyotard the postmodern sublime work is that which is 'white' in the manner of one of Malevich's squares; it operates by 'making an allusion to the unpresentable by means of visible representations'.[16] But it avoids conventional figuration. In Amey's piece, the sublimity provokes a pleasurable humour arising from the pain of the hunt or quest as made visible in the figure of the dog itself, a figure which is never fully articulated. But what is the painting in quest of? Here, we find that the work transgresses the very bounds of painting, and enters more fully into another mode, the linguistic or discursive. The humour of the piece lies in this linguistic functioning. Both as a work which exists fundamentally in the mode of the portrait (assuming that the dog is a belated part of the actual work itself, assuming, that is, the presence of the dog in the frame), and as one which makes ironic and parodic gestures towards the anti-narrative triptychs of Bacon in his *Three Studies of Isabel Rawsthorne* of 1967 or the *Three Studies of a Male Back* in 1970, the painting makes a linguistic joke. It is, as it were, the refusal of portraiture, for this dog is disobedient; it refuses to 'sit' for the painting, preferring to dance over it. The subject of this 'portrait' has escaped, leaving Amey with only the ghostly immaterial trace of its presence to inscribe. It points not only to the unpresentable, but also to the unportrayable and to the impossibility of portraiture or of 'sitting', the impossibility of the stable recuperation of a recognisable subject (or object) in postmodern work. Any attempt at such a recuperation is now possible only in the mode of a kind of parody, as in the paintings of Carlo Maria Mariani or those of Robert Ballagh. Parody, of course, is itself fundamentally a mode of

transgression, not only using but simultaneously abusing a con-
vention.[17]

Postmodern art typically is 'out of bounds' or undisciplined,
and it questions every manner of binding or of framing; its aim is
the emancipation of art from the institutional space of the
museum, and the opening of art to history. This is the most
fundamental transgression of all, of course, attacking the very
possibility of the commodification of art by making it not only
coterminous with historical experience but also constitutive of
such history. It is this which Marxism has failed to appreciate or
understand when it attacks postmodernism as simply the blatant
manifestation of consumer capitalism in a brute form.[18]

1.3 AURALITY

Jean-Jacques Beineix's film, *Diva*, opens with a sequence in which
a postman secretly records the previously unrecorded voice of the
Diva of the title at a concert. It is vital to the plot that the Diva
('Cynthia Hawkins') has never allowed her voice to be recorded,
for in a fundamental sense this means that she has never heard
herself sing, except in the disfiguring tones of her own inner ear.
In the plot, a number of capitalist villains who want to commodify
the art of this singing would like to possess the postman's tape of
the voice. Accordingly, he is hounded all over Paris in a series of
sequences which parody the *film policier*, as the hunt is on for the
voice of the Diva. The plot is complicated by the introduction of a
second (and eventually third) tape which, for reasons of personal
safety, a corrupt police officer is also determined to retrieve. The
film, fundamentally, becomes the quest for a voice, and the
labyrinthine movements and turns of its plot mimic formally
the labyrinthine ear which is striving to contain the voice, to hear
or understand/comprehend it. The postman, Jules, a Joycean (and
now also Derridean) figure if ever there was one, tries to keep the
voice on the move, lending it to an oriental girl, Alba, and the
guru-like Gorodish. After many byzantine complications, it is
retrieved. At the close, the voice is returned, safely, to Jules (who
by this time has become involved in a parodic 'affair' with the
Diva), and the film returns to its opening sequence. As in dance,
the characters return to their 'home' or starting-point, but it is now

a different place. This time, the hall in which the Diva sang is empty, save for the Diva herself and Jules. They stand together, hand-in-hand, on the stage on which she previously sang, and listen as Jules plays back the tape. The journey or odyssey of the voice is now complete: the film opened with the voice proceeding out of the mouth of the Diva, and at the end we return to the voice again, this time as it figures in the ears of the Diva, who hears herself sing, as she remarks, for the first time. The film is about the movement of a voice from a speaker's mouth into her ear; it is a dramatisation of the Derridean *s'entendre-parler*, but one which demonstrates the huge detours and relays that a voice has to travel in order for it to be 'heard' by its speaker, who is always anachronistic in relation to it. The Diva has, as it were, finally caught up with her own voice, and comes to inhabit it for the first time, having now heard it.

This brief analysis of the film demonstrates its fundamental trope, which is to turn away from the specular which dominates film, to turn away from the gaze, and to concentrate instead upon the aural, to stress the necessity of listening to and in cinema. A similar effect is to be found in Wenders's *Paris, Texas*. In this film, Travis returns to the scene of his conception, the Paris, Texas of the title; but this is a location of which he has no memory. All he has is a photograph of a patch of land which is, apparently, 'his' place. The return is made in an effort to find his estranged wife, Jane, whom Travis discovers working in a peep-show. Here, they make contact of a sort; but it is crucially important that they do not see each other, communicating instead through the aural means of a telephone link. Travis turns away from the one-way mirror in which he could have watched Jane; Jane, in her booth-room, cannot see her 'customers' through the same mirror.[19] Once more, in this postmodern cinema, the specularity of the gaze is ceding place to the importance of an active listening, to the prioritisation of aurality.

In popular cinema, James Brooks's *Broadcast News*, offers a similar trope. In this film, a TV presenter, Tom Grunick (William Hurt) finds himself in the difficult position of having to cover an extremely important news item. Grunick's main TV strength is his appearance, not his intellect. The intellect is shared between his Executive Producer, Jane Craig (Holly Hunter), and the journalist

Aaron Altman (Albert Brooks) who completes a kind of parodic *ménage-à-trois* in the film. Altman sits at home to watch the programme from which he has been explicitly excluded, and telephones information to Jane concerning the news item being covered. She, in turn, speaks directly into the ear of Grunick through his ear-piece, feeding him precisely the right information just before he needs to speak it. Meanwhile, Altman at home and watching, remarks to himself that 'I say it here; it comes out there' on the TV screen. In this, we have exactly the same kind of scenario as operated in *Diva*, but here complicated explicitly by the question of gender and authority: this voice is mediated by the female Executive Producer. There is, further, that element of anachronicity which is of importance in opening the postmodern work to its historicity, for there is a slight delay between the journalist phoning the information and it being relayed back to him after its labyrinthine detour through the medium of the TV studio and telephone links. But most obviously of all is the sheer stress on aurality, upon the ear which, all through this sequence, is explicitly highlighted on screen. What we are watching in this film is the mediation of the labyrinthine ear in its activity of listening.

A seeming counter to this stress on aurality is the tendency in postmodern art to silence.[20] Ever since John Cage's notorious 'silent' musical piece, there has been some interest in what might be called 'hearing what is not actually there' in music. Cage's piece allows us to hear the profound noise amidst which we live and which we usually fail to hear. As in Beuys, this works to alert us to the presence of art (here in the form of music) all around us; it breaks the barrier between the music hall and the street-sounds outside.

It is unlikely that one could provide a more 'minimalist' piece of music than Cage's, but in what has become known as the minimalist music of Reich, Glass, Riley, Adams and others, the extremely slight modulations which are made as the work progresses make it very difficult to assimilate and recognise. It is always difficult to recall the precise moment when the modulation of a chord takes place during a rendition of the piece. While listening to this kind of work, then, one tends to begin to hear what is not actually there, as one foretells or forehears the modulations anachronistically, out of their proper timing. This is the case in almost all minimalist work; but the same can be found in heavily overladen pieces of music as well, as in some Stockhausen or Berio. Silence, as well as overladen information, has the ability to make one freshly aware of one's ears.

In Simon Jeffes's piece, 'In the Back of a Taxi', written for the Penguin Cafe Orchestra, a Cagian silence is interwoven into the music itself. Near the end of the piece, there is a pause, lasting some forty-five seconds, before the music returns for its final twenty-five seconds. In listening to this piece, one is encouraged quite literally to hear what is not there, for during the silence there is a kind of challenge to hear the continuation of the music while one awaits its sudden return; and, of course, one hopes to be still in time with it, though this is, needless to say, extremely difficult. Anachronicity is again written into this heightened aurality.

Hearing what is not there is akin, of course, to what Hartman calls the 'madness' of hearing inner voices, a madness shared, in literature by almost all of Beckett's narrators. But in literary criticism as well, there are some fine examples of 'hearing what is not there', in a mode of criticism which can only be called fully postmodern. Among these would, of course, be the textual analyses, with all their attention to puns, of writers such as Derrida or Hartman himself; but the kind of reading I am describing can perhaps be found in its most cogent theoretical form in the hermeneutic of Julia Kristeva. When she reads Sollers's novel, *H*, Kristeva hears, as it were, the semiotic rhythms of the work rather than its surface symbolic words. As she proceeds through a page of this work, she is all the while hearing echoes of sounds and figuring them together in a complex semiotic weaving of a kind of primal aurality. In this, quite clearly, she is hearing what is and is not there for she is attending not to the discursive symbolic order of the text,[21] but rather to its semiotic, a sound which, as it were, remains itself immaterial and simply ghosts like a faint echo the text's articulated symbolic order. As she reads the discourse, she interweaves a semiotic figure through it. Once more, then, as in Amey's work, there is a transgression between discourse and figure, this time in the interests of aurality, of hearing what is not there.

Aurality, then, in postmodernism, replaces specularity as a dominant determining mode of perception. But this is an aurality marked by transgression and by anachronicity; it is, as it were, the aurality which figures in the silences which punctuate ritual; it attends not to the produced symbolic order of things, but rather listens to hear the seductive ritualistic noises which mark the labyrinthine meanderings of the processes of ritual. It thus combines with the seductive and transgressive aspects of postmodernism. Further, it adds an even more explicit historicity to the postmodern work, for the aural sense is predominantly a temporal, diachronic one while the visual is primarily spatial and synchrnonic. As it works in the manner of Kristevan hermeneutic (fundamentally akin to psychoanalytic hermeneutic, of course), it has the effect of altering the work which it strives to hear; this aurality is thus also marked by a tendency to heterogeneity or alterity, for its major transgression is in its tendency to hear what is not there, to make the work which is the object of its aural perception different from itself.

1.4 Flight

I indicated earlier the tendency of the postmodern work to operate in a mode of deterritorialisation, a kind of escape from all forms of rootedness. This can now be extended to include the area of the museum space itself, which becomes postmodern in what might seem to many to be the paradoxical nature of its flight from culture. For some time, the museum as an institution has been questioning its function. No longer can it be regarded merely as a kind of repository of the good and the beautiful, for its boundaries, its doors, have been broken down. Where it could work as a framing device, separating art from history, postmodern transgression has tended to knock down its walls, to turn the museum space inside out as it were. This is, of course, nowhere more apparent than in the effect of the architecture of the Centre Pompidou in Paris by Renzo Piano and Richard Rogers, where the building has, in a fundamental sense, been literally turned inside out. Those parts of it which would usually be concealed from view are now integrated in the exterior part of the frame. Further, the building's huge *parterre* allows space for a whole series of performing acts (clowns, mimes, fire-eaters, magicians, street-theatre, dancers, musicians, 'strongmen', and so on). Those who come to see the exhibitions must first negotiate their way through all this street-theatre, all this 'live art'. The boundary which marks the entry to the Centre is now unstable: are we 'in Beaubourg' when we enter the *parterre*; if so, are we 'in it' when we enter the surrounding streets of Paris from where it can be seen; if so, are we 'in it' from the moment we enter Paris itself; and so on, indefinitely. Even if we do manage to enter the building, we must climb those moving staircases which are on its outside and which allow an even better view of the circus below, and in which we are thoroughly visible, 'on display' ourselves. Beaubourg is not a mere stable repository where art or culture is located; rather Beaubourg is a seductive space which draws, as a magnet will draw iron filings, art and culture all around it in the streets of Paris. It moves its art onto the surrounding streets, making history itself as important and as visible as the art which the building is itself supposed to contain. Rather than being a container of art and culture, it allows culture to take flight from the museum space, emancipating it in the manner of Beuys, Long and the other artists discussed in these pages.

The effect of this architecture, then, is to open the streets, or everyday historical life, to the possibility of art. The same can be found in most postmodern buildings, where a labyrinthine eclectic melange of different styles from the past make one's negotiation of the building itself a work of performance art. In the architectural theory of Norberg-Schulz, architecture as the 'built environment' is thought of in profoundly phenomenological terms. Its main concern is the establishment of one's spatial relation with the surrounding 'lived space'. But in postmodern architecture, a walk through a building is not so much the negotiation of 'lived space' as it is the engagement with 'lived time', for one moves from one period of civilisation to another, stepping from one architectural style to a different style from a different historical moment. This can be seen in, for example, the Brant House in Bermuda, designed by Robert Venturi, John Rauch and Denise Scott-Brown, where classical styles sit alongside more modern ones. In these buildings, one is neither rooted in space (postmodern buildings are notoriously difficult to find one's way around in), nor is one rooted in time. They are the site of a full deterritorialisation or flight from the metaphysical tendency to self-presence and to all those forms of thinking — 'nominalist' or 'identity' — which aim to work as the counter to historical mutability and change.

This tendency to flight is articulated even more directly in another Paris museum, the Musée d'Orsay. This is built on the converted space of an old railway station: movement and flight in a radiation from the centre is inscribed into its very founding condition. Although it is the site for a range of works from a broad span of history, this museum's architectural embodiment and display of them converts them all in some sense into works of postmodernism. It breaks the frame of all the work exhibited within its space, but perhaps nowhere more so than in its extensive collection of Impressionist work. This is most aptly hung in Orsay, for the simple reason that it was painted not only in the heyday of the railway, but was also itself an art of flight. The Impressionists, painting under the differing conditions of light, often outdoors, produced a body of work whose determining condition is the flight from stability in every sense of the term. Their objects typically shimmer and have no definite fixed boundaries; they are unrooted in the paintings or even in the nature from which many of the paintings derived.

Culture, as a metaphor if not also as a fact, is itself concerned with the establishment of roots; in its most basic form, agriculture, it tends to a set plot of land in which any change is marked by the sign of threat: the threat of famine or of drought. Postmodernism fundamentally makes a movement away from the earth, or at least away from rootedness. In this sense, it is rather nomadic, concerned only with a locality insofar as that locale can be made to figure in a wider 'interlocal' framework. Localities are to be transgressed in postmodernism; movement is of its essence, for its art is most crucially historical, contaminated by anachronism. The establishment of cultures allows for the production of identity, be it a national identity or a personal biographical one. In its tendency to heterogeneity, postmodernism acts as a counter to this form of culture. This, of course, does not in any sense mean the neo-Hegelian 'end of art'. It simply means the end of art as reified commodity exhibited in a sacred shrine called a museum from which most people are barred by reasons of finance, ideology, or because they are deemed ideologically to lack the specific 'intellect' required for understanding. Postmodernism, in fleeing the culture of 'representation', opens art out, emancipates it from its commodification. It also emancipates the makers of art, therefore, from all forms of identity. As in dance, it allows the historical makers of art (people in general, those 'outside' Beaubourg) to lose identity in a sublime or ecstatic movement outwards, in a movement towards alterity, towards the establishment of an indefinite configuration with those other artists involved in the dance. As Yeats rightly asked, in this condition 'Who can tell the dancer from the dance?'

POSTSCRIPT

Clearly, there are a huge range of artists and of significant contemporary movements in the various arts which are not discussed here. This introduction makes no claims on comprehensiveness. What it does strive to do is to offer a mode of thinking 'the postmodern' through a number of specific examples of phenomena drawn from a wide range of the arts, serious or populist. The major claim I make for it is in its *theoretical* comprehensiveness. Its four categories (seduction, transgression, aurality and flight) understood in the precise terms in which they are outlined here (with their sub-categories of deterritorialisation, immaterialisation, heterogeneity, eclecticism, historicity, sublimity, anti-totality, and so on) offer a frame within and through which postmodernism can be cogently thought. My contention would be that these are appropriate, in one way or another, for the many artistic — and, indeed, political — movements which characterise the postmodern condition. My hope is that this book itself constitutes an exercise in postmodernism, and that it can be read as such.

II

Excess and Extravagance

2

Theory, Enlightenment, Violence

2.1 POSTMODERN HERMENEUTIC AS A COMEDY OF ERRORS

Traditionally, hermeneutic has been tragic in condition and orientation. It depends on the notion that texts are obscure, with secret *topoi* in the dark tropics of their discourse, demanding epistemological sleuths for their illumination or demystification. Ricoeur writes, for instance, that:

> on the one hand, hermeneutics is thought of as the manifestation and the restoration of a meaning which is addressed to me in the manner of a message, a proclamation or, as it is sometimes called, a kerygma; on the other hand, it is conceived as a demystification, or a reduction of illusions.[1]

Both the theological and the politically demystifying aspects of this formulation constitute the tragic orientation of hermeneutic. We have the interpreter as Oedipus, faced with the enigmatic and secret riddling text of the Sphinx at the gate of the city. In identifying the correct answer to the Sphinx's riddle as 'man', Oedipus is really naming himself. The riddle, 'What is it that walks with four legs, three legs, and two legs, yet always speaks with the one voice?' is answered, in this specific instance, by the response 'me, Oedipus'. It is, then, not some kind of transcendent truth or essence which reveals the city of light behind the text; rather, it is a profoundly secular, historical act of self-identification and self-nomination. The narrative of Sophocles can then slowly produce a meaning or identity for this name, constructing the truth of 'me, Oedipus'. The hermeneutic train all the

way from Thebes to Frankfurt has implied the presence of a reality
or ground which lies behind, alongside or in front of texts. The
emancipatory aspect of hermeneutic depends on the interpreter
being 'in touch with a reality obscured by "ideology" and dis-
closed by "theory" '.[2] The 'Elect', 'Reason', or 'Theory' itself have
all occupied the position of Oedipus, and taken on the function of
'illumination' of the 'city of light' which is obscured by the dark
text. The terminus of this trajectory would seem to be in the early
reader-response work of Fish. In revealing the secrets of the texts
which he examines, Fish watches them self-destruct, exactly like
Oedipus before the self-consuming Sphinx; and, interestingly,
'the' reader of his mode of criticism turns out to be, paradigmatically, himself. The interpretive manoeuvres turn out to be an
act of self-identification and self-nomination in exactly the same
'subjectivist' mode of Bleich:

> The reader of whose responses I speak, then, is this informed reader, neither
> an abstraction nor an actual living reader, but a hybrid — a real reader (me)
> who does everything within his power to make himself informed.[3]

But it is this 'information' or shaping of the name, Fish, Bleich or
Oedipus, that the interpretation then narrates and substantiates.
Oedipus's original solution, though an act of enlightening demystification, proposes in turn its own mystery: who is this 'Oedipus'? And the narrative proposed by Sophocles 'enlightens' this
secret in turn. In the case of Fish, this narrative aims to be more
clearly historical; the act of interpreting proposes a story of what
Fish is *doing* as the text self-consumes under his pitiless truth-
telling gaze. In that of Bleich, one's ontological presence is what is
at issue. The tragedy of Oedipus — or of Fish or Bleich — is not
that his identity is different from itself, or other than he thought
(that would make the narrative a comedy of errors), but rather that
he believes that there is an essence of his identity, a truth of
identity, which is not historically constructed but is rather merely
'revealed'.

The tragic hermeneutic is, as it were, geo-political: it aims to
reveal the *polis*, the city of light, as a non-historical, non-secular

space. Revelation or illumination of this space is, as Oedipus finds out, blinding and apocalyptic, spelling the end of change and of history.[4] The postmodern condition of hermeneutic is, I shall argue here, oriented towards a chrono-political mode, a mode of interpretation which is radically historical. Insofar as it is thus historical and constituted by change, self-difference or narrativity, this mode of hermeneutic lacks the possibility of an absolute knowing and an absolute self-consciousness. Consequently, the truth-claims of the propositions made in the name of such a hermeneutic will tend towards illegitimacy rather than verifiability. It will be, in terms advanced by Gerald L. Bruns, inventively rhetorical rather than philosophical, and to that extent, pragmatic.[5] The question addressed here, however, relates to the possible positive aspects of this. Marx's famous eleventh thesis on Feuerbach indicates the limitation of philosophical interpretation: 'The philosophers have only *interpreted* the world, in various ways; the point, however, is to change it'.[6] In the field of cultural practice, rhetorical interpretation might contribute to this task.

There are three stages to my argument in this chapter. First, by following a specific chain of euphemisms in modernist poetry and interpretation (Stevens and Freud), I indicate that modernist and postmodern hermeneutics are based not upon simple demysification but, on the contrary, are concerned to produce secrecy, in the form of secret narratives. Secondly, this production of secret narratives is construed as a mode of symbolic action, demanding interpretation in turn, but demanding in this a mode of interpretation which will itself be historical action:[7] this interpretation is concerned not so much with epistemology as with ontology, not with the production of knowledge as such but rather with the effecting of a mode of historical being towards the text. But just as absolute knowing and absolute self-consciousness are problematised in this kind of interpretation, so also the very agency of the interpreter is questioned. Can we know what will be the result of our pragmatic and rhetorical interpretations? This raises the third issue, of the historical efficacy of a cultural practice of rhetorical interpretation, with respect to modes of historical and political change effected by the seemingly more direct form of violence.

2.2 HELIOTROPISM: THE LINGUISTIC TURN IN THE LANGUAGE OF FLOWERS

We do not prove the existence of the poem.
It is something seen and known in lesser poems.
It is the huge, high harmony that sounds
A little and a little, suddenly,
By means of a separate sense. It is and it
Is not and, therefore, is.
　　　　　(Stevens, 'A Primitive Like An Orb')

As flowers turn toward the sun, by dint of a secret heliotropism the past strives to turn toward that sun which is rising in the sky of history. A historical materialist must be aware of this most inconspicuous of all transformations.
　　　　　(Benjamin, 'Theses on the Philosophy of History')

In a footnote in *Marges*, Derrida indicates that the flowers of rhetoric have always had a specific coloration or turning, being always metaphors for doomed youth or for the passage of time. But the very historicity of this is not attended to by Derrida. Since the *Fleurs du Mal* of Baudelaire, the modern language of flowers can be seen to take a new turn, not towards the violence of the (en)light(enment) of the sun, but rather towards the darkness visible of secrecy and obscurity; it is only in death that such flowers bloom.

In what follows, I shall attend in particular to the text of 'The Poems of our Climate' by Wallace Stevens:

I
Clear water in a brilliant bowl,
Pink and white carnations. The light
In the room more like a snowy air,
Reflecting snow. A newly-fallen snow
At the end of winter when afternoons return.
Pink and white carnations — one desires
So much more than that. The day itself
Is simplified: a bowl of white,
Cold, a cold porcelain, low and round,
With nothing more than the carnations there.

II
Say even that this complete simplicity
Stripped one of all one's torments, concealed

The evilly compounded, vital I,
And made it fresh in a world of white,
A world of clear water, brilliant-edged,
Still one would want more, one would need more,
More than a world of white and snowy scents.

III
There would still remain the never-resting mind,
So that one would want to escape, come back
To what had been so long composed.
The imperfect is our paradise.
Note that, in this bitterness, delight,
Since the imperfect is so hot in us,
Lies in flawed words and stubborn sounds.

When Harold Bloom considers this poem, he makes one basic
misprision to construct its genealogy:

Stevens writes: 'simplified', but he means 'reduced', and what he reduces is
Keats's Grecian Urn, with 'a bowl of white,/Cold, a cold porcelain, low and
round' replacing the 'silent form . . . Cold Pastoral' of Keats's vision.[8]

The poem does begin in a cold climate, with its central cold bowl;
but another genealogy is available. It is stressed that the bowl is
clear, brilliant and white 'With nothing more than the carnations
there', and yet 'one desires/So much more than that'. Bloom
arrives at the 'Cold *Pastor*al' via a mediatation on *Pater* (as always
for the Oedipal Bloom, many 'fathers' ghost these texts), whose
relation to *fin-de-siècle* decadence allows Bloom's second misprision which reads the line in the manner of a Wildean dandy as
'one desires/So much *less* than that'. But a something *more* is
specified in the text, a supplementary excess which is precisely a
kind of imperfection. It is, one might say, the staining of the water
in the white bowl as in Blake's 'Introduction' to *Songs of Innocence* where 'I made a rural pen,/And I stained the water clear,/
And I wrote my happy songs'; the excess of staining here being
instrumental in allowing the bard to write at all. The identity of
the 'pater' for the poem, then, is not so clear.

In characterising the poet as aesthetic flower-arranger, Bloom
notes 'an overtone of fleshly regret in those "pink and white
carnations"' such that 'this still life does not decline life'. This

allows us to begin to identify the bowl, and with it the source of
authority for the poem, more precisely. There is an equation of
three elements: bowl, cold, and light in the room or chamber. This
makes the bowl a *locus* or *topos* of light, precisely a bearer or
carrier of light: Lucifer. The light is described as a 'newly fallen
snow', and is thus like an angelic Lucifer, falling in the guilt of
some original crime or transgression: a transgression against
authority which aims to give Lucifer his own authority. Desire and
evil accrue around the description of the bowl, the *topos* of light
in the chamber/room/camera (*obscura*). Might this 'chamber-
bowl' not simply be a porcelain chamber-pot, to be stained by
something fleshy, something falling in Kristevan 'abjection'?[9] In
any case, it assumes the burden of a guilt associated with flesh,
with the historical reality of the material, carnal functions of the
human body.

If Stevens does indeed desire more than water or carnations, is
he not asking for some kind of 'production' (of faeces/penis/baby
in the Freudian triad), that is, for some historical motion in this
too still life? Such a production is equated with crime; it is the
criminal production of or revelation of something secret, private
to the flesh and body of the poet. The fall involves a fresh
compound, an incarnation of an evilly compounded and now,
being born, vital I. It is as if Stevens is trying to produce himself as
poet, to give birth to himself as a 'figure of the youth as virile poet'
(to borrow the title of one of his essays) in the production of his
fleshy 'supplement'.

* * *

A BOTANICAL MONOGRAPH

This, clearly, is being done in the language of flowers, and there
are indeed flowers, carnations, in the bowl already. One sixteenth-
century formation of this word is 'coronation', suggestive of the
roundness of both flower and bowl here. One kind of carnation
with low, rounded flowers is sweet-william. Interestingly, the
French for carnation is *œillet*, and sweet-william is referred to as
œillet de poète. The English equivalent of this coronation-flower,

however, is not the carnation as such, but rather the narcissus, of which there are three main botanical types: daffodil (with the trumpet-shaped flower known to Wordsworth), jonquil (used in perfumes, and, in its form as 'gillyvor', known to both Ophelia and Perdita in Shakespeare), and the 'poet's narcissus' (with a ringlike cup as its flower). The flowers in the bowl, then, are the *locus* of a heliotropic transformation: not so much carnations, losing their colour or trope of pinks and whites and becoming more obliquely, more darkly, narcissi. The bulbs of the narcissus, further, were considered to be medically useful in the herbarium, as a cathartic, an enema or an aid to (tragic) production. The aesthetic flower-arranger or re-arranger uses the language of flowers (a language which brings Ophelia's desperate death as she tries to find its 'words', as she tries to speak it) to create himself as a figure of virility.

* * *

The bowl in Stevens's poem reflects snow, and thus acts as a mirror of some kind, making the analogy with Ovid's narrative of Narcissus and Echo more explicit. The *topoi* and climates of the two narratives, that proposed by Stevens and that of Ovid which ghosts it, are similar. In Ovid, the secret pool where Narcissus stops is 'always cool', matching Stevens's coldness at the start of the poem. But as Narcissus looks into the pool, he gazes 'in his lovely face where a rosy flush stained the snowy whiteness of his complexion': a staining of whiteness in the rosy language of flowers, and a passage towards heat, clearly echoed in Stevens. Narcissus desires himself and here things hot up, 'kindling the flame with which he burned', 'fired at the sight of himself'.[10] At this point, he reaches knowledge, specifically an absolute epistemological recognition of himself, a revelation of his own identity as 'other', just like Oedipus, and he undergoes his 're-arrangement' or metamorphosis, consumed by fire and water.

The 'climates of our poems' are now clear. Stevens moves from cold to hot, from a cold bowl to a point where 'delight,/Since the imperfect is so hot in us,/Lies in flawed words and stubborn sounds'. Through imperfection, we go from cold to hot, like Lucifer who falls in imperfection or crime, and also like Narcissus who falls through a similar transgressive 'authorisation' of him-self. Beneath the *camera obscura* that is the dark-room or *topos* of this poem, then, there is another scene or *topos* in which a secret narrative link is proposed among the three figures of the evilly compounded vital I: Stevens, Lucifer, Narcissus. The source or authority for this 'com-position' is, therefore, not a single identity but rather a 'com-pound': the 'truth' behind the name of enigmatic Stevens is not just another single identity, certainly not the name of Keats alone. Rather, the interpretation here reveals a problem-atic relation among three names. That is, it reveals the skeleton of a historical narrative, in which the interpreter constructs a narra-tive link among the three names, and shows how they can be construed as part of the same configuration or story. That story or secret narrative here may have something to do with Oedipal self-authorisation. The 'truth' behind the face and signature of Stevens is not just another 'topic' (identified variously as Keats, or Blake, say), but rather is a secret narrative: a setting apart of three names in one secret relation.[11]

The poem, according to this mode of interpretation, is itself precisely composed in flawed words and stubborn sounds or echoes. The nymph Echo, of course, edits what she hears, giving a 'separate sense' in her repetitions. Her speech itself offers a criticism, a critical edition and interpretation of the texts she hears. Stevens's poem renders his relation to his criminal mythic forebears secret by 'flawing' the word 'narcissus' and replacing it, in the euphemistic linguistic turnings of the language of flowers, with the word 'carnation': a fundamental misprision of these blooms.

The perhaps troubling point about this manner of interpretation of the text is that it seems to be willing to change the text in order to suit the interpretive propositions: criminally to fix the evi-dence. This is a problem, however, if and only if the aim of interpretation is purely epistemological, only if the interpreter aims to reveal the truth of the text, its geo-polis of light behind its opaque gated surface. But what is revealed in the mode of hermeneutic advanced here is not a 'knowledge' and certainly not 'the truth' of the poem; rather, what is produced is something more historical, in that it is a narrative situation among a set of symbolic names. The text, thus, becomes not an icon or document which exists geo-politically, as a ritual object which has stepped out of time and history; rather, it becomes an arena of *action*, an arena in which temporal change or historicity is its very mode of being: a chrono-political history, therefore. The interpretation of the text does not propose its meaning as any substantive entity; rather, it proposes that in the hypothesisation of the narrative links among its spectral names the reader is involved in the historical production of meaning, that is, in meaningful action. 'Meaning' here is something that a consciousness *does*, not something that a text or consciousness *has*, intrinsically. But this would be to admit, necessarily, that this hermeneutic does not propose epistemological enlightenment; rather, it simply produces more obscurity, or a condition of secrecy (the secret narrative) as the very condition of its act of interpretation. It mystifies in the act of demystification.

This, then, proposes the historicity of interpretation in that interpretive analysis becomes interminable. Such a condition is, it might seem, the necessary consequence of understanding the notion of authority in these matters in terms of 'production' rather than 'creation' or revelation of meaning; for the same state of affairs applies in Macherey's position when he writes of the *roman énigmatique* of Anne Radcliffe:

The mystery novel, at least as it exists in the hands of A. Radcliffe, seems then to be produced by the confluence of two different motions: the one inaugurates the mystery while the other clears it up. All the ambiguity of the story resides in the fact that these two motions do not, properly speaking, follow one upon the other (in which case they would cancel each other out only at the end), but rather accompany each other inextricably, the one (but which?) constantly contesting the other: and perhaps, contrary to Breton's thought on this, it is the revelation rather than the mystery which emerges reduced from such an adventure. Thus the time of the story is like an interlude, after which everything will be able to begin again as before. But this interlude is properly endless: the mysteries never stop appearing, never stop disappearing.[12]

The difference between this Machereian position and the one I am outlining here is that Macherey synchronises the movement of de- and re-mystification; a procedure allowing him to outline the geo-political component of the texts to be analysed, and a procedure by which he produces or brings to light the 'truthful' propositions lying in the dark spaces of the text where it cannot know itself, those spaces to be identified by Jameson as the text's political unconscious.

The same position is also iterated by Ricoeur in his considera-tion of Freud on Leonardo. It seems at first glance that Freud achieves a demystification, a revelation of the smile of the mother behind Leonardo's smiling Mona Lisa. But in fact, the painting has · created what is supposedly hypothesised behind it, as its ground or truth, for the first time: this reality revealed did not pre-exist the painting, but was in fact created there:

> if the artist's brush recreates the smile of the mother in the smile of the Mona Lisa, it must be said that the smile exists nowhere other than in this smile, itself unreal, of the Mona Lisa . . . thus it is not something more familiar that would explain the mystery of the work of art; rather it is a deliberate absence which, far from dispelling it, redoubles the initial mystery . . . Leonardo's brush does not recreate the memory of the mother, it creates it as a work of art . . . The work of art is thus at one and the same time both symptom and cure.[13]

Ricoeur here shares Macherey's stance of synchronic under-standing; but the example of Freud's Oedipal reading of Leonardo's work does begin to bring into play an element of diachronicity in interpretation: it is here as if the present work of painting done by Leonardo is, instead of creating a future, creating a past, the enigmatic source of the present work itself. But Freud in fact offers a greater purchase on the notion that inter-pretation produces not only mystification as well as demystifica-tion, but a narrative progression and movement between these two hermeneutic states.

Psychoanalysis would appear to be a modernist version of Schleiermacher's preferred mode of hermeneutic, the 'technical' interpretation whose aim is to reveal the 'content as what moved the author and the form as his nature moved by that content', as opposed to a 'grammatical' exercise of an analysis of what the author's language can mean.[14] However, in Freud's hands, psycho-analysis constantly slips into a grammatical mode of hermeneutic; and yet that 'grammar' in turn reveals a 'technical' content, having firstly concealed it or made it secret. This, as in Stevens, does not reveal a single identifiable human nature under the material analysed, but rather a narrative situation comprising a number of technical consciousnesses.

More explicitly than in Stevens's poetry, the psychoanalytic exercise problematises the status of the text with regard to its commentary. As Freud elaborates his procedure in *The Interpretation of Dreams*, it becomes apparent that the text which is the ostensible object of study (the various dreams) is already contaminated with criticism or with other texts, through the processes of displacement and condensation. These texts, then, are 'stained', the scene of a writing, as Derrida indicates. Freud's practice is to use the dream as reported (which apparently is his text for analysis) in order to restitute the fundamental text which is his real goal, the historical reality proposed by his articulation of the dream-thoughts. One crucial factor here is motivation: the Freudian interpreter takes a text and 'motivates' it, in the sense that she takes the text's substantive images (like proper names) and construes them in a motivated narrative formation. The dream, Freud argues, cannot represent the conjunctions which would themselves constitute its narrative motivation; it is the task of interpretation to restore 'the connections which the dream-work has destroyed'.[15] The basic manoeuvre in this is one of 'verbalisation': not only does the interpreter bring to articulation the substance of the dream thoughts,[16] she also links a set of substantives (nouns or proper names) by action-words, verbs, in order to construct a symbolic action or narrative situation which lies within the text of the dream as reported.

We now have a number of possible locations for 'the' text, and with them a number of possible narrative situations. We have, for example, the text as produced by the dreamer in relating it orally; the 'same' text as transcribed by patient and/or Freud; we have the restitution of the ground-text of the dream-thought, as construed and transcribed by Freud; and we have the texts as presented in *The Interpretation of Dreams* where they have undergone overt censorship.[17] The material to be interpreted has, of course, already undergone criticism and editing through the psychic censorship: it is, then, a critical edition of something more fundamental. In every location for the text here, Freud is having to criticise an already critically edited text in order to reveal the fundamental criminalities or transgressions which the psychic censor (and which the conscious Freud) wants to keep secret. The practice,

then, is always an interpretation of an interpretation (the interpretation of the dream is work carried out upon a text which has
already been interpreted and modified by the censors). More than
this, the practice is *an interpretation of an interpretation of a text
which has yet to be written*, for the interpretive procedure produces, for the first time, the text which it aimed merely to reveal. ·
It is, in some ways, like Stevens's ultimate poem. Freud writes this
text himself in *The Interpretation of Dreams*, where his own
interpretations not only produce and constitute his text, but also
where they undergo further interpretation both by himself and by
a reader such as Carl E. Schorske who produces the narrative of
Freud's desired act of parricide from the materials of this text.[18]

We have a further issue here. The production of the secret
narratives linking Freud with his patients raises the question of
agency and authority over the texts. Following the question
'Where is the text?' we must now pose the question 'Whose text is
this anyway?' That is, the question of authority, of what axiomatically grounds a text, arises. Who is the agent of the text, and who
is its patient? Is authority in *The Interpretation of Dreams* pure
and identifiable as that of the singular 'Sigmund Freud'; or has it
been produced intertextually and interpersonally, through the
relations of Freud with patient and reader. Is it thus contaminated,
promiscuously deflowered, a 'gillyvor' or one of nature's historical
bastards, a rhetoric of grafted flowers, grafted texts?[19]

There are a large number of dreams reported by Freud in which
flowers figure prominently. I want to link two such dreams: 'I
arrange the centre of a table with flowers for a birthday' and 'The
Dream of the Botanical Monograph'.[20] In the first of these, dreamt
by a woman whom Freud describes as 'normal', there is a
revelation of sexual frustration at the likely deferral of her
marriage. The woman elaborates on her dream and three factors
assume special importance. First, the flowers are specified as
'lilies of the valley, violets and pinks or carnations'. The carnation
works here exactly as in Bloom's reading of Stevens, becoming a
euphemism for something carnal, fleshy (a 'colour', which is the
woman's first association with the word 'carnation' is itself an old
word for trope or figure). Secondly, 'violets' rapidly slips into
'violates', and thus weaves a scene of euphemistic rape (*le viol*)
into the analysis. Thirdly, the flowers are decorated with green,

crinkled paper which looks like 'velvet'. There is a chain of linguistic turns here, hinted at but unstated by Freud. I can list the linked words, or tropes, here, placing in parentheses those which are hinted at but unarticulated in Freud's text.[21] The text moves from 'valley' to (*vale* to veil to) 'violet' to 'violate' to 'velvet'; but this velvet is itself rapidly displaced as 'a reference to pubic hair' and is hence suggestive (of vulva). By this method, which looks more like the grammatical questioning of a language than the technical questioning of a consciousness or unconscious, the text of the dream-thought can be elaborated, going from flowers (violets) to the genital violation: 'If I were he, I wouldn't wait — I would deflower my fiancée without asking her leave — I would use violence'.[22] The woman as 'patient' here, it seems, wants to stop 'waiting'; that is, she wants to stop being a patient. It is as if the analyst himself, for these are his words, wished her to become an 'agent', thus casting himself in the role of patient, waiting for something to happen in this historical situation of the analysis.

Other matters complicate this interpretation. The woman is associated not with the table but with the flowers at its (her) centre; and, as the analysis progresses 'her reserve gave place to an evident interest in the interpretation and to an openness made possible by the seriousness of the conversation'. She is, in short, rather like a heliotropic flower, opening or blooming in this dialogue as she turns not towards the light of the sun/son, but towards that oedipal father, Freud the enlightener. It is this relation that the interpretation both reveals and conceals, as a secret narrative. The velvet paper mutates easily, by the same linguistic chain, into ('vulvar') leaves or folds, like paper pages to be turned, *conversed* with, manipulated by Freud. These folds can then be 'read' or opened out for the 'pleasurable suffering' which this 'normal' woman is supposedly anticipating and secretly desiring immediately. At this point, it should also be noted that she is reported as having 'a feeling of happiness' (*und habe ein Glücksgefühl empfunden*) associated with the dream; might this be at the expectation of a joy of some kind, and thus 'a feeling of *Freude*' (in which case, *Glücksgefühl*, 'happy feeling', would be a displaced euphemism for *Freude*, 'joy'; and would thus bring Freud's proper name into a ghostly relation with the text and its 'patient'). The situation, after all, is one in which the language of the woman, as her flowers of rhetoric and of sexuality, is arranged and re-arranged (terms analogous with coition in Freud) by the analyst. She is, as it were, deflowered in the language of flowers, as the analyst proleptically interprets her dream. The analyst as *voleur* here manipulates and steals the woman's flowers, violating them as he metaphorises them as euphemisms of her vulva; his interpretation unfolds or makes bloom her vulva for his linguistic or oral 'arrangements'. This text, then, proposes another narrative situation than that revealed by the overt interpretation. As Freud 'reveals' one situation (the woman's desire for immediate inter-course with her fiancé), he also proleptically constructs another secret narrative situation, with a narrative which links analyst to patient in a secret, 'criminal' or at least transgressive relation. This latter narrative relation, of course, is not just a dream but is based in material historical conditions between analyst and patient, between Freud and the women whom he subjected to analysis. That is to say, the interpretation in its revelation of the 'grammatical' sense of the woman's dream is instrumental in constructing another narrative by prolepsis, and this latter narrative is one which is enacted historically, at least at the level of symbolic action (the ideological relations between Freud and his patients). The dream text, then, is not just the scene of a writing but also the scene of a crime: one mystification is replaced by another, as Freud's enlightenment contrives to obscure his historical, critical and criminal relation to his patients.

What Freud 'jokingly called my favourite flower, the artichoke' makes a related appearance in 'The Dream of the Botanical Monograph':

I had written a monograph on an (unspecified) genus of plant. The book lay before me and I was at the moment turning over a folded coloured plate. Bound up in the copy there was a dried specimen of the plant.[23]

Proceeding on Freud's own principles, that a joke is serious and that a dream is the fulfilment of a wish, we can specify the monograph more precisely. Freud himself identifies it as his 1884 paper, 'On Coca', a paper whose authorship he wishes, in the analysis, to keep secret. This secrecy is itself instrumental in allowing him to establish a historical link, expressed in the mode of a secret narrative relation, among three proper names and three historical identities: Koller, Konigstein, and Freud himself (not to mention Freud's father who, according to Schorske, ghosts the whole text). This relation is clearly akin to the similar 'trinity' constructed by the secret narratives underpinning Stevens's poem discussed earlier. In the elaboration of Freud's analysis, however, another text supplants the centrality of 'On Coca'. It is the text which Freud wishes, like Stevens, to produce or complete, the one we are now reading, *The Interpretation of Dreams*. That is, it is a text which Freud wants to identify, in the sense that he wants to stabilise its identity, integrity or definition, by completing it:

I saw the monograph which I had written *lying before me*. This again led me back to something. I had had a letter from my friend [Fleiss] in Berlin the day before in which he had shown his power of visualization: 'I am very much occupied with your dream-book. *I see it lying finished before me and I see myself turning over its pages*'. How much I envied him his gift as a seer! If only *I* could have seen it lying before me![24]

This not only establishes a further relation, a narrative identification of Freud with Fleiss; it also identifies the text in the dream as *The Interpretation of Dreams* itself. The text which is the ostensible object of analysis and demystification is the text which has not yet been articulated. This is the condition of all postmodern interpretation, and one which guarantees its problematic status in historical terms. A reader does not so much demystify the secrets of a text; rather, she interprets those secrets prior to their transcription, and thus in fact constructs a secrecy or a mystification through her own authority or authorisation of such secret narratives as are produced by the interpretation. All such interpretation, then, is proleptic in condition.

The page being turned, or troped, within this dream is a 'folded coloured plate', and thus like a 'green, crinkled paper' (substituting 'coloured' for 'green', 'folded' for 'crinkled', and 'plate' for 'paper'); and it is this which Freud associates with his favourite flower, the artichoke. The turning of the page brings to mind the violation of a book in a narrative from Freud's childhood (and here the father re-appears), a book which Freud pulled apart 'leaf by leaf, like an artichoke'.[25] The reading of books, and the writing of them (demystification and mystification) are for Freud acts of such violence or violation. The act of interpreting, a cultural or symbolic action, implies or proposes a real historical narrative involving material action or violence. What Freud later calls his 'intimate relations with books' is thus like a description of this deflowering act of criticism (demystifying the flowers of rhetoric); but his interpretations of the dreams of others are equally acts of deflowering, rhetorically or symbolically, in dream, or in history. The deflowering of the leaves of a book or, euphemistically, the deflowering of the folds of skin, that carnal palimpsest which constitutes the material and historical scene of Freud's phallocratic writing and interpreting (the body of woman), constitutes precisely the cultural actions of reading, writing and interpreting. It is by such acts of interpreting, in the realm of symbolic action, that Freud produces or constructs the historical and material text of *The Interpretation of Dreams*.

Two things follow. First, *The Interpretation of Dreams* is, by condition, radically incomplete in that it demands its own successive reading, an act which involves its reader in the construction of secret narratives and the establishment of the cultural and political relations which constitute lived history. Such critical reading, according to the violent tenets of operation in *The Interpretation of Dreams* itself, must be iconoclastic, a 'violation' of the text's own flowers of rhetoric.[26] Freud's is not a substantive text, but rather the site of a 'texting' or weaving.[27] It is not a symbol or icon, but rather a site for iconoclasm, and for an iconoclasm whose purpose is to produce those secret narratives which constitute history. As Ricoeur has it, in discussing Marx, Nietzsche and Freud:

these three masters of suspicion are not three masters of scepticism; they are certainly three great 'destroyers'; but this must not mislead us; destruction, says Heidegger in *Being and Time*, is a moment of completely new foundation, and that goes for the destruction of religion insofar as that is, in Nietzsche's words, a 'platonism for the people'. It is beyond 'destruction' that one poses the question of knowing what would be the meaning of thought, reason, even faith.[28]

This is the second complicating consequence of the analysis: the production of historical action itself is linked to violence, a violence either historically enacted or deferred and maintained in the realm of desire or dream. In the woman's dream discussed here, the secret narrative produced by way of analysis is that of a psychoanalytic violation of the patient woman, a crime in which Freud as Tereus steals the tongue and flowers of rhetoric of the woman as Philomel. The question here is whether such 'symbolic' action — textual intervention — is ever 'historical' or materially substantive: can interpretation change the world, or must we revert to the seemingly more direct form of violence in material terms? How historical is the entire realm of cultural activity?

2.3 AGAINST AGAINST THEORY: PRAGMATISTS PLAYING PATIENCE

I have been advancing a theoretical assumption about the status of the text in the foregoing argument. This is that the text is not stable, but static, in the ancient sense of a *stasis*: a text at civil war with itself, whose boundaries thus appear stable while internally being riven with dissent.[29] This would be, in itself, no advance on Burke's idea of the text as symbolic action, nor on Derrida's textual *différance*, nor on Macherey's texts which allow the production of an identity just where they do not cohere or know themselves. What I hope to add to this notion of the *stasis*-text is historicity. All preceeding grammars of criticism proceed on the tenet that the text is the *site* of a civil war, and thus concern themselves with the spatial geo-political dimension of the text, with identifying precisely its topics or *topos*. For such criticism, the text, grammatically, is regarded as substantive noun, the site of a nomination, and demystification proceeds by revealing or pro- ducing the proper name which identifies the text.[30] Here, I propose a notion of the text as verb, so to speak, and thus as a space characterised not by its spatial identity or difference but rather by its *temporal* difference from itself; that is, a text conditioned by its historicity or by the temporal dimension of its civil war with itself. This shifts, potentially, the arena of political debate in a manner suggested by Paul Virilio, from geo-politics to chrono-politics:

Geography is replaced by chronography ... The new capital is no longer a spatial capital like New York, Paris or Moscow, a city located in a specific place, at the intersection of roads, but a city at the intersection of the practicabilities of time, in other words, of speed.[31]

The *stasis* of the text in the model proposed here is thus one measured not by space but by historicity; and, as a result, *narrative becomes the privileged mode of textuality*, replacing the primacy of lyric in New Criticism and since.

There is a corresponding shift in interpretation from epistemology to ontology, from producing or revealing the truth or a knowledge about a *topos* or space towards construction of a historical mode of being through the cultural activity of interpretation and narration. The parameters of argument here operate between a 'topical' criticism (based on subjects for discussion or discourse) and a 'pragmatic' criticism (based on deeds rather than 'mere' rhetoric). These parameters also mark the distance separating the tragic trajectory of an Oedipus, whose deeds are based upon a topical knowledge and a truth of identity, from an archetypal 'comedy of errors', in which there is no truth of identity (nor of anything else), and the subjects of narrative stumble or err from one local deed to the next, with no 'topical' method or 'way'. There arises, then, the fundamental textual conflict, a 'conflict of interpretations', a conflict between competing narratives and their tellers. The question becomes directed to the issue of legitimation of such narratives, narratives we live rather than live by, historically; and directed also to the issue of who has the authority to tell the narratives, or who has *agency* over the *patient* audience.

This, together with the seeming 'illegitimacies' of some of my interpretive manoeuvres on Stevens and Freud, addresses the problem of legitimation in interpretation; but now this legitimation is not merely related to epistemological results and evidence but also to the legitimation of what might be called our 'narrative action', our historical behaviour or ethic. This is the ground of the conflict between Habermas and a pragmatist such as Rorty.[32]

Habermas characterised many poststructuralists as neoconservative in that they offer no rational basis for choosing one mode of historical action over another; in Rorty's words, 'that they offer no "theoretical" reason to move in one social direction rather than another'.[33] Habermas's position is thoroughly imbued with an epistemological impetus, and the legitimation of his stance is based upon the truths established by the discursive formation of the consensual rational will. He writes:

What rationally motivated recognition of the validity claims of a norm of action means follows from the discursive procedures of motivation. Discourse can be understood as that form of communication that is removed from the contexts of experience and action and whose structure assures us: that the bracketed validity claims of assertions, recommendations, or warnings are the exclusive object of discussion; that participants, themes and contributions are not restricted except with reference to the goal of testing the validity claims in questions; that no force except that of the better argument is exercised; and that, as a result, all motives except that of the cooperative search for truth are excluded. If under these conditions a consensus about the recommendation to accept a norm arises argumentatively, that is, on the basis of hypothetically proposed, alternative justifications, then the consensus expresses a 'rational will'.[34]

Here, a social practice is consequent upon the production of knowledge or of method (what Lyotard might call 'metanarrative'); that is to say, however, that the production of this knowledge is assumed to take place outside of history or of social practice itself in the first instance; and the epistemological insight becomes the ground for ontological states or historical practices. In this, it is sufficient for the control of history or for a social practice that an agent knows itself fully. This is a legacy of Habermas's involvement with the whole Frankfurt School attempt to wed Marx to Freud. As Frederick Crews pithily put it, that School assumed that 'If the Western proletariat was not arising on schedule, its unconscious must have been in thrall to the oppressor'.[35] It is thus sufficient in this 'enlightened' project, the 'project of Modernity', to come to self-consciousness in order to assume a positive agency over history. Habermas follows Weber in thinking that such full and rational self-knowledge is theoretically possible, and that it is a guarantor of the legitimacy of a social action or practice based on the better arguments of Marxism.

The 'conservatives' who are the target of Habermas's attacks, such as Lyotard and Deleuze, certainly seem to be more pragmatic than epistemological. Such thinkers have not given up on theory as such, but they have rejected the idea of 'Grand Theory' and with it the related idea of 'Universal History'. Lyotard's postmodern position, of 'incredulity towards metanarratives',[36] puts him into the camp of those who prefer the local historical action, a pragmatics based not upon conformity with a methodical and fully-known metanarrational programme, but rather upon a less ambitious 'narrative knowledge'. Deleuze, especially in his work with Guattari, rejects the specific metanarrative of Oedipus as told by Freud. Metanarrative is rejected by Lyotard on three interrelated grounds. First, its totality, teleology and absolutist status renders it non-historical; subscription to a metanarrative would suggest that we are but fulfilling a prophecy and finding an allotted space in a non-secular version of 'history': it is thus geo- and not chrono-political. Secondly, its basis in a monotheology and dogma, as a totalising non-secular system, is alien to the secularity and materiality of a Lyotardian paganism or Deleuzian nomadism.[37] Thirdly, and most importantly, metanarratives are 'terroristic' and violent: they construct normative parameters within which one language-game or discourse is authorised through a silencing or disenfranchising of every other proposition made from the stance and vocabulary of a different language-game. For Lyotard, who wants to retain the notion of the cultural and historical specificity of language-games, and their resultant heterogeneity, the real 'terrorist' is the system-maker or speaker who, like Robespierre, subsumes all language-games under the rubric of his own, thus silencing the dissenting voices of any minority, ethnic or otherwise. Lyotard argues that there are *only* such minorities.[38] His position becomes antidemocratic for the reason that democracy, or rule by the many in the form of bourgeois democracy, is marked by violence. To the extent that he rejects violence as a mode of resolving the historical conflicts of narratives or interpretation, Lyotard is trying to save politics, for the violence which silences is, as Arendt has pointed out, anti-political, spelling only the end of politics.[39] In the postmodern condition, this salvaged politics is chrono-political.

Insofar as he wants to maintain the possibility of dialogue (albeit with massive logical problems, given the absolute heterogeneity of language-games), Lyotard approaches the 'New Pragmatism' of Rorty and others in the Dewey/James American tradition who take a stance more or less 'against theory'. For Rorty, historical change is nothing much more than a different way of talking about things; one narrative of how the world wags is superseded in time by another, to which we all more or less subscribe. Truth here is replaced by 'what is better in the way of belief', the Jamesian phrase much cited by Rorty: epistemological certainty is replaced by pragmatic efficiency. One of the major problems with the New Pragmatic position, however, as elaborated by Rorty, is that in junking the idea of truth, and specifically of a truth lying dormant behind an ideological veil, Rorty then proceeds as if he has also conjured the disappearance of ideology as well. History has been a progress towards the position in which Rorty and his cohorts now find themselves, and the adoption of a 'frank ethnocentrism' whose legitimacy is not doubted is made axiomatically correct.

Such a stance, of course, is an imposition of Rorty's language-game on every other possible language-game, all of which are now considered from the parameters set out by Rorty's favoured discourse. Lyotard refers to this as 'soft imperialism ... the conversational imperialism of Rorty'.[40] The pragmatic 'liberal' idea of free conversation and opposition of ideas not only ignores the ideological, historical and cultural formation of those ideas in the first place, but also leaves Rorty in the rather imperialist position which seems to be the logical terminus of all individualistic politics. For while Rorty argues that 'obscure mixtures of opposed values' are better than the 'clear hierarchies' of Cartesian philosophy, the historical obscure mixture of opposed views is read as having led, inexorably, to where Rorty now stands in his brave new world of American neo-pragmatism, in the current version of the Leibnizian Optimistic position that 'Whatever is, is RIGHT'.[41] In his adjudication between Habermas and Lyotard, Rorty writes that:

> whereas Habermas compliments 'bourgeois ideals' by reference to the 'elements of reason' contained in them, it would be better just to compliment those untheoretical sorts of narrative discourse which make up the political speech of the Western democracies. It would be better to be frankly ethnocentric.[42]

This perhaps unduly Optimistic stance with respect to the 'Western democracies' becomes more 'frankly ethnocentric' (or imperialist, depending on how you look at it, on what language-game you speak) when he argues, in the context of debate with Lyotard, that 'We await ... the time when the Cashinahua, the Chinese and (if it should prove that there are any) the Martians will take part in the same social democratic community. ... We pragmatists believe that this moderate ethnocentrism is inevitable and fully justified'.[43] This, it is vital to note, is not argued on *a priori* grounds, but on the more Optimistic grounds that Rorty's ethnic group at this historical moment has found 'what is better in the way of belief'. To the extent that it judges all other competing discourses from precisely that racial point, it sees them as deviant, 'foreign', or as wayward questings after some other kind of (less valid) truth. This 'liberal' stance, favouring conversation among equals, turns out to be indeed more imperialist, and its democracy is, in its frank ethnocentrism, not egalitarian at all: it is literally 'rule by the many' over the minorities to whom, according to Deleuze and Lyotard, we all belong.

It is important that Rorty and his anti-theoretical new pragmatists are merely 'awaiting' or 'expecting' (*attendre*) the moment when all will share their views and language; for there is a second self-contradiction in this position, relating to the impossibility of historical agency. Historical shifts between language-games, or pragmatic ways of talking about things, turn out to be undirected. The pragmatist, the critic who has shifted ground from epistemology to ontology, from knowledge and truth to deeds, turns out in this version to be surprisingly devoid of the capacity for enacting such deeds. As Rorty puts it, 'the notions of criteria and choice (including that of "arbitrary" choice) are no longer in point when it comes to change from one language-game to another'; and he goes on to discuss the historical and cultural shift of beliefs in the wake of the Copernican 'revolution':

we did not decide on the basis of some telescopic observations, or on the basis of anything else, that the Earth was not the centre of the universe, that macroscopic behaviour could be explained on the basis of micro-structural motion, or that prediction and control should be the principal aim of scientific theorising. Rather, after a hundred years of inconclusive muddle, the Europeans found themselves speaking in a way which took these interlocked theses for granted. . . . We should not look within ourselves for criteria of decision in such matters any more than we should look to the world.[44]

These historical changes seem to just happen: Europeans find themselves talking in different ways; Romantic poets find themselves writing a language different from earlier verse, and so on. By logical analogy, of course, Rorty must now simply find himself preaching the New Pragmatism, neither by choice nor conviction, but more or less unconsciously, modishly, fashionably — or, one might say, ideologically. If we should not look within ourselves for criteria in such matters of historical or cultural (or verbal) change, then it becomes odd to speak at all of 'what is better in the way of belief': belief as such has become a difficult category and one which, logically, has no place in Rorty's pragmatism. Similarly, while historical change just happened in the past, now it must stop as Rorty 'waits' patiently for others to catch up with his ethnic group's arrival at the end-point of such a historical narrative. But Rorty, of course, is not so passive or patient, and pretends to be capable of actively bringing about historical (or verbal: much the same thing to Rorty) change. He does not merely find himself speaking one thing, but tries to persuade others to speak it too:

Interesting philosophy is never an examination of the pros and cons of a thesis [never epistemological], but, implicitly or explicitly, a contest between an entrenched vocabulary which has become a nuisance and a half-formed new vocabulary which vaguely promises great things . . . The method [of effecting change from one to another] is to redescribe lots and lots of things in new ways, until you have created a pattern of behaviour which will tempt the rising generation to adopt it, thereby causing them to look for appropriate new forms of non-linguistic behaviour.[45]

Rorty then goes on to conform to his own precepts by refusing to argue, and preferring to try to make his favoured vocabulary look attractive: a cultural 'soft imperialism' which tries to sell itself as attractive commodity or tool to other ethnic groups not as 'advanced' in history's narrative as Rorty's own.

At each point in history, someone, somewhere, is telling the narratives which become dominant and shape the imagination, not to mention the specific power-relations, of a linguistic group. The New Pragmatism's self-contradiction here seems to arise from its ignorance of the power and authority which is formed in narrative situations: someone tells the story, for whatever pragmatic purpose, and another hears it; one is the 'agent' of the narrative act, the other its 'patient'. In Rorty's espoused view, it is as if we have all become the 'patients' of history, denied the possibility of agency: an odd definition of pragmatism. If historical change has 'just happened' until now, with people finding themselves speaking in tongues or speaking in puzzling new vocabularies, then why should this arrangement suddenly stop in order to allow an 'enthusiastic' Rorty and others to shape history by selling us a new and attractive vocabulary? Two possible answers come back. Either this ontological pragmatic patience turns out to be epistemological after all, and we can now control history because we *know* how it is shaped; or (a more sinister response), having learned the lessons of an imperialist history, we now impose our discourse on everyone else from all other ethnic groups (including Martians), and simply deem illegitimate or illegible any other language-game which fails to conform to our precepts and vocabulary. The result of this is a justification of a kind of state terrorism (if not cosmic imperialism: remember those Martians), a rather tragic narrative of the postmodern world of violent and/or cultural imperialisms.

But in the modernist and postmodern state of affairs, the situation in narrative is rather different. First, in the example of Freud, there is a confusion of the positions of agent and patient: the patient tells the story, and the agent then 'appropriates' it in whatever way she can.[46] This leads to the agent being an agent of parody or satire, rather than the straightforward agent of an original narrative: she rehearses the story by grafting its flowers of rhetoric into another vocabulary or, in short, by parodying it and thus proposing a comic, rather than tragic, narrative as the postmodern condition of understanding. Secondly, the Rortean new pragmatist position depends upon a consciousness having some kind of epistemological selfconsciousness. But it is worth pointing out that the modernist exercises in self-conscious art arise precisely from doubts about the very possibility of a consciousness reflexively knowing itself. As Ricoeur indicates, considering the three modernist precursors, Marx, Nietzsche and Freud, a common denominator seems to be:

the decision to take, from the start, consciousness in its entirety as 'false', thereby taking up, each in a different register, the problem of cartesian doubt in order to take it into the very heart of the cartesian fortress. The philosopher schooled with Descartes knows that things are doubtful, that they are not as they appear; but he does not doubt that the consciousness is not as it appears to itself; in it, meaning and consciousness coincide; since Marx, Nietzsche and

Freud, we doubt this. After doubt cast on things, we have entered the sphere of doubt cast on consciousness.[47]

The postmodern realisation of this, after Wittgenstein and Derrida, produces a variant on the existentialist notion that the self is radically split or *pour-soi*. That variant is described by Ricoeur in terms which indicate the shape of the modernist and postmodern consciousness as founded on separation, on self-difference and thus on secrecy from itself, or criticism:

I am lost, 'astray' amidst objects and separated from the centre of my existence, as I am separated from others and am the enemy of all. Whatever may be the secret of this 'diaspora', of this separation, it implies first of all that I am not in possession of what I am . . .[48]

It is just such a self-critique, or such a condition of criticism, that the quietist 'patient' pragmatic position of Rorty cannot accommodate, and which it denies. While there may be a great deal of anti-methodical pragmatic scepticism in Rorty's philosophical practice, there is implied a political stance of the metaphysics of 'frank ethnocentrism' and a corresponding unhistorical geo-politics (as opposed to chrono-politics) which seems to be beyond doubt, even beyond argument. The pragmatic 'postmodern bourgeois liberal' works on the assumption that loyalty to its own society is 'morality enough, and that such loyalty no longer needs an ahistorical backup'.[49] But a historical backup might still be felt to be necessary, as Lyotard knows. The relation of knowledge to state, or to politics, requires legitimation:

scientists must cooperate [with the prescriptions of the State] only if they judge that the politics of the State, in other words the sum of its prescriptions, is just. If they feel that the civil society of which they are members is badly represented by the State, they may reject its prescriptions.[50]

Criticism, dissent or decision — that is, policy-making and politics — here remain possible. More importantly, criticism of, and separation from, one's own narratives makes the politics of this case more akin to a chrono-political state, if the distance of the subject from its own narratives is a temporal or historical separation. There is thus a proliferation of narratives, and of the heterogeneity of language-games, which makes communication extremely problematic; but at least such a position has the virtue of not forcing Lyotard into a 'frank ethnocentrism', patiently waiting for the tardy races to catch up with his development.[51]

2.4 FOR A CHRONO-POLITICAL THEORY OF INTERPRETATION

Much has been written on the violence associated with interpretation and with authority, even specifically the authority informing the act of writing itself.[52] If interpretation is seen as a mode of enlightenment, then the equation of light with violence offers itself as a possibility: too much light produces the tragedy of blindness. Derrida writes of this in 'White Mythology', and relates it to a political, even a racial, issue. Examining a passage in Anatole France's *Garden of Epicurus*, Derrida comments on the *metaphor* (carrying across) of a metaphor from west to east, so to speak, and comments:

Metaphysics — the white mythology which reassembles and reflects the culture of the West: the white man takes his own mythology, Indo-European mythology, his own *logos*, that is, the *mythos* of his idiom, for the universal form of that he must still wish to call Reason.[53]

The East, of course, is where the sun also rises; that is, where the light at the end of the metaphorical tunnel finds its origin and ground. This metaphysical discovery of origins, either of history (Hegel) or of language (Rousseau) in the East is instrumental in establishing that racial violence described by Said in *Orientalism* and elsewhere.

Enlightenment, then, may not be so neutral or even positive as it seemed; as Newton showed, there is more to light than meets the eye. Light-as-origin, ground or truth (as base of physics research, as biblical origin, or as origin of language) is already invested with the colours of an originary violence of some kind; there is a subsequent sense in which violence and light (or enlightenment) can be seen to be coterminous. If there is to be a politics of interpretation, then to what extent should it be invested with enlightenment or violence as grounding or authoritative principles?

Hans Blumenberg traces a change in the attitude towards truth
in the history of western philosophy. 'That life was pleasanter for
one who knew than for one who sought knowledge was a premise
Aristotle took for granted'; but this eudemonic epistemology
underwent more or less complete reversal in the age of enlightenment, when 'Lack of consideration for happiness became the
stigma of truth itself, a homage to its absolutism'.[54] Truth in the
modern age is 'harsh', founded on a mode of violence. This finds
its modern political counterpart in the notion that 'the interest of
the whole must automatically, and indeed permanently, be hostile
to the particular interest of the citizen',[55] who thus finds an
'enemy within' the self. One way of avoiding such a criminalisation of the self (a criminalisation only according to the dominant
ideology, of course), is to take a strophic turn away from the sun
and from its white mythology and to release the dark tropics of
discourse into their full obscurity. Perhaps we moderns have all
been, like Hamlet, 'too much i'the sun', too much in the violent
light of the white fathers and their imperialist discourse or
missionary truths.

The idea should not be entirely shocking, for it has a respect-
able, if forgotten, history. As Bruns points out, the ancient world
certainly saw secrecy as a prime condition of understanding as
such; and when he considers the example of Origen's Hexapla,
Bruns indicates precisely the problem which attends us here. The
Hexapla gave six versions of Scripture (for which read *ecriture*)
side by side, all with some claim to authority, originality or the
'light' of truth:

The Hexapla illustrates nicely the problem of the scriptures: you cannot enter
into an understanding of them until you know that you have actually got them
in front of you, but it is difficult to say when you have actually got them.
Scripture is a text whose versions are replicas, not of an original text, but of
one another, as in a family where there are resemblances countermanded by
disagreements brought on by tangled lines of descent.[56]

This is the condition of a writing which denies nomination,
refuses to enlighten us as to the 'name of the father', so to speak; it
is thereby outside the Law, in its Lacanian sense, both illegible
and spawning illegitimate versions. The relation of these versions
to one another is like that obtaining in a comedy of errors rather

than a tragedy of revelation and self-nomination or self-identification. Error, as much as secrecy, becomes a condition of hermeneutic. This error, further, is 'criminal' in the eyes of the white fathers, the acknowledged legislators behind the law of the imperialist enlightenment of the dark tropics of discourse; but the 'criminality' remains fully justified if we wish to reject the parameters of an imperialist mode of politics and and imperialist mode of conversation or social understanding (that 'soft imperialism' of Rorty, as Lyotard characterises it).

This postmodern hermeneutic, then, based on an ancient model, proposes that the interpreter actually constructs a secrecy in some sense, providing not an allegorical revelation of the 'true' story behind the text's dark and veiling words, but rather a satirical version of that text. It reveals the text precisely as it is not, thereby construing an interpretation whose founding impetus is that of parody, and whose orientation is proleptic. As Bruns again indicates:

> More than one critic has satisfied himself that satire is a species of comedy, but it is also possible to imagine it as a species of tragedy as well, and it is equally possible to imagine it as generically unstable: something that is liable to break out at any moment, like an act of terrorism.[57]

But in its parodying of the text, it is not so much perpetrating an act of historical violence (which would *simply* silence the text), as an act of violating the text in the rhetorical language of flowers.

Violence, as Arendt points out, has a special place in politics: it can mean the end of politics in that violence as such is characterised by that which reduces opposition or criticism to silence: 'Where violence rules absolutely, as for instance in the concentration camps of totalitarian regimes . . . everything and everybody must fall silent'.[58] Such a silencing establishes, at most, a geo-politics, a system which is itself beyond the possibility of change and which is unhistorical. The parodic mode of hermeneutic which I am advancing here violates the text in a certain sense, but this violation is an act whose aim is to bring the text not to light but to speech. Ricoeur sees this as part of our condition of 'modernity', which leaves us oscillating between two trajectories in hermeneutic:

on the one hand, to purify discourse of its excrescences, to wipe out the idols, to go from inebriation to sobriety, to draw up once and for all the accounts of our poverty; on the other hand, to make use of the most 'nihilistic', destructive, iconoclastic movement, in order to *let speak* that which once, that which each time was *said* when the meaning appeared brand new, when the sense was full . . . we today are those who have not finished disposing of *idols* and who have hardly begun to understand *symbols*. Perhaps this situation, in its seeming anguish, is instructive: perhaps extreme iconoclasm belongs to the restoration of meaning.[59]

This iconoclasm, in the form of my own hermeneutic 'graftings' of the language of various flowers above, is thus instrumental, in the modern and even more in the postmodern condition, in promising a futurity of speech, bringing speech to articulation and audition. It seems prepared, as with nearly all modernist movements, to involve itself in the Nietzschean 'active forgetting' of a past, a forgetting attacked by marxists such as Eagleton and, in the specific context of legitimation, attacked also by Gillian Rose. But Rose's argument, that as a result of this forgetting 'the world remains not only unchanged, but also unknown',[60] need not follow. The 'active forgetting' here is itself instrumental not only in problematising knowledge as such, but also in producing a *different* knowledge; that is, knowledge in the mode of *recognition* (knowledge as what we always already knew) is replaced by knowledge in the mode of the *question* (knowledge as the 'shock of the new', knowledge as *thinking beyond system or ideology*).

The position I am advancing looks like a return to Feuerbach; its prolepsis relates specifically to his 'anticipative' epistemology. In Blumenberg's characterisation of this, 'The knowledge drive does not want to push forward into the inaccessible, which is anthropologically irrelevant, but rather to anticipate what is possible for man, which is the future'.[61] In Marx's first thesis on Feuerbach, the substance of the attack is that Feuerbach is, in the terms I advance here, merely geo-political and not chrono-political:

The chief defect of all hitherto existing materialism — that of Feuerbach included — is that the thing [*Gegenstand*], reality, sensuousness, is conceived only in the form of the *object* [*Objekt*] or of *intuition* [*Anschauung*], but not as *human sensuous activity, practice*, not subjectively.[62]

By shifting attention to the practice itself, Marx also shifts attention from the 'objective' to the historical. With this in mind, a proleptic or anticipative practice of the production of future meaning, such as I am advocating here, becomes crucial to a materialist historical hermeneutic. But it follows from this 'active forgetting', from this heliotropic transformation of the past and its 'objects', that there can be no *law* of interpretation for the hermeneut who wants to take her poetry from the future.[63] A genuinely chrono-political criticism must be, above all, trans-gressive of law, criminal, able to forge a future through the interpretive parodying of historical narrative, document, text.

In the terms of materialist politics, however, it follows that while criticism may be criminal in its iconoclastic parodic ges-tures — 'violating' texts to bring them into proleptic speech — such a cultural practice, such a criminality, remains entirely *gestural*. It is, if I may parodically paraphrase Jakobson, a 'vio-lence perpetrated on poetic language'; and this violence of crimi-nality, precisely because it remains merely gestural, replaces a more materialist violence of changing the world and writing the poetry of the future by the direct action of silencing that future's poets and critics, of collapsing the heterogeneity of their discourse into a totalising and 'true' (or merely predictable) answer to the riddle posed by the Sphinx. The white light of truth in inter-pretation proposes only the possibility of tragedy and violence; the dark secrets and errors of comedy allow the production of an unforeseen poetry of the future. Postmodern hermeneutics, then, is useful precisely to the extent that it releases poetry into its full comic, parodic obscurity.

This position clearly favours the avant-garde in cultural and political practices, and aligns it overtly with postmodernism. But this is not due to any mindless optimism with regard to the future. Rather, it is a position which thinks of the avant-garde as that impetus to continue history by making the future *different* from the past, by making it strictly unrecognisable and thus potentially unknowable. In cultural practices, I think postmodernism and the avant-garde as that radical form of experimentalism which, in painting, say, attempts to paint the unrepresentable; or in music, to play the inaudible and so on. In the specific examples of that critical practice adduced in the present chapter, the strategy has been to 'hear' what is not there in the texts — and then to criticise it. The political analogy for this would be simply that attempt to hear the voices of those who, in totalitarian regimes and bourgeois democracies alike, have largely gone unheard: those 'minorities' to which we all belong. Andreas Huyssen argues that modernism identified itself by a well-worn principle of exclusion; it insisted on the autonomy of the art-work and excluded mass-culture from its domain, ultimately separating culture itself from the everyday material life. However, this did not go uncontested:

The most sustained attack on aestheticist notions of the self-sufficiency of high culture in this century resulted from the clash of the early modernist autonomy aesthetic with the revolutionary politics arising in Russia and Germany out of World War I, and with the rapidly accelerating modernization of life in the big cities of the early 20th century. This attack goes by the name of historical avantgarde . . .[64]

Huyssen argues that this avant-garde, especially in its specific forms of Berlin Dada, French Surrealism and Russian Constructivism, strove to establish a different relationship between 'high art' and mass culture; in brief, this avant-garde strove to 'hear' what mass culture was saying, strove to hear what went unheard, what remained strictly inaudible within the language-game that characterised the autonomy aesthetic of modernism. It is this attitude, of hearing and representing the inarticulate or unrepresented within culture and social life, that I am characterising here as a genuinely postmodern — and postmarxist — tendency. Understanding as such — and especially understanding as an assumed knowledge of the ways of the world — has been too easily assumed; it is crucial that the social becomes obscure, unknown, quite simply so that it may in time be heard — and be heard in time.

═══ 3 ═══

Photography as Postmodern Cartography

Photography, it is usually assumed, impinges on the history of art to the extent that it affects other visual arts: it threatens to outdo the supposed desire for verisimilitude in painting, and it is proleptic of cinema. This underestimates the cultural importance of photography, that modernist 'truly revolutionary means of production', in the words of Benjamin. Coburn considered this 'most modern of the arts . . . an art that must live in skyscrapers' as a mode whose revolutionary impetus was doomed to redundancy with the passage of time which would make it into the 'classic' of tomorrow as a dominant aesthetic ideology found ways to accommodate its revolutionary potential. Contrary to these propositions, I shall argue here that photography- is better understood as a *post*modern art whose revolutionary potential is more attuned to postmarxism, rather than to classical marxist notions of revolution. Photography, I shall show, contributes to a major shift in the geopolitical axis of the cultural mapping of the world; but this revolutionary effect is not governed by any particular programme or metanarrative; rather, the revolution proposed by photography lacks a specificity of direction and threatens the dematerialisation of historical fact itself. In short, it dissolves the certainty of historical linearity, not to mention the supposed materiality of historical evidence which it is conventionally thought to document.[1]

There are three theoretical components to the argument of the present chapter. First, photography is seen as a counter to certain fundamental aspects of Comtian positivism. Far from offering a faithful documentary record of historical 'fact', it obscures the certainty of that fact; rather than preserve or return to us a world of hard objects and material objectivity, photography 'immaterialises' or 'deterritorialises' such a world, as Lyotard or Deleuze might phrase it.[2] This allows for a different construction of history from that proposed by linear narrative; here, that alternative will be seen to be tied to a feminist alternative to the dominant ways of thinking history in our culture. Secondly, the notion of photography as illustration or clarification of the enigmatic 'texts' of the world is explored, and the idea of photography as 'enlightenment' is found to have been instrumental in the production of an imperialist metaphysics. It is here that the photographic gesture ('you press the button, we do the rest,' boasted Kodak in 1900) contributes to the shift in the cultural axis of the world, a shift in which America proposes itself as geo-politically central and as the locus of enlightenment and of theory.[3] Thirdly, I argue for the postmodern revolutionary potential of photography, *contra* Deleuze; but in this I indicate that photography is only revolutionary insofar as it is read precisely as postmodern and not merely as a modernist art-form (a reading which arises from the historical 'accident' whereby photography is developed technically at roughly the same moment that those cultural practices which characterise modernism take shape).

3.1 PRODUCING THE GHOSTLY: THE NEGATION OF POSITIVISM

Conrad's *The Secret Agent* is an interesting exemplification of how the principles of photography make their way into the cultural realm of the literary as well as the visual. It is a detective-story with a difference: rather than having a sphinx-like enigmatic crime which provokes an agent to an act of enlightening revelation, this novel is concerned more with the production of secrecy and obscurity around the writing of the crime, which seems to be its main concern. One central enigma is the character of Stevie whose idiomatic world of graphic circles is never understood. Stevie, like the Sphinx, also spectacularly self-destructs, the victim of a crime of revelation (in which his interior, his insides, are literally fully revealed), and in this he is a precursor of some

postmodern art.[4] Stevie's obscurity is firmly linked to the character who is in some way responsible for his 'revelation', the
'Professor'. As 'Professor', this character's status is precisely that
of one who reveals, professing or confessing or witnessing clear
statements or propositions. Where Stevie is introspective, the
Professor is, by definition, expansive; however, it is of course
Stevie himself who becomes literally the most 'expansive' character in the text when the bomb he carries explodes at an untimely
moment. The nub of the relation between these two characters is
nothing other than photography.

When Barthes wrote of photography he suggested its link to
modernism. Considering an old photograph, he remarks '*because
it was a photograph* I could not deny that I had been *there* (even if
I did not know where)', and he goes on to suggest 'That the
Photograph is "modern," mingled with our noisiest everyday life,
does not keep it from having an enigmatic point of inactuality, a
strange stasis, the stasis of an *arrest*'.[5] In such comments, Eliot is
ghosting this text, the Eliot who, like Barthes in *Camera Lucida* is
concerned with a mythic personal history and who writes when
striving to elaborate that history:

At the still point of the turning world. Neither flesh nor
                                    fleshless;
Neither from nor towards; at the still point, there the
                                    dance is,
But neither arrest nor movement . . .
                Except for the point, the still point,
There would be no dance, and there is only the dance.
I can only say, *there* we have been: but I cannot say where.[6]

Eliot's suggestion that 'To be conscious is not to be in time' is
modified by Barthes who writes that 'As a living soul, I am the
very contrary of History, I am what belies it, destroys it for the
sake of my own history'.[7] Such 'untimely histories' as these are
relevant to *The Secret Agent*.

In the Conrad novel, the Professor owes his freedom from arrest
or stasis precisely to the machinery of photography, and also to
the fact that he confesses or professes his secret. More than
Isherwood, he is a camera of sorts, with the shutter firmly open. It
is crucial that he professes one secret, vital to him that the police

are cognisant of his mode of self-protection. It is revealed to Ossipon, and to us, that the Professor protects himself by making himself into a walking time-bomb. The operation of this device is simple:

'. . . I am seldom out in the streets after dark,' said the little man, impassively, 'and never very late. I walk always with my right hand closed round the india-rubber ball which I have in my trouser pocket. The pressing of this ball actuates a detonator inside the flask I carry in my pocket. It's the principle of the pneumatic instantaneous shutter for a camera lens . . .'[8]

The Professor must make this 'secret' into common knowledge. However, his 'revelation' is not itself productive of enlightenment within the text at all; rather, it contributes to the production of an obscurity. The next time we see the Professor he is 'Lost in the crowd' where:

miserable and undersized, he meditated confidently on his power, keeping his hand in the left pocket of his trousers, grasping lightly the india-rubber ball, the supreme guarantor of his sinister freedom.[9]

Either the Professor is uncannily prophetic of Ginna's film, *Vita futurista*, with its section on a 'Study of new ways of walking',[10] or, as is more likely, Conrad's text here produces obscurity and secrecy. In which pocket — the sinister left or the dextrous right — is the Professor's ball? Or does this proto-cameraman have a pair of them?

The nexus of 'secrecy/confession' is directly related to the new means of the revelation of reality, the camera lens. Further, the object of the proposed bomb-outrage of which Stevie is the hapless and untimely victim is the Greenwich Observatory. Two elements are thus scrutinised together: first, observation as such, the tyranny of the optical gaze as supposed guarantor of valid truth is questioned; and secondly, the further complication of the proposed attack on the centrality of Greenwich (the centre of 'observation') to the world. The world is mapped, both spatially and temporally, in relation to the 'zero degree' of the Greenwich 'meridian'. The proposed attack on the tyranny of the optical gaze is more important than it may at first seem, for it is an attack on the history of an imperialist geography which is centred on

Greenwich. But the Observatory remains in place; and in this, it is related directly to the scopophiliac and dangerous 'camera' as controlled by the diorchous and secretive Professor. The untimely detonation of the bomb serves to suggest that the text proposes an *alias* (another time) and an *alibi* (another place), another mapping of the world than that which is centred on the Greenwich Observatory, which can be thought as functioning in the manner of the Panopticon analysed by Foucault.[11] The positive anarchic act is negated in the dark box or *camera obscura* which is not only Stevie himself but also the glass-encased copal varnish can which he mishandles. Even this can makes the necessary links between the camera and imperialist vision for us: like the camera, it is glassy while copal, coming from the tropics, offers us the reminder of Greenwich's relation to the tropics through active imperialism.

'Profession' as such is tainted; as the Professor himself says, '"You can't expect a detonator to be absolutely fool-proof"'.[12] This is important because of the proximity of a professional or, better, 'confessional' art to the tenets of positivism. Positivism assumes that the world reveals or 'confesses' itself to its beholder. Photography, or the mechanical and technical principles which underpin and undermine the bombing in *The Secret Agent*, acts here as a counter to the very possibility of a positivist art-form. This argument runs against the usual understanding of these matters. Freund, for instance, relates the realist movement in painting, especially in Courbet's work of the 1850s, to a positivist aesthetic, which, she argues, is founded in the appearance of the camera:

Rejecting imagination as nonobjective and prone to falsification because of its subjectivity, they [Courbet and the Realists] declared that one can only paint what one sees. Accordingly, one's attitude toward nature was to be totally impersonal, to the point where the artist should be capable of painting ten identical canvases in succession without hesitation or deviation.[13]

Freund argues that 'The camera defined a reality which the photographer could alter, but never basically transform'; but she also indicates one of the single most salient features of the camera and its technology when she writes that 'the lens of the camera revealed things that no one had ever noticed before. The everyday realities of the visible world suddenly became important'.[14] In fact, however, it was precisely the *invisible* world that photo-graphy suddenly made accessible and important — even visible. As the shutter-speeds of the camera became faster and faster, so the minute intricacies of the world became visible for the first time. The photograph revealed what the human eye itself did not note. Eadweard Muybridge's sequence-photographs and Etienne-Jules Marey's chronophotographs late in the nineteenth century revealed the intricacies of animal locomotion; the hitherto invisible movement of the world became visible through the agency of the camera lens. But this in some ways controverts Freund's thesis, for the camera now affects how the world is perceived. Those very 'positives', positive facts and observable phenomena, on which positivism was based, come under pressure now from the photographic 'negative', to borrow the serendipitious terminology established by Herschel in the 1840s. Photography made it clear that observable phenomena were not necessarily positive facts; and the world suddenly becomes in some sense hardly observable at all, endowed with the rather shimmery mobility which photography revealed. This, furthermore, is not merely an effect of faster shutter-speeds; a similar ghostly movement is apparent in earlier photographs where the long-exposure times necessary for the taking of the photograph produced results in which there were traces of movement apparent, giving a ghostly image or trace left on the print.[15]

The link of photography to the ghostly or to death is treated extensively in Barthes's *Camera Lucida*. It is important that the central photograph in that study, the 'Winter Garden' photograph of the mother, is not reproduced and remains, so to speak, invisible in the text dominated by the sentiment produced when Barthes considered this image of the now dead mother. The 'illustration' remains in the dark, as it were. But Barthes points out that every photograph is invisible in a sense: 'Whatever it grants to vision and whatever its manner, a photograph is always invisible: it is not it that we see'.[16] This is partly due to the fact that Barthes sees the photograph as the locus of an *apophrades*, the return of the dead whose materiality is somewhat dubious, theatrical at best.[17] Further, Barthes follows in the steps of the sphinx-like Stevie, explicitly attempting to make the text of *Camera Lucida* itself into a kind of invisible photograph, the 'archaic trace' of itself, a 'certain but fugitive testimony' to the *disappearance* of photography.[18]

When Barthes constructs his photographic terminology, he prefers the word 'Spectrum' to denote the ostensible object of a photograph 'because this word retains through its root, a relation to "spectacle" and adds to it that rather terrible thing which there is in every photograph: the return of the dead'.[19] Representation as *apophrades* in a self-consciously 'modern' art-form, however, is not entirely new. When Swift and Pope satirised the 'moderns' in the eighteenth century's confrontation between the rival claims on truth and knowledge of antiquity and modernity, one dominant characterisation of the modern writer was of someone barely conscious. Journalistically 'writing to the minute', moderns (according to the satire) pretended to allow nature to speak through their more or less dead, more or less hallucinating bodies: as 'enthusiastic' preachers, they lose their own consciousness to that of the gods who fill them; as 'dunces', they are asleep and liable to hypnotise their public. It is this notion of modernity as a death of or as a loss of consciousness that is extended in the twentieth century's interest in spiritualism, automatic writing, the unconscious or twilight zones (celtic or otherwise) of existence; and there are obvious similarities to the position described for Rorty and the neopragmatists in my previous chapter. This culminates in the twentieth century in Barthes who thinks of the object of a photograph as a spectral, ghostly figure from the dead, and in Derrida's meditation on the '*spectres*' of Marx. A self-conscious modernity is intimately linked to a ghostly 'immaterialisation' or 'deterritorialisation'; and, in at least one eighteenth-century precursor, these are also linked to theory itself.

Within a fortnight of its original daily appearance, Addison had confirmed in *The Spectator* his belief in ghosts and the supernatural, a theme which recurs time and again in subsequent papers despite an early disavowal of superstition. But more importantly, Addison, like Barthes, conflates the notion of the ghostly with that of theory itself, confusing them in the term 'spectator' which is common to both. Like a prefiguration of Hillis Miller, Addison finds that the theorist is already a kind of apophatic ghost/guest in the house of textuality, negating the ontological materiality of house, guest and spectator herself in the act of theoretical criticism.[20]

In the opening paper of 1 March 1711, 'Mr Spectator' comments on his own taciturnity, and pronounces himself a creature of writing rather than of speech:

> When I consider how much I have seen, read and heard, I begin to blame my own Taciturnity; and since I have neither Time nor Inclination to communicate the Fulness of my Heart in Speech, I am resolved to do it in Writing; and to Print my self out, if possible, before I die.[21]

This stance assures him of anonymity, which he prefers to publicity 'for the greatest Pain I can suffer, is the being talked to, and being stared at'. But though he himself abjures being the object of the gaze, his own mode of being is almost entirely visual, nearly photographic. He claims that 'my Pleasures are almost wholly confined to those of the Sight', such scopophilia, paradoxically, granting him admittance to 'the fair Sex',[22] to whom he addresses the substance of these papers. But 'substance' is part of the problem of these 'speculations'; in a sense, the papers themselves are as 'insubstantial' as Barthes's *Camera Lucida*. Addison characterises himself as pure onlooker, uninvolved in material reality. This makes him a kind of prototype of one kind of 'theorist':

> Thus I live in the World, rather as a Spectator of Mankind, than as one of the Species; by which means I have made my self a Speculative Statesman, Soldier, Merchant, and Artizan, without ever meddling with any Practical Part in Life. I am very well versed in the Theory of an Husband, or a Father, and can discern the Errors in the Oeconomy, Business and Diversion of others, better than those who are engaged in them. . . .[23]

Addison, as spectator rather than species, looks on and is not looked at; *The Spectator*, as spectator, is invisible as well as silent.

Pondering his ever-increasing readership, Addison recommends the paper

> to the daily Perusal of those Gentlemen whom I cannot but consider as my good Brothers and Allies, I mean the Fraternity of Spectators who live in the World without having any thing to do in it; and either by the Affluence of their

Fortunes, or Laziness of their Dispositions, have no other Business with the rest of Mankind, but to look upon them. Under this Class of Men are comprehended . . . in short, every one that considers the World as a Theatre, and desires to form a right Judgment of those who are the Actors on it.[24]

For the later 'Spectator', Barthes, the world also became a theatrical scene of beholding, where every action became a semiotic role in a figure discerned by the theatrical onlooker. But the Spectator as theorist, and as quasi-invisible theorist, fades into a ghostly figure more explicitly in these papers. On 14 March 1711 *The Spectator* concerned itself with ghost-narratives. Having found suitable lodgings in London, where he can come and go as if unseen, Mr Spectator sits quietly in a dark room, near the fire (thus becoming a 'focal' point in the photographic narrative), where he overhears women telling each other ghost-stories. One of these women becomes more and more disturbed, to the point where 'I heard one of the Girls, that had looked upon me over her shoulder, asking the Company how long I had been in the Room, and whether I did not look paler than I used to do'. This prompts a hasty departure, and reflection on ghosts. But here, he describes ghosts precisely as 'spectators':

For my own Part, I am apt to join in Opinion with those who believe that all the Regions of Nature swarm with Spirits; and that we have Multitudes of Spectators on all our Actions, when we think our selves most alone: But instead of terrifying myself with such a Notion, I am wonderfully pleased to think that I am always engaged with such an innumerable Society . . .[25]

This 'innumerable Society', of course, is in fact the readership of *The Spectator*, who are, strangely, insubstantial and ghostly precisely in their very extensiveness. Addison is advised by his printer that three thousand copies of the paper sell every day. But there are not merely three thousand readers; rather, since he computes that each copy is read by some twenty people, the readership is sixty thousand. Fifty-seven thousand, then, fail to make the financial 'speculation' involved in actually purchasing the paper; they are, in a sense, its invisible readers, readers who remain 'invisible' in that they are not financially 'realised' or represented. There is no 'material' engagement between Addison and this audience; 'spectating' in this cultural communication 'immaterialises' both spectator and invisible audience or readership.

A number of propositions are now available. First, there is a confusion between Spectator-as-Theorist and Spectator-as-Ghost which facilitates a rhetorical equation of theorist with ghost in *The Spectator* papers. Secondly, theoretical speculation itself becomes characterised as an 'immaterial' activity, a ghostly act of scopophilia carried out by a ghostly writer. Thirdly, there is the effect of such 'speculation' on its audience; they, in turn, become 'immaterialised' in the act of reading the theory, disappearing into the insubstantial realm of speculation or the Barthesian spectrum itself. Such a situation is articulated all the more precisely in the twentieth century, through the medium of photography: photography is just such a 'speculation', a theoretical practice which immaterialises those involved in its means of production.

As already noted, early photographs produced ghostly traces of movement in the 'spectrum' due to long exposure-times. This affected modern art. Scharf points out:

Like the human optical system the camera too has its own kind of persistence of vision; but unlike the eye it retains more. The eye is incapable of seeing more than the most immediate continuity patterns of moving objects; the camera can preserve the whole spectrum of animation.[26]

Scharf claims this as the single most obvious influence on the paintings of Corot and Monet wherein the traces of movement provide a ghostly aura around the otherwise defined shapes on the canvas. A kind of 'indefinition' produced by the camera lens led to the immaterialisation and deterritorialisation evident in Impressionist painting.

Faster shutter-speeds eliminated this effect in photography; but many artists and moderns kept it in their work, producing what can be regarded as the first 'cinematic' photographs wherein an 'invisible' world or aura surrounding fairly defined forms began to ghost the images. Apart from the earlier slightly unfocussed photography of Julia Margaret Cameron which had a similar effect, this reaches its most advanced state in the Futurist 'photo-dynamism' of Bragaglia. Bragaglia adopted a Bergsonian parlance to suggest that he was capable of capturing on film the interstices of time and duration. This was not just an extension of the work of

Muybridge and Marey, according to Bragaglia, but something different which allowed him to 'capture the complexity of movement, rhythm, reality and dematerialization'. In his own words:

> To put it crudely chronophotography could be compared to a clock on the face of which only the half-hours are marked, cinematography to one on which the minutes too are indicated, and Photodynamism to a third on which are marked not only the seconds, but also the intermomental fractions existing in the passages between the seconds.[27]

This area, broadly equivalent to the Proustian '*intermittences du coeur*', was a favourite territory of modernist artists, concerned with what happened not at the level of material and historical action itself but rather with what happened in that area 'between the acts', an area whose material status becomes dubious, having no strict temporal or historical 'moment'. Such an area is one of 'between-ness', indeterminacy or *mediation* itself. As such, it obsessed those artists who were all extremely conscious of their own cultural medium, making art about art. It is important for the present argument, however, that this photodynamic form (whose results look very like those early photographs with their ghostly traces of movement elsewhere and from another time) presents — if we take Bragaglia at his word — not a material historical action in its moment but rather an 'immaterialisation' of historical action as such. It takes the historically and temporally real, and renders it ghostly, places it in a time 'between the acts', a time which has no material correlate or substance. The question being asked by such art relates to the substantiality of an action which has no secular moment in which it may 'really' exist.

Proust's great novel, *A la recherche du temps perdu*, starts in a cinematic 'dark room' or *camera obscura* where a magic lantern show goes on; its narrative also begins from a moment of negation, as Marcel suffers from the kiss withheld by his mother. Woolf begins *To the Lighthouse* on a contrary note, an affirmation that a voyage to the lighthouse (a *camera lucida*) will take place the following day. It is important, however, that such affirmation is itself immediately negated here, for one of the things dramatised in this novel is the confrontation of painting and photography: in a sense there is no return to the *camera lucida*. The text opens with James cutting out photographs from an illustrated catalogue, and it will close with Lily Briscoe 'completing' her painting at the end. But there is more to the confrontation of painting and photography, both theoretically and historically, in this novel.

To the Lighthouse has a broadly neo-classical format in temporal terms. Despite its huge modernist temporal interstice in the 'Time Passes' section, it is organised around a notional period of twenty-four hours. It starts in the evening with James's request to make the visit to the lighthouse the following morning; the interstitial section, though tracing a number of years, describes that temporal passage as if it were the dream-time of a single night only, with the fall into darkness and dreamy entropy or decay followed immediately by a dawning re-birth; and the third section then opens, in the morning (and now as if the following morning) with a trip to the lighthouse about to take place. The initial negation of the text's opening affirmative word, 'Yes', turns out to have been a mere deferral and to have enacted the positive nature of the original affirmation.

That temporal organisation gives a structure of *light-dark-light* to the novel. It has been noted many times that this echoes the flashing of the lighthouse itself, but the importance of the sequence is more significant than mere mimetic form. The central dark section is, above all, a darkened house, a *camera obscura* through which the text has to pass before the 'negative' at the start can be 'positively' realised at the end, in substantial action and in the successful development or completion of an image. In a sense, then, the novel itself approximates closely to the structural form of photography. Lily, it will be remembered, has difficulty in completing her painting, partly because people move, and partly because she has doubts about its validity as a representational mode. It is all the more important, then, that she takes up her work again in the third section, that 'following morning' where we are in the realm of the *camera lucida*, the lighthouse itself. The original *camera lucida*, of course, was an instrument which aided not photography but rather drawing. But Lily's success in this third section seems to owe little to painting itself; on the contrary, the very painting begins to assume the form of a photograph. First, Lily herself begins to 'stroke', like the light of the lighthouse:

she made her first decisive stroke. The brush descended. It flickered brown over the white canvas; it left a running mark. A second time she did it — a third time. And so pausing and so flickering, she attained a dancing rhythmical movement, as if the pauses were one part of the rhythm and the strokes another, and all were related; and so, lightly and swiftly pausing, striking, she scored her canvas with brown running nervous lines which had no sooner settled there than they enclosed (she felt it looming out at her) a space . . .[28]

Flickering herself now, offering intermittent lights in this enclosed dark space, Lily assumes the position of Mrs Ramsay earlier, as a central element in the text of which the lighthouse is a symbol. Her painting, moreover, now mimics the organisation of the novel: light-dark-light, for the dark line is her shifting the tree closer to the middle of the canvas as she had earlier planned to do. The centrality of this dark arborescent line is confirmed at the end of the text, as she completes her work while the others reach the lighthouse:

There it was — her picture . . . It would be hung in the attics, she thought; it would be destroyed. But what did that matter? she asked herself, taking up her brush again. She looked at the steps; they were empty; she looked at her canvas; it was blurred. With a sudden intensity as if she saw it clear for a second, she drew a line there, in the centre. It was done; it was finished.[29]

It is almost as if painting here has become, like the literary text, modelled on the photograph as a play of light in a dark space; and this 'photo-text', developing in the 'Time Passes' section, is one which contains the flow and passage of time or history, extremely like the ghostly photodynamism of Bragaglia or, much more appropriately here, like those slightly out of focus photos by Julia Margaret Cameron. Like the photographic work of both these practitioners, *To The Lighthouse* provides a photo-text taken in that intermittent moment 'between the acts', in the flicker, so to speak.

I suggest, however, that it is more apt to compare the text to the work of Julia Margaret Cameron for the simple reason that the real figure ghosting the novel is this early woman photographer, who was Virginia Woolf's great-aunt Julia. While writing the text, Woolf was also occupied in researching and writing a preface for a collection of photographs by this great-aunt after whom the partly visible ghost of *To The Lighthouse*, Woolf's mother Julia Stephen, was named. Cameron's own name echoes in the figure of Cam in the novel; but there are many other more important ways in which the photographer haunts the text.

At the dinner which occurs near the end of the novel's first section, candles are lit and the room becomes transfigured, assuming for itself the form and figure of the lighthouse which is supposed to be in the distance, elsewhere:

Now all the candles were lit, and the faces on both sides of the table were brought nearer by the candle light, and composed, as they had not been in the twilight, into a party round a table, for the night was now shut off by panes of glass, which, far from giving any accurate view of the outside world, rippled it so strangely that here, inside the room, seemed to be order and dry land; there, outside, a reflection in which things wavered and vanished, waterily.

Some change at once went through them all, as if this had really happened . . .[30]

If the text is in one sense the history of the house or family, and of Woolf's own house or family, then we have here a version of the *Annals of My Glass House*, which happens to be the title of a brief piece in which Julia Margaret Cameron related her attempts, successes and failures, at photography. Woolf is asserting a lineage or tradition for herself, a house for herself, stemming not simply from her mother Julia Stephen but also indirectly from her great-aunt whose favourite photograph was precisely a portrait of a 21-year-old Julia Stephen taken in April 1867.

Woolf was interested in Cameron's photography for some time prior to and during the composition of *To The Lighthouse*. In January and March 1923 she insists in letters that Vita Sackville-West should come and look at 'my great-aunt's photographs of Tennyson and other people'.[31] She had already conceived her play, *Freshwater*, based on incidents in Cameron's life and on her relations with Tennyson, G.F. Watts and Ellen Terry, sometime in 1919. It was in 1923 that she made her first draft of the play, to rewrite it for its actual performance some twelve years later, and significantly with her painter sister, Vanessa Bell, playing the role of the photographer Cameron. But it was in 1926, while at work on *To The Lighthouse*, that she was most concerned with her forebear, asking Bell for letters and photos to aid her in preparing the book which eventually appeared as *Victorian Photographs of*

Famous Men and Fair Women, containing Cameron's photographs and with prefaces by Woolf and Roger Fry. While thinking on this book, she also considered the development of Bell's painting, following her exhibition at Leicester Galleries, and precisely the same kind of confrontation between painting and photography occurs in her thought:

What I think is this: there is a divinely lovely landscape of yours at Charleston: one of flashing brilliance, of sunlight crystallised, of diamond durability. This I consider your masterpiece. I do not think the big picture of Angelica etc. in the garden quite succeeds. I expect the problem of empty spaces, and how to model them, has rather baffled you. There are flat passages, so that the design is not completely apprehended. Of the smaller works, I think the blue boat by the bridge is my favourite. Indeed, I am amazed, a little alarmed (for as you have the children, the fame by rights belongs to me) by your combination of pure artistic vision and brilliance of imagination. A mistress of your brush — you are now undoubtedly that; but still I think the problems of design on a large scale slightly baffle you. For example the aunt Julia photograph.[32]

It is interesting in the light of this to record, further, Woolf's feeling about her own work — writing — at this moment; for there is a close echo in what she finds successful and what distasteful in her current novel:

how lovely some parts of the *Lighthouse* are! Soft and pliable, and I think deep, and never a word wrong for a page at a time. This I feel about the dinner party and the children in the boat; but not of Lily on the lawn. That I do not much like. But I like the end.[33]

Lily on the lawn, Angelica in the garden; it is as if they are both found lacking in comparison with Cameron's photographs, or even, indeed, with Vanessa Bell's photographs. Further, the end of *To The Lighthouse*, with its assertions of the value of the photogenic (where both painting and text succeed as they approach the condition of the photographic as described earlier) lends credence to the argument that Woolf in this novel strives to construct a lineage for herself stretching back to Julia Margaret Cameron through the mediation of representations and photographs of her mother, established by both Cameron (in her many portraits of Julia Stephen) and by Woolf herself (in her textual portrait). This 'amazing portrait of mother', as Bell called it, produces a heritage that significantly by-passes Leslie Stephen and returns instead to Julia Margaret Cameron's roots in India. In her identification of her own graphic art with that of her sister in the dislike of their management of lawn-scenes, Woolf finds a common heritage for the two female children of Leslie and Julia Stephen, and one which involves a *clinamen* or swerve from the direct (and masculinist) linear historical line of supposed descent. It is important that this photographic heritage, in making this historical swerve, also involves a geographical swerve, locating roots in colonial India where Cameron was born as Julia Pattle. *To The Lighthouse* is, in a sense, Woolf's own 'Passage to India', and its writing is informed by her reading of Forster's novel, as recorded in her diary in December 1925.

But this search for an alternative lineage based on gender is not, strictly speaking, a search for 'roots' or even for rootedness. Thinking in terms of a female lineage and a lineage that swerves towards the colonised races involves Woolf in precisely an erasure of the notion of 'roots' as such, together with its concomitant notions of the certainty of identity and stability of personal or familial boundary. It involves an implicit attack on the law of the stable name of the father.

What Woolf found in common with Julia Margaret Cameron in their respective arts was an effect that can only really be described as *immaterialisation*. In her accurate description of Cameron's photographs, she points out that:

She used to say that in her photographs a hundred negatives were destroyed before she achieved a good result; her object being to overcome realism by diminishing just in the least degree the precision of the focus.[34]

This is exactly how Woolf at this time saw the development of her own work. In November 1926 she is looking forward to starting *Orlando* (as yet untitled). The project as such is not entirely clear, but its fundamental orientation is:

Yet I am now and then haunted by some semi-mystic very profound life of a woman, which shall be all told on one occasion; and time shall be utterly obliterated; future shall somehow blossom out of the past. One incident — say the fall of a flower — might contain it. My theory being that the actual event practically does not exist — nor time either.[35]

The 'actual' or historical here is threatened by immaterialisation or deterritorialisation. According to Benjamin this is precisely a central effect of the mechanical reproduction of photography, for, as he writes, 'From a photographic negative, for example, one can make any number of prints; to ask for the "authentic" print makes no sense'.[36]

The very reproducibility which is the condition of photography constitutes an attack on the notion of an 'origin' which 'grounds' representation; the 'root' of the photographic representation becomes un-grounded or deterritorialised and lacks the specificity of a presence. History, as a continuous series of such ontological presences, is in turn supplanted by an immaterialisation of itself in the age of mechanical reproduction. In postmodern understandings of history, it is not that history does not exist, nor is it that it is entirely forgotten; rather, history haunts the postmodern critic all the more, but in a ghostly shape, as a form or figure whose material ground can no longer be regarded as easily accessible. Further, as suggested earlier, the postmodern critic is herself or himself threatened with precisely similar deterritorialisation, ghostliness: this is, in fact, the condition of 'speculation'. It is also, of course, exactly the condition of photography.

It follows from this that photography is better considered not as Coburn's 'modernist' art-form, but rather as a postmodern art-form *par excellence*. It focusses not on the reality of a presence but rather, as was tangentially suggested by Barthes, on what is absent, what is *not* there. The most 'typical' photograph, literally, is precisely the blurred image, the Cameron- or Bragaglia-like picture 'in motion', so to speak. The 'spectrum' of the photograph is akin here to Virilio's description of the city: a stasis that contains movement and speed. Virilio's comment can be applied more or less directly to the photograph:

La cité n'est qu'une halte, un point sur la voie synoptique d'une trajectoire, ancien glacis militaire, chemin de crête, frontière ou rivage, ou s'associaient instrumentalement le regard et la vitesse de déplacement des véhicules, comme je l'ai dit il y a longtemps, il n'y a que de la *circulation habitable* . . .[37]

Movement, speed and displacement are all inscribed in the typical photograph: its spectrum reveals not what is there as presence but rather it reveals what is always already elsewhere; it produces 'presence' only if that term is understood as carrying the sense of 'ghostly' presence.[38] The similarity of this structural aspect of photography with many postmodern critical practices should be obvious, as more and more critics attend to a text's 'unsaid', to its significant absences or 'gaps', to what is, as it were, the *ghost* of the text which is their ostensible object.

When Coburn asserted the modernity of photography, he was most convincing when he showed it as a fundamentally post-modern form despite himself; for he suggested that it photo-graphed not what was there in reality but rather a world which could (or in some cases could not) be: a 'futurist' world of sorts. In his vortographs, he was concerned to make the world unrecognis-able, to immaterialise the material historical objects in his abstracted (mis)representations of them. Since the moderns in other arts were striving towards a future, he asked, why should not photography proceed in the same spirit:

Why should not its subtle rapidity be utilised to study movement? Why not repeated successive exposures of an object in motion on the same plate? Why should not perspective be studied from angles hitherto neglected or unob-served? Why, I ask you earnestly, need we go on making commonplace little exposures of subjects that may be sorted into groups of landscapes, portraits, and figure studies? Think of the joy of doing something which it would be impossible to classify, or to tell which was the top and which the bottom![39]

In other words, Coburn here thinks of the joy of doing something which cannot be generically rooted in the recognisable and always already known or predetermined; he prefers, in his abstract vortographic work, the immaterialisation of the historical object, together with its deterritorialisation as he leaves it with no clearly defined top or root.

Following her own exploration of the imprecision of representa-tion which is the postmodern condition of photographic writing, Woolf attempted a similar indeterminacy in her construction of Orlando, a character who defies territorialisation in terms of gender; and this follows on from her own strategy in *To The Lighthouse* where Lily fades into the position of Mrs Ramsay, yesterday flows into tomorrow, Virginia Woolf herself slides into Vanessa Bell whose children she envied, and these all fade in a cinematic shift or 'wash' into Juia Margaret Cameron, that shady ghost who understands the text.

Woolf's quest for a heritage which by-passes the name of the father is, in its clinamen, necessarily imprecise and can offer no historical certitudes; but her desire to construct this alternative history is clear. In a letter to Vita Sackville-West she asks for information regarding the legitimacy of a coronet, for 'I'm trying to prove my great Aunt's descent from a Neapolitan adventurer and a French Marquis. But I have no time'.[40] The French Marquis was Antoine Chevalier de l'Etang who was in the service of the Nawab of Oudh (now Uttar Pradesh). His daughter, Adeline, married James Pattle who was also in colonial service, and Julia Margaret Cameron was a child of this marriage. In *To The Lighthouse* itself, there is an odd passage which speaks indirectly to this history. Lily, watching Mr Ramsay and the others heading for the light-house, imagines Mrs Ramsay there before her:

thinking again of Mrs Ramsay on the beach; the cask bobbing up and down; and the pages flying. Why, after all these years, had that survived, ringed round, lit up, visible to the last detail, with all before it blank and all after it blank, for miles and miles?

'Is it a boat? Is it a cask?' Mrs Ramsay said. And she began hunting round for her spectacles . . . Shouts came from a world far away. Steamers vanished in stalks of smoke on the horizon.[41]

This odd object of vision, hovering imprecisely between cork, cask and boat, recalls an apocryphal story 'from a world far away', a story which survives when all else is lost, of the death of James Pattle, Cameron's father. It was said that he was a drunk and the greatest liar in India. When he died, he was sent home, pickled (literally, it seems) in a cask, and accompanied on this traumatic journey by his wife. This cask, it was also said, in a bizarre prefiguration of Conrad's Stevie, exploded and, as Quentin Bell puts it, 'ejected his unbottled corpse before his widow's eyes, drove her out of her wits, set the ship on fire and left it stranded in the Hooghly'.[42]

The passage in *To The Lighthouse* which indirectly alludes to this occurs during that fertile moment of influence or interfusion between Lily and Mrs Ramsay, which provokes Lily into making a photographic *instantané* or snapshot of the moment:

The moment at least seemed extraordinarily fertile. She rammed a little hole in the sand and covered it up, by way of burying in it the perfection of the moment. It was like a drop of silver in which one dipped and illumined the darkness of the past.[43]

Again, then, precisely at the moment when the apocryphal tale of James Pattle's death shadily ghosts the text, Lily contrives to make a dark box in the sand, with its hole or lens and silver which helps lighten and fix this dark moment of a past and shadowy history.

But the death of James Pattle, and Julia Margaret Cameron's oriental 'roots', lead both to the next stage of the present argument. Though Conrad's anarchists may have failed to shift the earth's geo-political axis in the bomb-outrage of *The Secret Agent*, and though Woolf may have been unable to state directly her alternatively-gendered heritage, photography itself supplies the necessary machinery for effecting such geo-political and gendered shifts in the cultural mapping of the world and its history.

3.2 BLACK MYTHOLOGY

It is important that the Professor's 'photographic' pneumatic balls are made of 'india-rubber', a product which comes from Brazil and more importantly in the present context from Malaysia, where the British had made heavy investments in rubber in the 1890s. It is at the end of this decade that Conrad engages directly with the issue of imperialist exploitation and its racial corollaries, in texts such as *Lord Jim*, set in Malay, and perhaps especially in *Heart of Darkness*, a textual voyage *au bout de la nuit*, an explicit journey into darkness and obscurity, five years prior to the writing of *The Secret Agent*. Interestingly, five years is a period known to the ancient world as a *lustrum*, meaning a purificatory sacrifice made after the quinquennial census in Roman ritual. *The Secret Agent*, then, as a novel which tries unsuccessfully to be a revelatory kind of detective-fiction might productively be seen as the product of Conrad's attempt to expiate Marlow's famous lie of 1902. But the single most important factor to recall here is that *The Secret Agent* fails to be a confessional text: confession is undone with the same kind of retreat into obscurity as we had in *Heart of Darkness*, a production of secrecy and enigmatic obscurity by those agents of secret narrative, Marlow and Conrad. Like the negating lie which closes *Heart of Darkness*, *The Secret Agent* is oriented away from the positivist impetus necessary to the validation of a confessional text. But *Heart of Darkness* is more important than this; in its concern with colonialism, the violent imposition of white 'enlightenment' on black 'savagery', it shared the period's ideological interest in the construction of a 'primitivism' against which 'civilised' modes of behaviour are to be defined.

A number of patronising modernists, like true 'White Fathers', assured themselves that the civilised could learn from the primitive (though it should be immediately indicated that what they were about to learn was, of course, what they had always already 'known': their own 'superiority' of development and superior political and ethical values). In a deconstruction of the opposition of the concepts of civil and savage these writers indulged in a spurious search not for the 'inner light' which had been the goal of their eighteenth-century precursors, but rather for the inner darkness or obscurity which they aligned with black races and which they assumed to be at the primitive or primary origins of human thought and culture. As Said has shown, the period was rife in the cultural construction of an 'orient'; but my argument here extends this. What we have in the modernist culture of this moment is a shift away from the cultural dominance of the sunny Mediterranean and its (en)light(ened) Greco-Roman values towards another geo-construction, not quite the Arnoldian Hebraism to this Hellenism, but rather a construction identified as the 'middle east' and 'Africa'. It is this construction, fairly clearly, which dominates political thought in the postmodern occident. It is as if the attempt to shift the earth's axis in *The Secret Agent* at the Greenwich Observatory had in fact succeeded; and I shall argue here that the photographic culture of postmodernism plays a crucial role in effecting this neo-copernican reovolution.

When Roger Fry wrote his 'Essay in Aesthetics' in 1909, he concerned himself centrally with what was to become a major obsession of his contemporaries: an interest in 'primitivism', dressed up as 'instinct' in the attempt to domesticate its nudity. In considering the question of appropriate responses to art, Fry pretends to find causal relations between perception and historical motor-response, and the vehicle of such causation is instinct: we see a bull, for instance, and instinct makes us flee. Such instinct was supposed to be natural, pre-ideological and pre-cultural; and this was thought to be a major part of its implied value. Art (and especially cinema), Fry argued, provided the same intensity of emotion as seeing a bull would do, but without the same motor-response, since, like Samuel Johnson, we all knew ourselves to be at the scene of an art-work and not at the scene of a crime. The discovery of instinct, then, which is supposedly primitive or originary, would be a counter to ideology and the falsity inhering in a consciousness suffering from the dross of cultural beliefs and prejudices which veil the area between the work of art and its perceiver. The discovery of instinct was like a dance of the seven veils in which the perceiver is supposed to come closer to the object of perception. But such a 'return to nature' is itself productive of ideology, of a 'black mythology' so to speak, for it tends to be instrumental in a racial (and gendered) stereotyping. The mysterious object behind the veils is an Other both sexually and racially for the white fathers in western theory.

Fry was impressed by eastern art, praising it highly in his review of the 'Munich Exhibition of Mohammedan Art' in 1910, for instance. At the same time, he articulated a theoretical position in reviewing M. Helen Tongue's book of *Bushmen Drawings*, where his interest in instinct finds a geo-political discursive location in the art of 'primitive' races. But most significantly here, it is thanks to photography that Fry appreciates the validity, even the 'civilised' status of such drawings which some time before would have been subject to ridicule at the hands of the art establishment of the civilised west. These Bushman drawings show movement or imply motion in their objects:

Most curious of all are the cases . . . of animals trotting, in which the gesture is seen by us to be true only because our slow and imperfect vision has been helped by the instantaneous photograph. Fifty years ago we would have rejected such a drawing as absurd; we now know it to be a correct statement of one movement in the action of trotting.[44]

These 'primitives', untainted by ideological acculturation, have always been closer to the truths of nature, truths which are revealed to our dim eyes only thanks to the light-writing of photography. But that is to say, of course, that the 'truth' sub-scribed to here is precisely the truth as revealed or constructed by the technology of scientific and industrial culture, a truth based on the ground of light and of lightwritings, the white mythology of heliocentric thought in the west itself.[45]

By the end of this decade when Fry reviewed the 'Negro Sculpture' at the Chelsea Book Club he is more aware of the vast implications of his interest in 'primitivism'. We can chart from here the beginning of the discursive shift in the mapping of 'civilisation' itself:

What a comfortable mental furniture the generalisations of a century ago must have afforded! What a right little, tight little, round little world it was when Greece was the only source of culture, when Greek art, even in Roman copies, was the only indisputable art, except for some Renaissance repetitions! . . . And now, in the last sixty years, knowledge and perception have poured upon us so fast that the whole well-ordered system has been blown away, and we stand bare to the blast, scarcely able to snatch a hasty generalisation or two to cover our nakedness for a moment.[46]

Here Fry strips himself bare to assert an identification with the producers of 'Negro Sculpture' against Greco-Romanism. The cultural events of the years since 1860 (that is, broadly since the supervention of photography) have effected a neo-copernican revolution, re-shaping once more the round and tight little world which we have known since the Renaissance rediscovered the ancient Greeks and their sunny Mediterranean light.

Lawrence was fond of the Lear-like nudity proposed by Fry, a nudity confused with the 'primitivism' and supposed innocence of the child from *Macbeth*, naked and newborn, 'striding the blast' (a Blast produced in these times, of course, by Wyndham Lewis). In 1921 precisely the kind of 'negro sculpture' of which Fry wrote with admiration turns up in *Women in Love*. In London's bohemian cafe, the first thing Minette discovers about Gerald Crich is that he had explored the Amazon where he found that the 'savage' people of the Amazon are 'too much like other people, not exciting, after the first acquaintance'. This revelation produces a telling relation between these two:

She looked at him steadily with her naive eyes, that rested on him and roused him so deeply, that it left his upper self quite calm. It was rather delicious, to feel her drawing his self-revelations from him, as from the very innermost dark marrow of his body. She wanted to know. And her eyes seemed to be looking through into his naked organism.[47]

The revelatory confession of self here is described in terms of an X-ray photograph, with Gerald stripped and photographed into the 'dark marrow' of his organism.

Savagery and nudity are aligned further when the party return to Halliday's flat to spend the night there. In the morning, Gerald comes upon Halliday and Maxim sitting naked before the fire, and Halliday is delighted to hear that Gerald has lived in a climate where 'one could do without clothing altogether'. Gerald, bemused, asks why clothing makes such a difference, and Halliday's reply is that nudity would provide an escape from the tyranny of the visual, from the scopophiliac (or photological) organisation of perception:

'. . . one would *feel* things instead of merely looking at them. I should feel the air move against me, and feel the things I touched, instead of having only to look at them. I'm sure life is all wrong because it has become much too visual — we can neither hear nor feel nor understand, we can only see. I'm sure that is entirely wrong.'[48]

Oedipus, of course, found another way to deal with the tyranny of the visual. But the argument here seems to go that a savage nudity would allow for a greater tactile sense, that 'blindness' would produce 'insight'; and correspondingly, there would be a greater materiality or sense of plastic freedom in art. This is precisely what Fry praised in his essay on 'Negro Sculpture'.

It is also what Maxim (the Russian) and Birkin both find in the example of west Pacific art in Halliday's flat, that carving that disturbs Gerald so:

One was a woman sitting naked in a strange posture, and looking tortured, her abdomen stuck out. The young Russian explained that she was sitting in child-birth, clutching the ends of the band that hung from her neck, one in each hand, so that she could bear down, and help labour.[49]

The carving reminds Gerald of an actual foetus, consolidating a link between the carving and Minette, who is also pregnant and has a neckband at which she tugs. Minette also has a slightly affected speech-impediment, and 'spoke her r's like w's, lisping with a slightly babyish pronunciation' which makes her infantile.[50] She and Gerald share a room, or as she would think it, they share a 'woom'/womb. When Gerald stares at the carving, then, he sees in its blackness a kind of negative image of Minette, an image of her as in a Man Ray rayograph; he thus returns the 'compliment' of seeing her as in an X-ray negative when he contemplates the naked organism of Minette in the black and obscure object of desire that sits inside her, literally like a foetus. The carving works like a photograph; Gerald, though looking in its direction, sees not it itself but rather a naked Minette with this black image inside her. The 'logic' in the argument that primitive nudity provides an escape from scopophilia is controverted here: this instance of black, 'savage' nudity merely encourages the scopophiliac and photological attitude of Gerald. The comprehension of the art itself is entirely photological. The carving is praised because it 'reveals' or exposes the condition of pregnancy, and we have a 'development' of the black negative carving in the vital white form of Minette who, as we already know, will model for the photographer Frederick Carmarthen to make some money for herself.

The two chapters in which the totem figures prominently, 'Crème de Menthe' and 'Totem', are distinguished by an obsessive haze or mist which renders all boundaries indeterminate. The description of the cafe not only looks like a description of a smoky cinema, but it also contains a number of elements which figure in my present argument:

Gerald went through the push doors into the large, lofty room where the faces and heads of the drinkers showed dimly through the haze of smoke, reflected more dimly, and repeated *ad infinitum* in the great mirrors on the walls, so that one seemed to enter a vague, dim world of shadowy drinkers humming within an atmosphere of blue smoke. There was, however, the red plush of the seats to give substance within the bubble of pleasure.[51]

The pleasure-dome, like Coleridge's in *Kubla Khan*, seems to promise vision but becomes instead 'The shadow of the dome of pleasure', where things fade into insubstantiality. In the cafe, all is threatened with immaterialisation, especially in that endless reduplication in framed mirrors like reproduced portrait photographs — or like the postmodern seriographs of Andy Warhol, say.

Minette then speculates on the financial rewards of photography; that is, she thinks of 'realising' herself as a counter to this immaterialisation. But perhaps most importantly, there is a description of Birkin in the cafe which is uncannily proleptic of Benjamin's thoughts on the effect of film on the actor, thoughts which have profoundly influenced the postmodern consideration of the relation of an image to its original in the *société du spectacle* as delineated by Debord or Baudrillard.[52]

Birkin 'looked muted, unreal, his presence left out', and this ghostly presence/absence of Birkin in the cafe, his immaterialisation before Minette, is itself reiterated before the carving. The carving suggests a loss of consciousness when Gerald stands before it: 'it was rather wonderful, conveying the suggestion of the extreme of physical sensation, beyond the limits of mental consciousness'. When Gerald asks Birkin for his opinion on it, Birkin has already begun to fade far away as he contemplates the deterritorialising and immaterialising object:

> Birkin suddenly appeared in the doorway, in white pyjamas and wet hair, and a towel over his arm. He was aloof and white, and somehow evanescent. . . .
>
> 'I say, Rupert!'
>
> 'What?' The single white figure appeared again, a presence in the room.
>
> 'What do you think of that figure there? I want to know,' Gerald asked.
>
> Birkin, white and strangely ghostly, went over to the carved figure of the savage woman in labour . . .[53]

The photological consciousness, the scopophiliac stare, produces an immaterialisation of both spectator and spectrum; they become as silhouetted magic lantern figures or images of themselves, groundless and insubstantial, ghostly.

Such 'speculative' activity is, of course, related to capital, to money which can 'realise' or make *en liquide*, currency, that which is not yet valid or current. Minette will pose for photographs to make money, for instance, which helps her 'realise' herself in fiscal terms, while 'de-realising' or imagining herself in 'specular' terms. But this is important in a wider consideration of the cultural prominence of photography. There are many precursors of the contemporary photograph, including the obvious machines of Daguerre, Niepce, Talbot and others. Freund points to another mode of representation, similar to photography in its speed and effects, and just as capable as photography was of putting portrait painters out of work. This was the silhouette which proved enormously popular in nineteenth-century France. M. de Silhouette did not invent this method; but his name has an interesting link to this photology under discussion. As Freund points out, he was a Finance Minister who raised taxes in 1750 to 'realise' France in fiscal terms and bail it out of a desperate situation. For a time it looked as if he would be successful, and his popularity and stature rose accordingly; but the debts in question proved too large and as repayments fell behind schedule, so his popularity and stature waned, then plummeted:

A new style in clothing appeared: narrow coats without pleats and breeches without pockets. Without money to store in them, what good were pockets? These clothes were said to be styled à la Silhouette, and to this day, anything as insubstantial as a shadow is called a silhouette; in a short time, the brilliant Controller General had become no more than a shadow of himself.[54]

Silhouette was but a silhouette of a Silhouette, a man without aura. He became like a photograph of himself, lacking substance and ground: immaterialised and deterritorialised.

This had been seen before in those proto-photological *Spectator* papers of Addison. *The Spectator* of 3 March 1711, for instance, relates a ghostly dream whose allegorical meanings focus entirely on public credit and financial speculation. Addison, like Birkin (and Pound, perhaps), falls into an unconscious dreamy state before being able to 'realise' the substance of an art-work which confronts him (in Addison's case, the dream-allegory). Both situations involve the attempt to realise the speculative and both see a realisation of self-presence as a corollary or consequence of that financial accreditation. But the photological nature of each situation simply reveals how unfounded, how deterritorialised and immaterial or ghostly are those engaged in such photological self-portraiture or self-identification. The scopophiliac speculator is constantly threatened by the historical immaterialisation of self; in the terms of capitalism, with the loss of financial assets; in photological terms, with loss of representability or even of ideological 'respectability'.

Addison's papers start by promising enlightenment. The opening epigram speaks directly of this:

Non fumum ex fulgore, sed ex fumo dare lucem
Cogitat, ut speciosa dehinc miracula promat.

This is lifted from Horace's *Ars Poetica*, where Horace is considering the kind of poet who 'does not mean to let his flash of fire die
away in smoke, but to make the smoke give way to light' in telling
tales of wonder.[55] Yet the entire proto-photological basis of the
Spectator as an organ of enlightened vision plays directly into that
tyranny of the *optics* which simply works to immaterialise, to
deterritorialise, to render the reality of itself, of its objects and its
readers foggy, smoky, like a London artist's cafe or like the coffee-
houses in which the paper was dreamed up and read in a tobacco
trance made possible by the speculations of a beginning imperialism and colonialism. The opening of the very first *Spectator* paper
proper, is extremely telling when considered alongside the cultural and geo-political shift for which I argue that the photological
attitude is partly responsible. The text opens:

I have observed, that a Reader seldom peruses a Book with Pleasure, 'till he
knows whether the Writer of it be a black or a fair man . . .[56]

This is the first consideration which Addison addresses in a list of
factors pertaining to a reader's acquaintance with the person of an
author. The similar confrontation of supposedly enlightening
whiteness with a smoky or hazy blackness recurs in twentieth-
century modernism; but with one crucial difference involving a
geo-political shift in the organisation of white and black space in
the world. The 'black mythology' aroused by the interest in
primitivism re-maps the cultural space of purity and negritude.
Greek sunshine and Oriental enigmatic smoke cede place to a new
configuration involving the middle east and Africa as counters in
the modernist and then postmodern geo-political configuration of
cultural thought and practices. Both *Heart of Darkness* and
Women in Love speak to this modification in the precise photological ways which I can now elaborate.

3.3 'MAKE MAPS, NOT PHOTOGRAPHS . . .'?

Marlow's tale in *Heart of Darkness* begins in the outdoors equivalent of Lawrence's bohemian London cafe where we saw the text

through a darkening photographic or seriographic glass. The misty darkness of the western port of London is the dominant feature, where 'Only the gloom to the west, brooding over the upper reaches, became more sombre every minute, as if angered by the approach of the sun'.[57] This west, then, is angered by an encroaching eastern or mediterranean light which darkens as it falls away to the west. Marlow's narration is directly related to this 'obscuring' mode:

Marlow was not typical (if his propensity to spin yarns be excepted), and to him the meaning of an episode was not inside like a kernel but outside, enveloping the tale which brought it out only as a glow brings out a haze, in the likeness of one of those misty halos that sometimes are made visible by the spectral illumination of moonshine.[58]

Conrad here begins a re-writing of the Arnoldian confrontation of Hellenism with Hebraism; and this involves a re-drawing of boundaries or maps. He thinks of the Romans in Britain on their imperialist exercise, when 'this also . . . has been one of the dark places of the earth', Britain owing its 'enlightened' status to that prior invasion of its ground or space:

'I was thinking of very old times, when the Romans first came here, nineteen hundred years ago — the other day. . . . Light came out of this river since — you say Knights? Yes; but it is like a running blaze on a plain, like a flash of lightning in the coulds. We live in the flicker — may it last as long as the old earth keeps rolling! But darkness was here yesterday.'[59]

Maps, especially geo-political and cultural maps, are not stable or naturally-fixed. Britain, source of supposed imperial enlightenment since at least the eighteenth century if not before, is itself illuminated by the flicker of a light that has passed from the Greco-Roman world towards it, and which will also run on through it and proceed elsewhere. There is no sense in which Britain or the 'enlightened' or civilised world is *by definition* a source or authorisation of light. Marlow traces the relay of this flickering torch that is 'enlightenment' from the Greco-Roman world through to contemporary Europe and on into Africa; and from this trading of the flow or current of the light the whole notion of imperialist 'civilised' enlightenment is shown to be based upon a lie, to be insubstantial (immaterial) and ungrounded (deterritorialised). Only the haze of an obscuring secret narrative can proceed from this ideology, and that is what Marlow produces, specifically in the closing lie to the Intended.

The geography of Marlow's encounter is significant. It is not a case of there being a light that can be identified as 'Greek' set against a darkness that can be similarly easily named as 'Oriental'; rather there is no locus of light that is fixed and immutable: 'We live in the flicker', like Lily Briscoe or Mrs Ramsay or those characters in the Proustian magic lantern. No geographic space has an *a priori* claim on light or on darkness; the map which Marlow looked at when he was a child has itself shifted its contours, been blacked in in different lines. In 1902 the mapping of the confrontation of light and dark involves Europe (specifically Belgium) and Africa (specifically Zaire, formerly the Belgian Congo). The polarities of this geo-political map or arrangement have shifted, and are now located around the Tropic of Cancer, with a suppositious light above it and the 'dark tropics' below. Such a shift is made possible because Marlow realises the insubstantiality of national or racial claims to light and dark. In the imperialist enterprise — the passing on of the flickering torch – no grounds, boundaries or identities of nations are stable. We may have thought of Britain or of Belgium as the territory from which we export light; but that light is not British or Belgian in the first place; it is not theirs to export, since it has merely been temporarily borrowed from a source elsewhere — Rome — which in turn had borrowed it from Athens, and so on, *ad infinitum*.

The confrontation of nations involved in the imperialist adventure, then, begins to assume precisely the same configuration as that between spectator and spectrum in the photographic interchange, which can be thought as a model for it. Conrad even describes its effect in similar terms, as the production of obscurity, of an immaterialisation or ghostliness in all the elements of his obscuring secret narratives, and of a deterritorialisation such that no boundaries are fixed but rather flow instead like those rivers which originally demarcate geographic if not geo-political boundaries, like the river Congo (or Zaire). This is but the precursor of that more explicit invocation of photography, light-writing, brought in to provoke a similar anarchist upheaval in the mapping of the world in *The Secret Agent*. The photographic mode of representation, and its effects on the cultural mapping of the world, are already partly responsible for this political orientation of the world and its shift around a Tropic of Cancer which becomes a locus of transgression and hence of authority. In later cultural terms, of course, that is the precise locus of Henry Miller's transgression against literature or the book as such.[60]

In Miller's forebear, Lawrence, there is another important geopolitical shift, again relevant to the photological impulse. Two somewhat mysterious characters appear and disappear in *Women in Love*, precisely during those photographic or scopophiliac personal relations mapped out above. In the cafe, the photographic stripping of Gerald and Minette by each other's gaze is interrupted, and their 'ghostliness' is bloodied as a consequence. Minette proclaims that she is not afraid of blood and when jeered at by 'a young man with a thick, pale, jeering face, who had just come to their table', she provides blood for the ghosts: 'For reply, she suddenly jabbed a knife across his thick, pale hand. He started up with a vulgar curse' and moves off, blood flowing from his hand.[61] At the moment when the characters are themselves becoming somewhat immaterial or ghostly in their photographic interchange, this other ghostly figure briefly appears. The scene moves from a marking with blood to a corresponding signification with a curse. But 'to mark with blood' (or, as Lawrence writes, 'blud', thereby drawing attention to the root-meaning of the word) is precisely 'to bless'; so the scene hovers uncertainly and uneasily, like the Hebrew word *darach*, between a blessing and a cursing,[62] and such instability or uncertainty, an undecidability about the roots of words and their grounding in this scene where they display their own deterritorialisation, draws further attention to the deterritorialised locus of the stranger's provenace. Gerald asks who he is:

'He's a Jew, really. I can't bear him.'

'Well, he's quite unimportant. . . .'

'They're all afwaid of me,' she said. 'Only the Jew thinks he's going to show his courage. But he's the biggest coward of them all, really, because he's afwaid of what people will think about him . . .'[63]

This character's diasporal deterritorialisation is matched almost immediately by that of a second ghostly or fleeting character back at Halliday's flat. This man is not pale, but Halliday's 'dark-skinned servant' who provokes surprise in Gerald because of his dapper clothes so that Gerald wonders 'if he were a gentleman, one of the Orientals down from Oxford'. But he is 'half a savage . . . Arab'. He is also a keen speculator of sorts, and is most certainly a counter to the notion that 'savagery', even 'Arab savagery' finds its enterprise in walking naked. He appears for two reasons: firstly, to make tea; secondly, to ask for money, to 'speculate'. Halliday speaks to him:

'What?' they heard his voice. 'What? What do you say? Tell me again. What? Want money? Want *more* money? But what do you want money for?' There was the confused sound of the Arab's talking, then Halliday appeared in the room, smiling also foolishly, and saying:
  'He says he wants money to buy underclothing. . . .'[64]

The expected Lawrentian confrontation, of white maleness (Birkin's ghostliness) against dark womanliness (the black totem), a confrontation symbolising civilised with savage, ideological with natural, is hereby complicated. The typical modernist decon-struction — which, if the opposition were thus simple, might apply to Lawrence — would be that the civilised can learn from the primitive to strip away the ideological dross of civilised manners to reveal the naked truth beneath. But the text and its photological manoeuvres do not allow for this; the geopolitical space of light and dark, of civilised and primitive, have clearly shifted.

The Arab who is 'half savage' but who wears civilised clothing becomes the dark component, countered by a 'pale' Jew who mingles with 'civilised' people in the cafe (the very civilised people, of course, who attack him in a savage manner). The modernist deconstruction of light and dark here proffers a literal displacement of the terms of the opposition and of the argument. Light and dark no longer settle on Greek and Oriental, but rather on wandering Jew and nomadic Arab, both rendered immaterial by the text and both in different ways deterritorialised. Once again, the mapping of 'enlightenment' against 'obscurity' has involved a re-drawing of boundaries, a different geopolitics in cultural thought.

These two examples, then, mark a shift in the way that *soidisant* 'western' thought orients itself, especially in political and cultural terms, in the twentieth century. The 'Other' of 'The West' is increasingly identified not as the 'eastern bloc' (the figure of Libidnikov the Russian becomes less relevant than the opposition of Arab and Jew, despite the proximity of this text to the moment of the Russian revolution), but as Africa and the Middle East. And, of course, the 'Self' which identifies itself against this geo-political configuration as 'The West' is, precisely, 'America', which sees both these areas as a threat to its own 'speculative' (theoretical and capitalist) identity. America now proposes itself, culturally, as a locus of enlightenment and speculation.

Coburn considered photography to be somehow specifically American in its very modernity, and he waxed lyrical about the streets of New York, a city best photographed in the dark, best revealed in its very obscure speculative immateriality and deterritorialisation:

Now to me New York is a vision that rises out of the sea as I come up the harbor on my Atlantic liner, and which glimmers for a while in the sun for the first of my stay amidst its pinnacles; but which vanishes, but for fragmentary glimpses, as I become one of the grey creatures that crawl about like ants, at the bottom of its gloomy caverns.[65]

Coburn in 1911 re-enacts the scenario laid out for Marlow in 1902 by Conrad. In these few brief years, the centre of photological enlightenment shifts from London to New York, partly because America had made photography its own art-form, an art that must live in and know itself among the skyscrapers of Chicago and New York.

Freund indicates that the daguerreotype, though popular in nineteenth-century Europe, became absolutely central to America at that time. It was in America that it attained the greatest currency and 'developed into a prosperous business':

In 1840 American society had not yet become rigidly stratified, and initiative was the passport to success. Between 1840 and 1860, the period of the daguerreotype's greatest popularity, America was shifting from an agricultural to an industrial society as the result of numerous technical advances: refrigeration, the invention of the reaper, new developments in mass production, the expansion of the railroads, and other products of American ingenuity. It was the period of rapid urbanisation in the East and of the gold rush and the frantic development of cities in the West. Proud of its success, the new country found in photography an ideal way to preserve and promote its achievements.[66]

This, then, was a period first of deterritorialisation (the shift away from agriculture, away from the soil or earth), secondly of a re-drawing of maps (the expansion of the railroads and shifting of the frontier marking the west), and thirdly a period of speculation (the gold rush). This, I insist, is precisely the condition of photography itself. It is not merely that photography 'records' this establish-ment of modern America; the photographic gesture is in large measure responsible for the construction of modern America in the first place. America is built upon photography.

This runs counter to the formulations of Deleuze and Guattari in 'Rhizome', the introduction to *Mille Plateaux*, where they insist that the map is rhizomatic while the photograph is rooted, a territorialising record of a material and fixed moment. But this is based on a misunderstanding of photography which is, in fact and on the contrary, paradigmatic of the rhizome; and it is in its rhizomaticity that we find its proper status not as a modernist art but rather as a postmodern cultural practice of cartography.

'Rhizome' constitutes an enormous attack on the 'language of flowers', though it itself is written and conceived in precisely a botanical register. Deleuze and Guattari proclaim that 'We are tired of the tree . . . We must no longer put our faith in trees, roots, or radicels; we have suffered enough from them'.[67] The rhizome is distinguished from all kinds of neo-Cartesian arborescent culture, from all the cultural thought which led eventually to structural-ism and its homological classifications and taxonomies which stratify or ground thought at all. Like the Futurists, Deleuze and Guattari were more interested in flight, in speeding away from any ground whatsoever; like Virilio, they are fascinated by the airport as the new 'city', the locus of a politics of transition, fluency, currency or speculative relations. The rhizome, though itself including 'lines of segmentation according to which it is stratified' becomes precisely rhizomatic to the extent that it flees such lines:

A rhizome never ceases to connect semiotic chains, organizations of power, and events in the arts, sciences, and social struggles. A semiotic chain is like a tuber gathering up very diverse acts — linguistic, but also perceptual, mimetic, gestural, and cognitive. There is no language in itself, no universality of language, but an encounter of dialects, patois, argots and special languages.[68]

This deterritorialisation of a language which refuses systematicity, which is based on heterogeneity and semiotic chains of connection, describes also the principles of cinematography, at least as they are adumbrated by Eisenstein for whom cinematography was 'first and foremost, montage'. In arguing this, Eisenstein distanced himself from Pudovkin and came very close to the rhizomatic formulations of Deleuze and Guattari; for montage is best considered not as an establishment of temporal continuity and mere conjunction but rather as the establishment of discontinuity, disjunction: 'montage is an idea that arises from the collision of independent shots — shots even opposite to one another: the "dramatic" principle'.[69] Photography itself, especially in its form as cinematography, is rhizomatically heterogeneous.

The rhizome shares even more than this with the photograph, however, for both are opposed to the principles of positivist thought. 'There are no points or positions in a rhizome, as one finds in a structure, tree or root. There are only lines',[70] and these lines of flight and deterritorialisation are never themselves determined or materialised. They have no specific origin (or root) and no end, but constitute an *intermezzo*, intermediary lines like those on a map (which have no material existence), subject to constant change and open to new but temporary 'arrangements' and re-arrangements.

The rhizome denies all identification or demarcation of boundaries; or, better, the rhizome is always and everywhere precisely the redrawing of boundaries. In itself, the rhizome is nothing; it has no positive or empirical existence but is always and everywhere merely a mediation, a temporary condition or 'arrangement'. In this respect, and in its denial of such positivist notions it shares the representational predilections of the photographic negative: both conspire to erase any positive or specific origin or telos, and with it any specificity for a ghostly spectator or spectrum. The photographic gesture works to immaterialise or deterritorialise both its subject and object, rendering them ghostly or speculative; it takes presence and relocates it at the level of representation, but in a representation which is itself, as Barthes has pointed out, extremely indeterminate. The point or *punctum* of the photograph is always in another place (*alibi*) and in another time (*alias*) than was thought at the moment of the photographic gesture. Photography, then, contrary to the general belief subscribed to by Freund, Deleuze, Guattari and others, does not 'record' the positive elements of an empirically historical and observable set of phenomena; rather, it generates a continual remapping of that history, producing or reproducing a material history in an immaterial and deterritorialised form, as a negative, as an obscurity, as an *unconscious*. In this respect, it is precisely rhizomatic:

> The important thing is never to reduce the unconscious, to interpret it or make it signify following the tree model, but rather to *produce the unconscious*, and, along with it, new utterances and other desires. The rhizome is precisely this production of the unconscious.[71]

And so, we might add, is the photograph.

There is a geo-political corollary to this. Deleuze and Guattari argue that the tree and arborescent thought dominate the west where the privileged relationship is with the forest and with deforestation for the cultivation of species of arborescent types (that is, for the cultivation of *species*, of that which can be looked at, scene of the photographic). This 'West' is the locus of a particular (agri)*culture*. The East, they write, presents another configuration, that of the relationship to steppe and garden (or desert and oasis) 'where the husbandry confined to closed spaces is set aside or put into parentheses or pushed back into the steppe of the nomads'. But what they have failed to add to this is that it is partly the photological culture of the west, its configuration of spectator and species, which is responsible for the geo-political shift of which they are aware and in which the 'west' becomes 'America', an America that has colonised the world. This new America contains both east and west, as a modern America where new maps are drawn:

> Nor are directions the same in America: the East is where the arborescent search and the return to the old world takes place; but the West is rhizomatic, with its Indians without ancestry, its always receding borders, its fluid and

shifting frontiers . . . America has reversed the directions: it has put its Orient in the West . . . It isn't India that serves as an intermediary between the Orient and the Occident, as Haudricourt believed, but America, which is the pivot and mechanism of reversal.[72]

Again, it is the cultural practice of photography which proves the pivot and mechanism of reversal at the level of representation or cartography. It is the photographic gesture, a specific gesture which has constructed this map of America as a modernist arena defined by speculation or by (in two other words close to 'speculation') theory and capital.

In considering *Hamlet*, Terence Hawkes finds another play, *Telmah*, struggling to make itself heard. The model for the kind of criticism which allows him to hear this ghostly other play is 'that of jazz music: that black American challenge to the Eurocentric idea of the author's, or the composer's authority'. The art of Louis Armstrong (or of his ghostly precursor, Fortinbras) is precisely the art of interpretation, argues Hawkes; and from this he makes the move to suggest that criticism is the only native American art, so that 'criticism makes Americans of us all'.[73] We might now add to this that it is not merely criticism but also photography and the photological ideology which has helped in the intellectual Americanisation of Europe. There would seem to be a configuration in modern and postmodern criticism whereby 'America' becomes either 'the West' or indeed 'the World' and identifies itself as locus of *culture*, that postmodern version of 'civilisation'.

There is a clear danger here that 'America' itself will escape our critique. A major postmodern task might thus be to find a criticism which can take 'America' into its ambit alongside those supposed 'other' eastern enigmatic modes of darkly tropical thought.[74] Since this dominance of the 'American' rhizome depends upon a particular photological version of realist representation (the modernist understanding of photography as technically superb mimesis), one first move in this critical direction should be a rethinking of representation as such, and specifically 'mimetic' or photographic representation which pretends to a positive accuracy. That criticism would be one which reneges on the idea of 'representing' the texts or cultural practices which are its ostensible object. To save the political component of criticism and to avoid being seduced by the American rhizome, we must learn to view the photographic not as a strict record or documentary evidence purporting to provide truth in the guise of enlightenment about specific material histories in certain stable terrains. Rather, it becomes important that we recognise the photographic as an obscuring mode of representation, the very production of an unconscious, of a *camera obscura* or dark nomadic territory whose maps have always still to be drawn and re-drawn.

Deleuze and Guattari oppose the map to the photograph, and urge us to 'make maps, not photographs'. But the photograph, properly understood as a postmodern immaterialising and deterritorialising mode of representation, is precisely a mapping itself. It is a machine whereby we can construct 'new desires', a machine instrumental in the immaterialisation and deterritorisalisation of that historically and materially grounded presence which, for the modernist world, thought itself as identity and self-presence. Thus understood, photography becomes instrumental not only in constructing 'the American rhizome', but also in setting it to flight once again; the photograph thereby allows us the political opportunity to re-map the geo-political configurations of the world. For America, it is apposite to note that the Tropic of Cancer cuts right through the boundary between itself and its 'back-yard', as it disarmingly calls Cuba and Latin America. But perhaps it is only because we take the *Rambo* movies as an index of some kind of truthful representation, however ideological, that America continues to resist the particular re-drawing of boundaries or of maps in which Latin America might become 'another country'.

III

Clews and Webs

4

Representing Postmodernism

'The things of the eye are done'
(Robert Lowell)

Representation as a theoretical issue is somewhat problematic;
and its problematisation has made it into a major area of contention in the debate around postmodernism. It is an important issue
here, for the arguments being carried on at the present time about
the value or otherwise of postmodernism have two crucial components, an aesthetic and a political. The idea of 'representation' is
central to both of these: in aesthetic terms, we have an art which,
whether figural or not, questions figuration and which typically
refers to itself or to art-history rather than to a prior state which it
merely re-presents; and in political terms, we have a 'West'
(whose major figure and figuration is the USA) which organises
itself around a notion of 'representative government', which it
calls 'democracy', but which lacks adequate theorisation.[1]

Conventional thought about representation is that it does not
require theorisation. As Arac writes, 'I shall not try to define
representation; we know well enough the different things we
mean by it. People do it all the time'.[2] In untheorised form,
representation is usually thought of as a 'making present again' of
something which is now not present, something unavailable or
inaccessible. It is an 'imitation', more or less adequate, more or
less precise, of something else whose ontological status is more
stable and assured, more grounded or foundational. The representation itself — in words, paint, music or movement — exists in
order to 'evoke' that supposedly prior presence, more or less

115

successfully. Representation, then, is deemed to be a kind of imagining, an 'imagination' of some presence or reality, whose essential status goes unquestioned, even if the representation makes it clear, in a typical 'enlightening' gesture, that its apparent or self-evident identity — its appearance — was or is deceptive.

This is a rather comforting notion of representation; in this form, it makes the world of nature accessible to human conscious-ness in more or less direct ways, and works to guarantee the subject's knowledge of the world. The representation merely 'figures' for us what we always already know: where the world can be 'cognised', the representation consolidates such ideological 'knowledge' by making it 're-cognisable'. It is perhaps because this notion of representation is so comforting that many theorists have tried to retain it, in the face of an aesthetics and a politics which are ever less 'representational'. I shall argue here that postmodern culture is antipathetic to representation, at least in this untheor-ised form; but will also suggest that this is no reason for aesthetic or political despair. On the contrary, I shall argue that the 'end of representation' typical of postmodern culture can have only beneficial socio-cultural and socio-political effects.

The argument has two major parts. In the first, I elaborate a notion of the relation between representation and history. The point here is not to reiterate earlier ideas of how to make representation more adequate to a prior historical reality; rather, I will outline what might be called the 'temporality of representa-tion' itself, whereby any specific representation will be seen to have an integral temporal dimension. It will be the relation between that temporality of the aesthetic representation and the temporality of an empirical secular history which will allow for a theorisation of the historicity of representation. But if representa-tion has such a historical component, if it is properly thought of as a historical event, then it must also be opened to questions of a political nature, concerning precisely the notion of 'representative government'. To address this in the second part of the argument, I turn to a particular aesthetic form, that of so-called 'confessional' poetry. Superficially, such a form appears to be extremely 'demo-cratic', representing the true interior self of an individual poet or consciousness at a particular moment in time. But I shall argue that to read the poetry in this way is to tread the dangerous path of the aestheticisation of politics; and to avert this, I shall propose a non-representational, more historical, mode of reading.

4.1 'BEWARE OF THE DOG!': THE HISTORICITY OF REPRESENTATION

But keep the wolf far hence, that's foe to men,
For with his nails he'll dig them up again.

(John Webster)

'Oh keep the Dog far hence, that's friend to men,
'Or with his nails he'll dig it up again!
'You! hypocrite lecteur! — mon semblable, — mon frère!'

(T.S. Eliot)

'By the dog!'

(Socrates)

In his 'Introduction' to *Postmodernism and Politics*, Arac is concerned to argue that postmodernists, or specifically post-structuralists, do not necessarily think that 'representation is bad'. As he rightly indicates, some notion of representation is absolutely crucial to that mode of Derridean deconstruction which is an important element in poststructuralist thought: 'The inescapability of representation is Derrida's deconstructive point against the metaphysical fantasy of pure presence'.[3] But this displacement of presence onto representation fails to resolve the issue of the relations obtaining between representation and something more 'archaic' (or arche-ic) which must remain as a something elsewhere, but a something which grounds or guarantees the status of the representation as literally a repetition of sorts, a 'mere' re-presentation.

It can be seen from this that representation is being implicitly considered in simply spatial terms, as a dis-*place*-ment of that which we had thought, in our metaphysical ignorance, as something present to itself in its proper place. In language borrowed from criminology, this might be called the *alibi* (literally 'elsewhere') of representation. To this must be added the question of the *alias* (literally 'at another time') of representation.

That temporal aspect of representation seems to be demanded by the very term itself, with its appeals to the 'present'. The word carries a meaning whose weight implies the status of a 'being before' (*prae-sens*) and hence *anteriority*; but it also simultaneously implies its less exalted status as a belated *posteriority*, for it is in one way a 'being after' (re-). Representation, then, seems to comprise something whose status is the 'being before' of a 'being after': in temporal terms, more precisely, the being-to-come or · coming-into-being of something whose very status is that of the not-yet-realised, always about to be ('being before'). This paradox is simplified when we recall that what is realised in representation is not in fact some putative prior essence in its essential self-presence, but rather the more vacuous, deconstructible representation itself. Put in these terms, representation bears an uncanny resemblance to the condition of the postmodern itself, at least insofar as that is formulated by Lyotard:

A postmodern artist or writer is in the position of a philosopher: the text he writes, the work he produces are not in principle governed by preestablished rules, and they cannot be judged according to a determining judgment, by applying familiar categories to the text or to the work. Those rules and categories are what the work of art itself is looking for. The artist and the writer, then, are working without rules in order to formulate the rules of what *will have been done*. Hence the fact that work and text have the characters of an *event*; hence also, they always come too late for their author, or, what amounts to the same thing, their being put into work, their realization (*mise en oeuvre*) always begins too soon. *Post modern* would have to be understood according to the paradox of the future (*post*) anterior (*modo*).[4]

The issues of postmodernism and of representation are fully imbricated one with the other. In attending to the 'future anteriority' which is of the essence of representation, we must see its *alias* as well as its *alibi*, its temporality as well as its displacement, its chrono-politics as well as its geo-politics.

Conventional thought on representation is that the representation refers or corresponds to something else, its prior referent; but it is not usually noted that such a relation between representation and prior referent can only be *ironic*, deceptive. This is clear from one of the earliest discussions of the problem. Plato in the *Cratylus* suggests that perfect representation is, in fact, by virtue of its perfection, no longer representation at all (*Cratylus*, 432b et seq.). There must be some perceived difference between that which claims to be representation and that which claims the status of the referent, the 'thing itself'. Otherwise, the object represented is no longer merely evoked but is actually there, present-in-itself. As Genette has it, 'perfect imitation is no longer an imitation, it is the thing itself'.[5] Representation, then, can only be representation if it is always already misrepresentation; like metaphor, it depends upon a *dis*similarity between itself and its implied referent. It is more accurate to suggest that it produces or establishes just such a dissimilarity or difference precisely at the moment of claiming an identity between itself and its referent; for it is in the moment of producing this 'alterity' of representation, this difference from a correspondent object, that it attains the status of representation as such and not as 'the thing itself'. Representation, then, is always misrepresentation and to the precise extent that it is decepetive and misrepresentative, it is also ironic, for misrepresentation such as this is the essence of irony.

We can approach the issue of the temporality of representation by way of de Man's ruminations on irony in 'The Rhetoric of Temporality'. In his consideration of Baudelaire's '*De l'essence du rire*', de Man finds that irony is 'a problem that exists within the self', for it demonstrates 'the impossibility of our being historical'.[6] The argument is that irony produces a radical discontinuity between consciousness and empirical history, and while it allows for temporal change within that consciousness, can find no way of establishing any contiguity between the consciousness and the world of exterior nature. There is, however, a blind spot in de Man's argument; and that blind spot is concerned precisely with a failure to theorise representation in the argument.

Baudelaire links comedy to a fall in both sacred and secular terms: '*Il est certain . . . que le rire humain est intimement lié á l'accident d'une chute ancienne, d'une dégradation physique et morale*'.[7] That fall is specified more precisely when Baudelaire provides a comic scenario, cited by de Man, of a man tripping and falling in the street:

Le comique, la puissance du rire est dans le rieur et nullement dans l'objet du rire. Ce n'est point l'homme qui tombe qui rit de sa propre chute, à moins qu'il ne soit un philosophe, un homme qui ait acquis, par habitude, la force de se dédoubler rapidement et d'assister comme spectateur désintéressé aux phé-nomènes de son *moi*. Mais le cas est rare.[8]

For de Man, it is this doubling of the self which is crucial, marking a distinction between the empirical or everyday self which stumbles and falls, and a contemplative, philosophical or 'linguistic' self (as de Man calls it) which can laugh at the falling self. The split reveals a more basic problem, but one which helps de Man effect the more radical split between the world of nature (or empirical history) and the consciousness of the linguistic self. In stumbling, the man in the case had been living in error, for he had presumed that there was an intersubjective relation between himself and the world of nature when in fact the essence of the self and the essence of nature are fundamentally incompatible and incommensurable. The fall produces a knowledge of that incommensurability, but (and this is the important point for de Man) this fallen man can effectively do nothing about it. If the man is philosophical and rapidly 'doubles' himself into the self that falls and the self that knows it, then what is actually produced is no more than *self*-knowledge. That is, the fall and doubling effect a break between the empirical or historical realm and the realm of consciousness, which is now (in its doublement) condemned forever to live in the 'linguistic' realm. The provision of this knowledge of the proper relations between self and nature is troubling, for de Man argues that the knowledge is gained at the cost of losing the world: once the production or ironising doublement of the linguistic self begins there is no way back to the empirical world, and consciousness, or self-consciousness is radically severed from empirical history.

Baudelaire makes a distinction between what he calls '*comique significatif*' and '*comique absolu*', which is the *grotesque* (and which de Man equates with irony). Baudelaire writes:

Le comique est, au point de vue artistique, une imitation; le grotesque, une création. Le comique est une imitation mêlée d'une certaine faculté créatrice, c'est-à-dire d'une idéalité artistique. Or l'orgueil humain, qui prend toujours le dessus, et qui est la cause naturelle du rire dans le cas du comique, devient aussi cause naturelle du rire dans le cas du grotesque, qui est une création mêlée d'une certaine faculté imitatrice d'éléments préexistants dans la nature.[9]

This, Baudelaire claims, is parallel to the difference between '*l'école littéraire intéressée et l'école de l'art pour l'art*'. But perhaps the single most important point to be noted is that this passage makes it clear that for Baudelaire, the site of '*le comique*' was precisely in an act of representation. In the case of the man falling, the doubling of the self produces a man who falls and a man who is present at the spectacle of the fall; that is to say, the comic is produced from an act of self-representation. It is not the case that the doublement innocently produces self-consciousness; self-consciousness is already dependent upon an act of self-representation. There are important implications in this, and in de Man's decision to circumvent it.

As with de Man's analysis of the structure of allegory, irony too is seen to have a temporality; but this temporality, thanks to de Man's severing of consciousness from history (a separation made possible only by his circumvention of the fact of representation) remains as a temporality removed from the world of empirical history. This irony originates for de Man precisely at the cost of the empirical self, allowing for a temporality only at the level of the linguistic self. That is to say, de Man here simply reiterates the Kantian and Husserlian point that consciousness can know itself but not immediately a world outside that self; the ironic consciousness is trapped within a repetitive series of acts of ever-increasing self-consciousness; but the more conscious of itself this self becomes, the more it severs its contact with empirical history. Theorists such as Starobinski and Szondi make what de Man calls the 'morally admirable' mistake of seeing the ironic moment of doublement as being prefigurative of the future re-establishment of a correspondence between the ironising linguistic self-consciousness and the empirical world of nature and history. But this is wrong, de Man argues:

irony engenders a temporal sequence of acts of consciousness which is endless. Contrary to Szondi's assertion, irony is not temporary (*vorläufig*) but repetitive, the recurrence of a self-escalating act of consciousness . . .
    The act of irony, as we know [*sic*] understand it, reveals the existence of a temporality that is definitely not organic, in that it relates to its source only in terms of distance and difference and allows for no end, for no totality. Irony divides the flow of temporal experience into a past that is pure mystification and a future that remains harassed forever by a relapse within the inauthentic. It can know this inauthenticity but can never overcome it. It can only restate and repeat it on an increasingly conscious level, but it remains endlessly

caught in the impossibility of making this knowledge applicable to the empirical world.[10]

The logical consequence of this, predictably, is that in a certain sense representation becomes impossible:

Allegory and irony are thus linked in their common discovery of a truly temporal predicament. They are also linked in their common demystification of an organic world postulated in a symbolic mode of anagogical correspondences or in a mimetic mode of representation in which fiction and reality could coincide. It is especially against the latter mystification that irony is directed . . .[11]

At this point, the argument falls into banality due to de Man's evasion of the function of representation in fully theorised terms. At one level, all he has shown is that signs are arbitrary and bear no necessary relation to empirically real or historical referents: language refers to itself in the first instance, and to non-linguistic entities only problematically, if at all. Moreover, on the specific point of the temporality of the ironising self-consciousness, all de Man has outlined is the existentialist paradox, that an essential, totalising or totalised self is unavailable. The conscious subject, by dint of its very consciousness, can never be fully present to itself, can never coincide with itself.

This restatement of Kant, Saussure and Sartre on the part of de Man weakens the originality of the argument significantly; but the fall into this reiteration of the same old stories is brought about by de Man's stumbling over the fact of representation. Following Baudelaire more rigorously, it might be pointed out that consciousness becomes conscious of itself (produces de Manic irony) only contemporaneously with an act of self-representation. It is the ontological status of this representation which is at issue here; for in seeing the empirical self falling, the linguistic self has produced irony not at the level of the consciousness divorced from history but precisely at the level of a quasi-textual representation. De Man is wrong to locate irony as a problem of the self; on the contrary, it is a problem of the *representation* of the self. In the case of the fall, the representation of the self falling, which enables the production of ironic selfconsciousness, does have fully empirical and historical status as Baudelaire at least knows:

qu'y a-t-il de si réjouissant dans le spectacle d'un homme qui tombe sur la glace ou sur le pavé, qui trébuche au bout d'un trottoir, pour que la face de son frère en Jésus-Christ se contracte d'une façon désordonnée, pour que les muscles de son visage se mettent à jouer subitement comme une horloge à midi ou un joujou à ressorts? Ce pauvre diable s'est au moins défiguré, peut-être s'est-il fracturé un membre essentiel.[12]

It is important to note, then, that de Man does not demonstrate the impossibility of representation; what he does show is that *perfect* representation, whereby a linguistic representation would be deemed to be the same as its historical correspondent, is impossible. But this is not exactly news; and other more interesting modes of representation remain a possibility. De Man's fundamental manoeuvre is similar to Derrida's in the attack on the metaphysics of presence; for what de Man does is to empty out the supposed presence of an empirical and social history onto the endless self-representations of a consciousness. That is to say, he shifts attention from presence to representation (from empirical to linguistic self), and within this latter realm of representation or ironic self-consciousness, what we have is self-reflexivity first and foremost. The mode of representation germane here is not one which asserts a relation between itself and some prior more 'self-present' correspondent in the world of nature with which it is fundamentally incommensurable; on the contrary, all representations are now ones which correspond only to other representations. What we can save from de Man's argument, then, is simply the temporality of this relation between representations.

There is, however, one further vital distinction to be made between de Man's position on irony and that which I am outlining here for representation. For de Man, the ironising self-consciousness is caught in an endless repetitive chain in which it endlessly repeats the *same* act of self-consciousness, only at ever-increasing degrees both of consciousness and of alienation from empirical history: it is not temporary but repetitive, he asserts. Representation, too, is caught in a similar chain whereby it escalates with self-consciousness in a temporal dimension, producing subsequent representations of representations without any single such representation ever being able to claim the status of full self-presence. But it is of the essence of representation to be always misrepresentation. It follows, therefore, that the temporality of representation, unlike that of de Manic irony, involves the production of a series of *mutations* in the consciousness which represents itself. Further, while de Man sees the ever-spiralling self-consciousness in existentialist terms, never coinciding with itself, but also never touching on empirical or historical selfhood, once we introduce representation into the spiral, we have regained access to the historical world, even if we can never claim to know that world to the same degree of mediacy with which we claim to know ourselves or our own consciousness. For self-representation, that act of representation which grounds the very linguistic consciousness of which de Man writes, involves the historical *enactment* of the self.

The consequence of this is that the series of self-representations in which we are now involved do not refer to a prior world as their ground; on the contrary, they construct a subsequent world in a series of presentations and representations of the self which deny that self any 'essence' or totality in the historical realm but which produce its existential provisionality. We do not just play the role of the waiter, in Sartre's famous example; in our self-representations, we produce and modify that role. Such modification has a temporal dimension, in the chain of endless representations in which we are involved; but this temporality is not one which exists at the level of the linguistic self or at the level of representation as a mere shadow of something more empirical or self-present; on the contrary, history is nothing but such self-representations. De Man's blind spot, in his evasion of the centrality of spectacle in Baudelaire's essay, leaves him with a binary opposition between the realm of ironising self-consciousness and an unironised and therefore self-present 'history' in which language and consciousness are logically redundant. Once representation is seen as the component that bridges the gap, we can construe history itself as being nothing more than the representational enactments of the consciousnesses whose interrelations make it up as empirical event. It is important, further, to note that this attention to the historicity of representations modifies more radically the de Manic position. For de Man, the escalating acts of self-consciousness are endless repetitions of the *same*: this is the existentialist production of a linguistic self in the mode of 'identity'. On the other hand, when representation is taken fully into account, and when it is recalled that representation is always already misrepresentation, the escalating acts of self-representation involve us in the existentialist production of a historical self whose status is not that of self-presence but of self-(mis)representation, a 'self' thus oriented to the mode of *alterity*. If the temporal representations are not in the strict sense constructing a self-present identification due to the necessity of misrepresentation across and through time, it follows that what is being produced here is, if still a self at all, only a self in the form of the Other. This 'self' is produced as that which is always different from itself; its identity is grounded in its difference from itself, its alterity with respect to itself.

Where de Man stumbles over representation, Plato had already evaded such a *faux pas*; and he did so by treating irony as a problem of the text (and therefore of representation) and not of a self divorced from text and history. In *Republic* (392 et seq.), Socrates makes a distinction between the modes of mimesis and diegesis, between the moments in a narrative when the poet speaks in the voice of an Other (mimesis: imitating speech) and those other moments when the poet speaks in her or his own voice (diegesis: narrating the story). His purpose is to enable an ethical argument about the preferred manner in which the Guardians will represent or enact themselves in the republic. Socrates here prefigures that enthusiastic modern, Oscar Wilde, as well as foreshadowing the Sartrean position outlined above, when he says:

have you not noticed how dramatic and similar representations, if indulgence in them is prolonged into adult life, establish habits in physical poise, intonation and thought which become second nature?[13]

Given this kind of premiss, and given that the Guardians of the hypothetical republic 'must from their earliest years act the part only of characters suitable to them', there is an obvious necessity for a strict policing of representations in the mode of mimesis. Socrates fears that if the Guardians act, in traditional enthusiastic and rhapsodic Greek manner, those roles which are deemed unsuitable for their function as Guardians, they will in some sense become identified entirely through such unsuitable roles and will

therefore not be 'proper' Guardians but only hypocritical or
actorly Guardians. Mimetic representation, it is feared, will corrupt the pure self-identity of the Guardian *qua* Guardian. The
conclusion of this kind of argument, as is well known, is,
logically, that the mimetic artists must be banished from the state,
leaving only diegetical narrators behind; and these can remain
only on the condition that they do not make too much use of
mimesis in their narratives. The banishment of mimesis is a
banishment of what can be seen as precisely a form of modernist
'enthusiasm' which involves the mimetician in speaking in the
voice of an Other rather than the Self. This enthusiasm is exactly
the mode of mimesis which worried Swift in *The Mechanical
Operation of the Spirit*, where it is satirised as a 'modern' mode
involving a loss of self-consciousness and the occupation of the
self by the voice of the other. It is also the same kind of
enthusiastic mimesis which shaped a subsequent modernist enterprise, in the allusions and citations of Eliot, the automatic
writings of Georgie Yeats and a number of Surrealists such as
Breton, Eluard and Desnos; and, some would add, the same mode
which dominates the postmodern mode through plagiarism,
parody or pastiche.[14] This Socratic argument, then, is an attempt
to banish what we have since learned to call 'modernism',
specifically understood as a mode whereby the Self is enacted
only at the level of representations (mimesis), and only in the
mode of alterity (only in the voice of, or representation as, the
Other). De Man's position on irony is exactly analogous to this: it
too fears and 'banishes' the historicity of representation; it too
construes selfhood only in the form of an endless act of escalating
repetitions of the *same* act of self-consciousness, producing selfhood only in the mode of identity or the Same rather than in the
mode of alterity and the Other or difference.

Diegesis, the representation of history, is deemed acceptable;
but mimesis, the historicising of representations, is dangerous to
the hypothesised ideal state. The impetus informing this position
is clear. In diegesis, a speaking subject is in control of a narrative
which guaranteees the identity and authority of the speaking
subject, giving, in circular fashion, that subject authority to
control and manipulate the shape of the diegesis. In mimesis, on
the other hand, the narrative is entirely in authoritative control

over the speaking subject, who speaks only in conformity to that narrative itself: 'I say it as I hear it',[15] as Beckett's narrators have it in *Comment C'Est*. In this latter case, it is the narrative which constructs history, for it shapes, constructs or dictates the empirical and historical life of its speaker, whose voice mimetically becomes the voice not of a guaranteed 'identical' Self but rather the voice of the Other. The historical subject thus produced represents itself not in the mode of identity but in that of alterity: it represents itself, in short, as other than itself, as something not identified by its own 'individuality'.

Two things are at issue, then: authority to shape and control history (or to be controlled by stories); and the historical or ontological status of representations themselves. Socrates seems to offer solutions to these problems: he argues that the subject should control history; and that self-presence in the mode of identity is to be preferred to self-representation in the mode of alterity. The net result of this is the argument that the individual self should be empowered to control history; the self-identical individual becomes the locus of meaning for empirical and social history.

I stress throughout that this is Socrates's argument, for the simple reason that there is a problem with it: Socrates 'says it as he hears it'.[16] The passage of *Republic* under consideration here is profoundly ironic; and this irony exists as a problem not at the level of the self but at that of the text. The very mode of mimesis which comes under most severe censure, to the point of banishment, is precisely the mode in which the attack is itself being made. We have here a *mimesis of the undoing of mimesis*; for Plato's text is itself thoroughly, almost enitirely, mimetic, an imitation of direct speech. It follows, logically, that if mimesis is to be banished, then *Republic* must be among the first texts to go; if it goes, then so does the argument it contains against mimesis, and hence it can in fact remain or be readmitted; and so on in a Moebius-spiralling paradoxicality or Lyotardian paralogy.

Such paralogy is, according to Lyotard, characteristic of the postmodern condition, and, in its mimetic dialogicity and self-ironising stance, *Republic* begins to looks rather like some central texts of modernism and postmodernism. Plato's writing against enthusiasm, on the grounds of its insanitising or unhealthy

impetus towards a modernist loss of consciousness and towards
the madness of the loss of individuality in ironising deceptions,
turns out itself to be thoroughly enthusiastic and modernist. In its
structure, it begins to approximate to the condition of that great
European modernist form, the *Künstlerroman*. Such texts end,
paradoxically, and Moebius-like, at the very point where they can
begin to be written. When we reach the 'end' of Joyce's *Portrait* or
Proust's *A la recherche du temps perdu*, the status of the text
changes; for it transpires that what we have been reading is not
the text in its self-present and self-identical condition. On the
contrary, what we have read is but the pre-text, a representation of
'the' text *avant la lettre*. The historical status of the text is thus
called into question, and it is in this respect exactly like de Man's
undertsanding of the ironic consciousness, always about to be,
never totalised or realised, its historical ontological status denied.
The paralogy of the *Künstlerroman* makes it into a pretext both
temporally and also in terms of its being a prefigurative 'excuse'
for a future confessional act of writing or provision of 'the' text. In
this potentially endless deferral of its own historical realisation,
the text is, temporally, always 'modern' in the banal sense, for it is
always 'writing to the minute', always 'about-to-be'.

Precisely the same can be said for Plato's *Republic* in its
ironising paralogical status, but with an important difference of
orientation. In the case of de Manic irony, historical referents are
dissolved into the endless play of acts of consciousness, but this is
a consciousness divorced from history by means of de Man's
evasion of the historicity of representations in which that consciousness enacts itself. In the case of Plato, the orientation is
exactly the reverse of this: we move from text to history, from
Republic to republic. The text turns out to be mere pre-text,
looking forward proleptically to the moment when the *Republic*
will be articulated or realised. But because Plato is also attending
to the historicity of representations, aware that the enthusiastic
reader of the dialogue (like its writer) is invited to speak in the
voice of alterity here, Plato's text looks forward to the *historical*
representation of the republic, its enactment as historical state
rather than its 'mere' textual articulation; for all being here is in
the mode of 'alterior' representation, not in the mode of self-
identical individuality. A *res publica* by definition, cannot exist in

the mode of individuality: it is public, and, as such, its citizens acquire their status through their relations to and with the other citizens who comprise it. The republic thus envisaged is comprised of subjects who exist in the mode of alterity. They do not find their subjectivity by speaking in their own voice, but on the contrary by always 'mimetically' speaking in the voice of alterity, the voice of the Other. This is exactly what Plato (or is it Socrates?) does. It follows that this argument about representation in the *Republic* is not only modern but also postmodern: it is written, so to speak, in the future anterior tense, working without rules or dogma in order to formulate the rules of what will have been done, of the republic that will have been established. That republic will have had an 'empirical' historical status, to borrow de Man's term; for all its citizens in their dialogical interactions with each other and with this pre-text of the *Republic* — that is, the polis which constitutes the republic itself — will exist through their historical representations of themselves; and those representations of themselves as historical enactments, will in turn be misrepresentations, for they will have represented themselves in the voices of their Others. In simple terms, this might mean that those who comprise the polis will do so by 'voting' (which means 'voicing') not, as it were, in their own voice and on behalf of themselves as individuals; on the contrary, they will vote or voice themselves on behalf of the republic which will always still have to be enacted or formed. Their 'votes' here would not represent themselves singly, but would be cast in the prosopopoeic voice of alterity, or mimetically. If I may paraphrase or misrepresent a perspicacious remark of de Man's, curiously enough, it seems to be only in using a mode of language which does not means what it says (i.e., representation) that one can actually say what it means or what others mean by it.[17]

When Genette considered this passage from the *Republic*, his fundamental manoeuvre was to deconstruct the opposition of mimesis and diegesis. He points out the problem with Plato's notion of mimesis as outlined by Socrates:

It can be said that verses 12 to 16 of the *Iliad* . . . give us a verbal representation of Chryses' actions, but the same cannot be said of the next five lines [the passage of direct speech: mimesis]; they do not *represent* Chryses' speech: if this is a speech, actually spoken, they *repeat* it, literally, and if it is a fictitious speech, they *constitute* it, just as literally. In both cases, the work of representation is nil; in both cases, Homer's five lines are strictly identical with Chryses' speech: this is obviously not so in the case of the five narrative lines preceding it, which are in no way identical with Chryses' actions: 'The word "dog" does not bite,' William James remarked.[18]

Genette can then challenge the distinction between the act of mental representation or *logos* and the act of verbal representation or *lexis*; for the direct speech or mimesis is, in these terms, not strictly a representation at all. On the contrary, as mimesis it disappears or is subsumed under the proper rubric of diegesis:

> the very notion of imitation on the level of *lexis* is a pure mirage, which vanishes as one approaches it; the only thing that language can imitate perfectly is language, or, to be more precise, a discourse can imitate perfectly only a perfectly identical discourse; in short, a discourse can imitate only itself. *Qua lexis*, direct imitation is simply a tautology.
> So we are led to this unexpected conclusion, that the only mode that knows literature as representation is the narrative [i.e., the diegesis], the verbal equivalent of non-verbal events and also . . . of verbal events, unless it vanishes . . . before a direct quotation in which all representative function is abolished.[19]

According to Genette, mimesis actually is diegesis, representation is 'narrative, and only narrative'. And the foundational moment which allows the performance of this deconstruction lies in the proposition, a 'cratylian' proposition already mentioned, that perfect representation is somehow an oxymoron. As Genette has it, 'perfect imitation is no longer imitation, it is the thing itself'.

Clearly, however, Genette as a *facteur de la vérité* here, as postman bringing the good news from Plato, is tempting fate somewhat when he himself quotes William James, a mimetic move in an argument demonstrating that mimesis is always already diegesis or a narrative with an empirical or historical status as 'the thing itself'. In the midst of Genette's narrative, we have a mimesis which itself contains a mimesis, for within James's comment is an internal citation of the word 'dog'. According to Genette's argument, the sentence from James has no status as representation but is 'the thing itself'; its intentional form can be authorised only by the consciousness identified as 'William James'. The sentence is marked not by a representation of James's consciousness; in Genette's terms, that consciousness informing these words is not represented but is rather there as a presence, as the thing itself. Within the citation, there is another citation, of 'dog'. By the same argument, this loses its status as mere sign or representation of a biting dog and begins to assume the historical status of the presence of the thing itself. This dog indeed bites, according to the logic, a paralogic, of Genette's argument. The argument collapses in irony for it disproves the very Jamesian thesis which is supposed to validate it. The problem with the argument is that it presupposes an originary speech which is not already representation; it presupposes the possibility of 'identity', of 'the thing itself'. But in language, the thing, the word, is never 'itself', never self-identical; it is always already representation, never presence. The argument assumes a realm of history which is somehow prior to representation; but history is nothing other than representations, a series of enactments or *mimesis*.

Arguments such as Genette's are dogged with the problem of history, when history is construed as something independent of representation. They flounder at the moment when they think representation in terms of correspondence between aesthetic entity (text, painting, music, dance, etc.) and historical or political entity ('reality'), which *can* be, but *need not* be, formulated in the mode of representation. Considered in these terms — as correspondence between aesthetics and politics — representation can only ever be an aestheticisation of politics: in de Man's case, in terms of the dissolution of history into the ironised self-consciousness of an individual; in Genette's case, in terms of the construction of a formal and stable narrative structure which 'contains' the historical. The problem here is that the correspondence theory thus understood proffers only a geo-politics of representation; that is, it sees representation as a displacement of presence, giving us only the alibi of representation. It thus 'spatialises' the temporal flow of historicity itself. The proper response to this would be first to acknowledge the ironic status of representation, whereby it must always be misrepresentation (or disguise, deception, impersonation); and secondly to historicise representation, not as a problem of individual consciousness and identity, but as a problem of textuality and alterity. Representation is better understood as that historical 'moment' or time wherein consciousness of self and of alterity is produced: and that production, tantamount to the production of the unconscious in the terms advanced by Deleuze and Guattari, is the stuff of material history itself.

For de Man, representation could only ever be self-representation, and its ironic component could only ever be an aspect of individual consciousness, or personality. In political terms, this is the basis of a certain kind of 'democracy', identified as that which underpins the bourgeois individualism of the so-called 'free democracies', paradigmatically America.[20] But the political question of representation is potentially more complex than this, especially if we shift from the de Manic position which is founded on the centrality of homogeneous self-identity towards a position based more on the heterogeneity of alterity. Do we represent the self or the Other; in whose voice do we speak or 'vote'? The issues here question the relations between consciousness and history or — in the phenomenological terms which linger all the way through de Man's work — between subject and object. Marx had a view on this in the *Eighteenth Brumaire*, when he argued that people make their own history but they do not make it just as they please, for they are haunted by the past which they inherit only more or less willingly.[21] The return of the dead to shape the present implies a certain heterogeneity in that which we usually understand as the homogeneous 'identifiable' self; such a theme is, of course, taken up in psychoanalysis as the return of the repressed. Michel de Certeau addresses the issue of heterogeneity in such terms, and here Genette's (or James's) dog begins to bite:

There is an 'uncanniness' about this past that a present occupant has expelled (or thinks it has) in an effort to take its place. The dead haunt the living. The past: it 're-bites' [*il re-mord*] (it is a secret and repeated biting). History is 'cannibalistic,' and memory becomes the closed arena of conflict between two contradictory operations: forgetting, which is not something passive, a loss, but an action directed against the past; and the mnemic trace, the return of what was forgotten, in other words, an action by a past that is now forced to disguise itself. More generally speaking, any autonomous order is founded upon what it eliminates; it produces a 'residue' condemned to be forgotten. But what was excluded re-infiltrates the place of its origin — now the present's 'clean' [*propre*] place. It resurfaces, it troubles, it turns the present's feeling of being 'at home' into an illusion, it lurks — this 'wild,' this 'obscene,' this 'filth,' this 'resistance' of 'superstition' — within the walls of the residence, and, behind the back of the owner (the *ego*), or over its objections, it inscribes there the law of the other.[22]

De Certeau's alterity here is the material of our historicity; it is exactly the same as the borrowed voices and figures from the past which 'bite' into our present activities in the manner outlined by Marx. In literary terms, of course, this alterity is nothing other than the inevitability of quotation and repetition, that repetition which, according to Derrida, was the undoing of Artaud's linguistic and theatrical project.[23] Such mimesis as this, itself integral to our historical existence, does not mean that it is impossible to be historical, as de Man argued; on the contrary, it is the very substance of our historical self-representation in the mode of alterity, or in a socio-political mode. However, it does mark the impossibility of our being 'authentic', and de Man here comes close not to the position of Sartre (to whom this term overtly alludes) but rather to that of Benjamin.

Benjamin's celebrated essay, 'The Work of Art in the Age of Mechanical Reproduction', certainly takes into account the notion of representation which is lacking in de Man's thoughts on the ironising linguistic self. It is concerned with representation in two central ways: the representation of the work of art which is now subject to its own reproducibility (representation *of* the work); and the representation and representability of the human self in film and photography (representation *in* the work), a representation in visual terms which is itself susceptible to its own reproducibility at the first level. There are two crucial points in the essay which have a specific bearing on the present argument. First, the effect of mechanical reproducibility, especially in the form of film and photography, is to produce a decline in the 'aura' or authenticity of the 'original' work of art, a loss of its 'authority' as an object from a more or less 'distanced' historical moment, its location within a 'tradition'; and secondly, the age of mechanical reproduction effects a huge 'popularisation' of the aesthetic, in the sense later elaborated by Beuys that potentially everyone is an artist, or, in that sense advertised by Warhol, that everyone is now a star — at least for a few minutes.

In the first of these points, Benjamin's argument prefigures that of de Man, albeit from a different overt politics. With ease of reproduction, 'exhibition value' begins to replace 'cult value' in art. It is easier to see, for example, a reproduction that is transportable from place to place than it is to make the visit to a cathedral elsewhere in the world to view an original fresco; the art comes to us, not we to the art. The result of this is that, increasingly, 'the work of art reproduced becomes the work of art designed for reproducibility',[24] and such 'errant', travelling art (art itself as *flâneur*) becomes displaced from its own specific historical or cultic moment: we may see the form of art, but have lost its content. That is, almost exactly as in de Man, Benjamin addresses the split between the consciousness of the subject perceiving the work of art, and the specificity and alterity of the work's own historical moment, its location in a tradition that is 'distanced' from the perceiving subject. Again, there is a dislocation between consciousness and a historicity which is other than that of the perceiving consciousness. What is lost here, for Benjamin, is the authority of that tradition; history itself is being actively 'forgotten', as the conscious subject sucks everything into the terms of its own self-consciousness (that is, construes an alien otherness in terms of its own restricted culture). Photography and film are in the forefront of this development, and their social significance must therefore be understood while accounting for their 'destructive, cathartic aspect, that is, the liquidation of the traditional value of the cultural heritage'.[25]

Reproducibility, then, affects the aura and authority of the alterity of history, argues Benjamin. In the case of film, this has a specific effect on the actor, who now acts for a mechanical contrivance (the camera) rather than being 'present' before an audience in a specific shared historical moment. In elaborating this argument, Benjamin points out that the effect of film is that 'man [the actor] has to operate with his whole living person, yet forgoing its aura. For aura is tied to his presence; there can be no replica of it'.[26] It is, however, when he backs this point up, or authorises it by citing Pirandello (of all people) to the same effect, that there appears a by now predictable logical hiccup in the argument. Benjamin quotes from Pirandello's novel, *Si Gira. . .* :

'The film actor,' writes Pirandello, 'feels as if in exile — exiled not only from the stage but also from himself. With a vague sense of discomfort he feels inexplicable emptiness: his body loses its corporeality, it evaporates, it is deprived of reality, life, voice, and the noises caused by his moving about, in order to be changed into a mute silence. . . . The projector will play with his shadow before the public, and he himself must be content to play before the camera.'[27]

In this mimesis of Pirandello, we have a mechanical reproduction of his work. Further, the footnote at this point advises us that this mimesis is itself cited from another reproduction of Pirandello's words, for Benjamin is quoting not from his source directly, but from *Si Gira* . . . , as 'quoted by Léon-Pierre Quint, "*Signification du cinéma*," *L'Art cinématographique*, . . . pp. 14–25'. This is a reproduction of a reproduction of Pirandello. Any aura, authenticity or authority which may have been invested in that text and its propositions are, according to the logic of Benjamin's position, lost. This dangerous mimesis, then, far from authenticating or guaranteeing Benjamin's argument, undercuts it with a mordant irony. Although Benjamin attends both to representation and to what I have termed alterity (his 'distance' of history), still the argument is based on an unproblematised notion of the individual consciousness. For Benjamin, there is the possibility of 'agreement' or accord between a consciousness from one historical moment and a consciousness from another (and even from another cultural tradition): that is, there is the possibility not only of a 'con-sensus' or *sensus communis*, but also the possibility of an identity based on self-sameness. Benjamin fails to take his argument to the rigorous extreme whereby distance (heterogeneity) is seen to be itself constitutive of each 'individual' consciousness. In short, while worrying about photography and its fixating power, he takes a snapshot of himself with Pirandello, fixed in nodding agreement with each other. Such a move 'identifies' the consciousness in the sense that it removes it from the flow of history (here, it removes both Pirandello's and Benjamin's consciousness from their historical specificity, finding their 'common ground'); it empties the space of the relation, the distance, between the consciousness and history. In the terms of my argument here, it is not extreme enough in the sense that it fails to historicise the consciousness, fails to acknowledge that its 'identity' is grounded precisely on its heterogeneity with respect to itself. Benjamin, paradoxically, fails to acknowledge the temporality of the representations in which a consciousness comes to know itself, and to know itself as different from itself. The move whereby he snaps himself and Pirandello together leads to precisely that aestheticisation of politics which is the ostensible object of his attack.

The reproducibility of the self effected by film leads, he argues, to the emptying of the theatres; in political terms, to the emptying of the specific 'theatre' of Parliaments. The politician becomes, like a film star, a 'stylistician':

The change noted here in the method of exhibition caused by mechanical reproduction applies to politics as well. The present crisis of the bourgeois democracies comprises a crisis of the conditions which determine the public presentation of the rulers. Democracies exhibit a member of government directly and personally before the nation's representatives. Parliament is his public. Since the innovations of camera and recording equipment make it possible for the orator to become audible and visible to an unlimited number of persons, the presentation of the man of politics before camera and recording equipment becomes paramount. Parliaments, as much as theaters, are deserted.[28]

The star and the dictator, Benjamin points out, are the true beneficiaries of this state of affairs.

But the real political problem lies not quite here; rather, it lies in the way representation is being thought. Politicians have always, perhaps inevitably, been concerned with stylistic matters, availing themselves of whatever technological means is at their disposal, all the way from the rhetorical delivery in stentorian voice at political rallies to invisible lecterns in a TV studio. This in itself is not the issue here. What is at stake is a particular mode of understanding representation as the base of democratic politics. Once again, with Benjamin, we have an argument which construes representation as mere reproduction of something elsewhere, something to which the representation corresponds and upon which it depends, something whose self-present ontology is more secure and foundational than that of the representation. Where others might call that self-presence 'reality', Benjamin refers to it as the aura or authentic status of an originary instant of the entity's historical being. However, at least where consciousness is concerned, there simply is no such 'originary' or authentic moment; at least there is no such moment in a past towards which representation nostalgically strives. For the consciousness is *always* nothing other than representation *with no ground* — without criteria — no basis in a prior presence. Representation is not one specific historical moment which refers back to some prior moment; if it were so, then representation would be self-identical, one self-identical instant. But it has already become clear that, as in irony, representation must always be misrepresentation and therefore heterogeneous with respect to itself. It is thus composed not as one temporal instant: rather, *a representation actually contains a historical dimension*. It is not just a displacement: representation is also an *anachronism*.

One political problem with bourgeois democracy lies in this misunderstanding of representation whereby it is construed as a merely geo-political phenomenon rather than being adequately *historical*. Political 'representatives', of whatever overt political persuasion, must (according to the misunderstanding of representation) think themselves as the figures in and through whom a prior historical truth speaks itself, and in which they find their common ground, their 'constituency' or authoritative identity. The problem with this is that it involves them precisely in the aestheticisation of politics; for it 'fixes' the historical moment which supposedly grounds them; and such an arrest of history (whereby a historical moment is thought to be more or less accurately 'represented' in the political representative's consciousness and speeches on behalf of her or his constituency) converts the heterogeneity of that history, its very temporal materiality, into a static 'photographic' representation, a form without material content. The category of representation understood in this way is a purely aesthetic term. The result of such an argument is that the entire history of 'Western bourgeois democracy', based on 'democratic representation' is, and always has been, the kind of aestheticisation of politics which leads, according to Benjamin, to war and to the supervention of fascism. Fascism, in these terms, is not an effect of the so-called stylisation of politics; on the contrary, it is an effect of an insufficiently theorised notion of political representation. What is called for, then, is an understanding of representation as a chronopolitical form; in short, for the historicising of representation as a counter to the representation of history.[29]

Benjamin himself approaches such a position when he describes the proleptic condition of art:

One of the foremost tasks of art has always been the creation of a demand which could be fully satisfied only later. The history of every art form shows critical epochs in which a certain art form aspires to effects which could be fully obtained only with a changed technical standard, that is to say, in a new art form.[30]

This is extremely close to Lyotard's understanding of postmodern-ism in art which is revealed in the art-work's future anterior status. It is also extremely close to my own formulations on a chrono-political representation. What happens here is that the temporality of representation, properly addressed, subverts the usual misconception whereby representation is thought as being simply 'belated', dependent upon a prior historical presence. Representation, once opened to its own historicity, becomes more fully proleptic rather than nostalgic. In Baudrillard's terms, repre-sentation becomes more adequately understood as 'simulation'. Here lies the importance of a second major point in Benjamin's essay, that we are all potentially 'stars'.

The age of mechanical reproduction blurs the distinction between consumers and producers. In newspapers, as soon as editors open their pages to letters from readers, the reader is in a position to become, simultaneously, a writer. In more obviously representational terms, and thanks to the coming omnipresence of the surveillance camera, 'Any man today can lay claim to being filmed'.[31] This leads to a kind of Wildean paradox where it becomes possible to suggest that one is only real while one is being represented; the locus of the representation becomes, para-doxically, the ground of the empirical history. The political analogy here is that one 'counts' only if one is genuinely enfran-chised. But to leave the matter at this would be simply to reinstate precisely the problem of ground and presence which, as we have seen, dogs and undercuts representation with that mordant irony of which Plato was already aware. Baudrillard makes the neces-sary step beyond this geo-politics of representation when he analyses the relation of what he calls the hyperreal and the imaginary. He considers Disneyland as a model of his orders of simulation. Disneyland, he argues, is understood as an imaginary representation in order to guarantee a reality elsewhere. If we accept that Disneyland exists only at the level of imaginary representation, then we can begin to think that there is a non-imaginary, a real, which lies outside Disneyland, in that space we call America:

Disneyland is there to conceal the fact that it is the 'real' country, all of 'real' America, which *is* Disneyland (just as prisons are there to conceal the fact that it is the social in its entirety, in its banal omnipresence, which is carceral). Disneyland is presented as imaginary in order to make us believe that the rest is real, when in fact all of Los Angeles and the America surrounding it are no longer real, but of the order of the hyperreal and of simulation. It is no longer a question of a false representation of reality (ideology), but of concealing the fact that the real is no longer real, and thus of saving the reality principle.

The Disneyland imaginary is neither true nor false; it is a deterrence machine set up in order to rejuvenate in reverse the fiction of the real.[32]

What we choose to call reality, in these terms, is nothing other than a hyperreality, based entirely on what we used to term 'mere' representation, an imaginary. The poles of reality and representation are here in some measure reversed, such that representation has become proleptic of a reality; but for Baudrillard, what is at stake in this is the loss of reality itself (elsewhere in his work considered as the realm of the Object) and the subsequent pretence whereby some reality principle is maintained. In this, there is a negativising moment (the production of the imaginary) which exists in order to positivise something else, something elsewhere, as 'real'. In a specific political case, Baudrillard links the Disneyland scenario with Watergate, which produces a political scandal — but one which is only imaginary — in order to maintain certain fundamental political principles about the reality of the Office of the President of the USA. Here we have the same operation as in Disneyland, 'though this time tending towards scandal as a means to regenerate a moral and political principle, towards the imaginary as a means to regenerate a reality principle in distress'.[33] Such operational negativity is a 'scenario of deterrence', meant to deter any fundamental historical and political change. It is at work everywhere, proving theatre by anti-theatre, art by anti-art, psychiatry by anti-psychiatry, capitalism by revolution, etc.:

Everything is metamorphosed into its inverse in order to be perpetuated in its purged form. Every form of power, every situation speaks of itself by denial, in order to attempt to escape, by simulation of death, its real agony. Power can stage its own murder to rediscover a glimmer of existence and legitimacy.[34]

The catharsis effected by such 'negation' suggests the proper characterisation of the scenario of deterrence as a *tragic* theatre. Against this, we can posit the characteristic postmodern form of parody, as a mode of comic politics.

The problem of representation, as I have outlined it here, lies in the notion of mimesis in which Plato started the argument. Throughout, we have seen how mimesis is inevitably an undoing of mimesis: quotation and allusion (themselves constitutive and necessary elements of any linguistic utterance) work to undercut that irony and temporality which is axiomatic to representation, for the simple reason that they are understood to reinstate a ground or presence which 'fixes' the representation as self-identical and specific to one identifiable historical moment, thereby collapsing history, divorcing the relevant moment from the historical. This notion of mimetic quotation, then, might be replaced by parody; for parody attacks the very principle of reality or of presence upon which most current understandings of representation are fallaciously and erroneously based. Baudrillard is again instructive here. He poses the question of whether the repressive apparatus of a society might not react more violently against, for example, a simulated hold-up than it would against a 'real' hold-up, for 'the latter only upsets the order of things, the right of property, whereas the other interferes with the very principle of reality'.[35] This simulation, in its attack on the principle of reality, also thereby questions the supposed reality of the law and its systems and apparatus of repression. Parody here is instrumental in suggesting that 'law and order themselves might really be nothing more than a simulation',[36] and it is this which the society which bases its self-representations in a principle of reality cannot bear, dare not even address.

Parodic simulation, in all its comedy, has a definite political purpose here. It does not merely re-arrange or re-distribute the orders by which a society knows itself: much more than this, it subverts any claim to reality at all. In so doing, it opens the question of a genuine politics, for what is at stake here is a struggle between simulations, none of which have any *a priori* claims to an absolute or totalising truth, for none of them can any more ground themselves in a claim as to their adequacy in representing a prior self-present 'real' state of affairs. Politics becomes no longer a nostalgia, but a poetry of the future, a proleptic politicising of aesthetic simulations, to parody and paraphrase Marx. As Baudrillard writes:

The simulation of an offence, if it is patent, will either be punished more lightly (because it has no 'consequences') or be punished as an offence to public office (for example, if one triggered off a police operation 'for nothing') — but *never as simulation*, since it is precisely as such that no equivalence with the real is possible, and hence no repression either. The challenge of simulation is irreceivable by power. How can you punish the simulation of virtue? Yet as such it is as serious as the simulation of crime. Parody makes obedience and transgression equivalent, and that is the most serious crime, since it *cancels out the difference upon which the law is based.*[37]

It might be more accurate to suggest that parody cancels out the reality- or truth-claims of the differences upon which the law is based. Law, legitimation, the entire order of socio-political historical being is opened to its own historicity by such parody. It is open to enact itself in a series of ironic (mis)representations of itself, but only of itself under the form of alterity. If it is advanced against this that all we have here is yet another claim to have reached the 'end of ideology', then the response must be that if that is so, it simply means that we have reached the start of politics; for we have undercut the notion of political representation, the notion of a democracy based upon a geo-political mode of representation, and have been able to articulate the argument that any such 'politics' is in fact the disappearance of the political or its subvention under aesthetics. In this position, we can begin to think our way beyond the reality principle, can evade the 'fascinating' mimesis which is nothing other than an aestheticisation of politics, and can start, for once, to politicise aesthetics. The 'end of representation' (or at least of our previous geo-political understanding of representation as mimesis) means the beginning of prolepsis, a writing of the poetry of the future which will escape the merely aesthetic realm and will reinstate history.

Postmodern (Dis)Simulation

Tauromachia and the Struggle for Europe

5.1 Introductory: For a Historical Consciousness

Arachne wove a picture of Europa, deceived by Jupiter when he presented himself in the shape of a bull. You would have thought that the bull was a live one . . .

(Ovid, *Metamorphoses*)

Belmonte's great attraction is working close to the bull. In bull-fighting they speak of the terrain of the bull and the terrain of the bull-fighter. As long as a bull-fighter stays in his own terrain he is comparatively safe. Each time he enters into the terrain of the bull he is in great danger. Belmonte, in his best days, worked always in the terrain of the bull. This way he gave the sensation of coming tragedy.

(Hemingway, *Fiesta*)

   the God Adonis bled
and lay beside you, forcing you to strip.
You felt his gored thigh spurting on your hip.

(Lowell, 'Caligula')

If we want a chrono-political understanding of representation, it is important to evade the mordant irony of the biting dog which harassed the Achilles' heel of previous theories of representation. Lowell begins to pull the offending teeth in his poem, 'Eye and Tooth', in *For the Union Dead*, where 'Nothing can dislodge/the house with my first tooth/noosed in a knot to the doorknob'. This poem, coming in the collection where we are told that 'The things of the eye are done', brings together representation and that biting tooth in a particular political context:

No ease from the eye
of the sharp-shinned hawk in the birdbook there,
with reddish brown buffalo hair
on its shanks, one ascetic talon

clasping the abstract imperial sky.
It says:
an eye for an eye,
a tooth for a tooth.[1]

This bird, in its 'imperial' sky, bears a striking resemblance to the American eagle; and it proclaims, mimetically and enthusiastically, a particular kind of 'justice' in that balanced cited phrase, 'an eye for an eye,/a tooth for a tooth. The phrase comes from Exodus, 21: 24ff.:

then thou shalt give life for life,
Eye for eye, tooth for tooth, hand for hand, foot for foot,
Burning for burning, wound for wound, stripe for stripe.
. . .
If an ox gore a man or a woman, that they die: then the ox
shall be surely stoned, and his flesh shall not be eaten . . .
  Or if it be known that the ox hath used to push in time
past, and his owner hath not kept him in; he shall surely
pay ox for ox; and the dead shall be his own.

These balances, at the verbal level at least, offer a particular kind of economy of representation, in which a mode of justice is advanced. In that economy of judicial representation, the punishment is, as it were, a perfect representation of the crime: life for life, eye for eye, ox for ox, and so on. This is similar to the economy of a liberal capitalism, where exchange-value is based upon the same notion of adequate representation, not only in the sense that one coat is represented by x pounds, but also in a more fundamental sense elaborated by Marx in his writings on the process of capitalist exchange. Since commodities cannot themselves go to market, they must be taken there by their 'guardians' who, in the exchange of commodities, recognise themselves as owners of private property:

This juridical relation, whose form is the contract, whether as part of a
developed legal system or not, is a relation between two wills which mirrors

the economic relation. . . . Here the persons exist for one another merely as representatives and hence owners, of commodities.[2]

This economy of representation, in its balanced form, implies a mode of equality in its justice. But it also presupposes that the 'representatives' are always already commensurable, if not homogeneous and equal, even identical. This is, of course, the basis of a liberal ideology, that ideology known and supervised by the American eagle.

This requires further exploration and explication. It is conventionally agreed that a specific sort of literary representation runs into difficulty at the turn of the twentieth century. Writers and artists, it is claimed, often give up on the project of representing truthfully or objectively an 'external' world, and are willing to lose that world in order to gaze deeply into their own redeemable soul or consciousness, or even unconscious. It is further supposed that this enables the production of a mode of truth or at least of authenticity in writing, a mode which has come to be thought of as in some way 'confessional'. Auerbach, in closing *Mimesis* with a consideration of Proust and Woolf, follows the movement to 'look within' in Woolf's celebrated phrase; but this internalised mode of writing is still thought of as in some way representational. It has, moreover, an explicit political component:

What takes place here in Virginia Woolf's novel is precisely what was attempted everywhere in works of this kind . . . that is, to put the emphasis on the random occurrence, to exploit it not in the service of a planned continuity of action but in itself. And in the process something new and elemental appeared: nothing less than the wealth of reality and depth of life in every moment to which we surrender ourselves without prejudice. . . . The more it is exploited, the more the elementary things which our lives have in common come to light. . . . In this unprejudiced and exploratory type of representation we cannot but see to what an extent — below the surface conflicts — the differences between men's ways of life and forms of thought have already lessened.[3]

The construction of *Mimesis* itself, of Auerbach's own text, was itself a kind of *bricolage*, a putting together of random materials, those materials being the texts which Auerbach had to hand while he was in Turkey, an exiled Jewish refugee fleeing Nazi Europe during the Second World War. Auerbach — due, it is true, to force of circumstance — writes of his modernist enlightenment after a migration eastwards. Said has drawn explicit attention to Auerbach's plight in another context;[4] but it is surely important here that Auerbach makes that appeal to something which under-lies 'surface conflicts'. In the introspective withdrawal from empirical history which we see occurring in modernist writing and repeated in Auerbach's own text, there is represented some-thing which transcends any particular historical moment, some-thing which endures and which was known to earlier historical periods as 'human nature', some internal essence which reduces empirical history, even the horrors of the Second World War, to the status of mere epiphenomena.

The politics of this appeal are clear. Auerbach has, at this moment, to make an appeal to an implied equality which is always already there in 'human nature' as a means of protesting against the atrocious Nazi destruction of 'western history', and specifically as a means of protesting against the racist inegalitar-ianism upon which Nazism based itself. Auerbach's liberalism has to assume a basic truth of human equality as an *a priori* given; an empirical history which manifestly questioned this could only be reduced in Auerbach's predicament, to the level of a myth, a fiction, or 'surface conflicts', rather than directly struggled against. Liberalism, especially in its American and Modernist mode, always works by assuming human emancipation and equality as givens, rather than by acknowledging them as values to be struggled for in the arena of history. That is, liberalism always loses the empirical historical world, dissolving it into an effect of consciousness which it usually calls 'human nature': to this extent at least, liberalism and phenomenology go together as aestheti-cisations of the political. That retreat into consciousness or into 'human nature' is, however, precisely the attempt to evade or to circumscribe empirical history that we have already examined in one of Auerbach's successors in a Sterling Chair at Yale, Paul de Man.

In literary history, the origin of such a retreat into an eternising notion of human nature dates not from the moment of Husserlian phenomenology but from the eighteenth century. Then, the neo-classical attempt to translate the idiom of an ancient culture into a

contemporary one was, among other things, an attempt to circumvent the vagaries of history by constructing at least one 'eternal',
non-historical and unchanging point of reference. This *point de
repère* was to be the identity of consciousness itself, a consciousness which was, in protophenomenological manner, somehow in
principle the same for Pope as it had been for Homer. The
construction of such a *tradition* (actually the collapsing of history
into 'tradition' or 'heritage'), which is central to all neo-
classicisms and which here involved the invention of human
nature, reduces empirical history to the level of the merest
epiphenomena, a series of 'surface conflicts' masking a deep
equality, identity and homogeneity. The dominant form of the
eighteenth-century satirical attack on the 'Moderns' correspondingly implies that the Modern was only too historical, caught up
in the fleeting evanescent moment, rather than doing something
useful and valid like tapping into some substantial and unchanging traditional or eternal truth. The invention of human nature at
this time allows for the circumvention of a troubled and troubling
historicity, an evasion of history carried out in the name of a
supposed truth. Further, it is this which allows for the liberal
assumption, shared later by Auerbach, that the struggle for equality or for emancipation has always already in some sense been
won. People no longer need to struggle in real historical situations
for their emancipation from oppression: all they need do is look
within to see their common cause.[5]

The particular mode of mimesis that we have in modernists
such as Woolf and Proust is precisely that which Socrates understood by mimesis: that is, an enthusiastic *loss* of identity or loss of
one's own presence or nature. The modernist text sees the
supervention of mimesis over diegesis (at least in the classical
senses of these terms), the paradigmatic writer here being Ivy
Compton-Burnet. It sees the supervention of precisely that mode
of enthusiasm which in the eighteenth century was attacked for
being too secular and therefore supposedly 'superficial', ignoring
the traditional base of human nature. Tradition, for the neo-
classicist, when adhered to in anything other than parody, guarantees an identity of individual consciousness, itself grounded on
the transhistorical identity of human nature which is considered
axiomatically to be always and everywhere the same. But for a

modern enthusiast such as Woolf, looking within at the atoms which fall on an ordinary mind on an ordinary day, the interest lies in the fact that as these atoms 'shape themselves into the life of Monday or Tuesday, the accent falls *differently* from of old'.[6] That is, looking within here does not produce identity across history; on the contrary, it allows Woolf to bear witness to difference, to temporal heterogeneity.

This, however, is not meant to suggest that enthusiastic mimesis is in any simple way more historical than an avowedly outward-looking representation which comes into disrepute at the turn of the twentieth century. The enthusiastic writer, while open to temporality, is not yet necessarily open to historicity; she or he is in the position described by de Man as that of the ironist, for the locus of interest in these writings is typically not empirical history itself but rather the temporality of a consciousness in its relation to itself, that is, an ironising self-consciousness. In the modernist retreat from history, we have a prefiguration of the world well lost elaborated in de Man's 'refuge in more theoretical inquiries into the problems of figural language'.[7] The historicity of representation when the very object of representation is itself understood as being non-historical (that is, when it is construed as a self or a human nature divorced from empirical history) must now be examined. This kind of self has become a central figure in twentieth century American poetry, and most especially in that mode of poetry usually referred to as 'confessional'.

5.2 POETRY AS ANACHRONISM

The phrase 'confessional poetry' was coined by M.L. Rosenthal in his review of Lowell's *Life Studies*, a volume which was revoutionary in its autobiographical and personalist stance and which secured Lowell's reputation as the leading American poet of the century. In the years between 1959 and 1964, certainly, this personalist stance in the poetry was understood, by Lowell himself as well as by his critics, to be the basis of its success. Asked by Stanley Kunitz why his poetry was now so highly regarded, Lowell replied 'It may be that some people have turned to my poems because of the very things that are wrong with me. I

mean the difficulty I have with ordinary living, the impracticabil-
ity, the myopia. Seeing less than others can be a great strain'.[8]
Lowell, however, certainly had not begun as a personalist poet. He
remained always aware that he was in many ways shaped as a
poet by the prevalence of the American New Criticism: 'The kind
of poet I am was largely determined by the fact that I grew up in ·
the heyday of the New Criticism. From the beginning I was
preoccupied with technique, fascinated by the past and tempted
by other languages. It is hard for me (now) to imagine a poet not
interested in the classics'.[9] This was written in 1974, as Lowell
looked back over his career; and certainly the fascination with the
past and with other languages confuses that view of the 1959–64
period poems as strictly personalist spontaneous overflows of
personal emotions, for the poems of this period are indeed
contaminated by translation, *imitatio*, other languages and past
histories and texts.

Lowell did, however, always consider himself in his work as a
specifically American, specifically modern poet, shaped by the
pressures of the New Criticism, that mirror-image of Russian
Formalism which was developed most fully by critics — largely
unacquainted with the Russians — in the universities and liberal
arts colleges of the southern states of America. But although John
Crowe Ransom and Allen Tate had persuaded the young Lowell to
come south in 1937 in what Tate at least saw as a politico-cultural
triumph for the right-wing secessionists, Lowell simply found in
the South his own political stance as a Northern Democrat, later
the supporter of Stevenson and the Kennedys. On 5 June 1960, at
the Boston Festival of the Arts, Lowell read the poem which in
many ways marks his leave-taking of this southern New Critical
tradition, 'For the Union Dead' — a poem which is a direct
political riposte to Allen Tate's 'Ode to the Confederate Dead'. In
the collection *For the Union Dead*, Lowell's confessional stance
becomes *apologia* not merely for a personal self but also for a
political self, for the identity of 'America'; and hence there is a
political as well as an ethical representation at work in this
revelatory poetry. Lowell represents not merely himself, but also a
political state with himself as its 'democractic' representative
figure, in the manner of Whitman. However, confessional poetry
involving representation of interior states of being, be they of a

human nature or of the politics of a country, is no more straight-forward than the representation of an empirical historical and external world. It too has a problematic historicity.

The New Criticism, as is well known, produced its most typical work when confronted with the lyric, even to the point of making the lyric a paradigm for all textuality. But at the turn of the 1960s, when Lowell was making a genuine break from the dominance of the New Criticism and discovering a political position at odds with it, his own poetry was beginning to operate not on the level of lyric so much as upon that of narrative which, as I argued above, has become the privileged form in postmodernism. His poems were now being organised in a series of interlocking relations with each other, breaking the framed bounds of the individual text or 'verbal icon', and opening themselves out to intertextual relations and cross-weavings with each other. That narrativity remained as a dominant shaping factor in Lowell's poetry right up until his death; but it had its originating moment in the 1960s, when he was writing *Life Studies*, *Imitations*, *For the Union Dead*. These poems, if 'confessional' at all, are not simply lyrical effusions revealing a depth of self at specific historical or personal moments: this confessional narrative poetry has a temporal and historical dimension which breaks the bounds of lyric as such. Where lyric operates most typically as an iconic representation of the identity of a consciousness at one isolated and particular instant, and identifies its consciousness by removing it from history, narrative poetry, as here understood, works by proposing the break-down of such identity and its replacement with a heterogeneity which marks the release of an 'unidentified' consciousness into the flow of historicity.

When de Man considers the *Confessions* of Rousseau, he repeats the manoeuvre of divorcing consciousness from empirical history which organised 'The Rhetoric of Temporality'. This manoeuvre now assumes the configuration of a recognisable 'liberal' attempt to construct a tradition of human consciousness, a consciousness always repeating itself in the mode of identity, divorced from historicity or from empirical conflicts or politics; it is a repetition of the eighteenth-century manoeuvre of the invention of 'human nature', the 'pli' in our understanding called 'Man', as Foucault has it. There are, according to de Man, two

modes in which confession exists, one empirical and one linguistic. Rousseau steals a ribbon, blames the theft on Marion, and then
confesses to this. But de Man points out that confession, 'stating
things as they are', is an attempt to restore an ethical balance
which had been disturbed by the crime; it involves the over-
coming of guilt and shame in the name of truth. This is imbricated ·
with an impetus of excuse which threatens to undo the act of
confession as such and at source:

> The only thing one has to fear from the excuse is that it will indeed exculpate
> the confessor, thus making the confession (and the confessional act) redundant
> as it originates. *Qui s'accuse s'excuse*; this sounds convincing enough, but, in
> terms of absolute truth, it ruins the seriousness of any confessional discourse
> by making it self-destructive.[10]

This is further clarified when de Man elaborates the distinction
between empirical history and verbal consciousness and the two
related and different modes of confession:

> The distinction between the confession stated in the mode of revealed truth
> and the confession stated in the mode of excuse is that the evidence for the
> former is referential (the ribbon), whereas the evidence for the latter can only
> be verbal. Rousseau can convey his 'inner feeling' to us only if we take, as we
> say, his *word* for it, whereas the evidence for the theft is, at least in theory,
> literally available.[11]

Verbal confession, that which is stated in 'the mode of excuse' in
order to restore that ethical balance which bears a striking
resemblance to the 'economy of representation' outlined earlier,
seems condemned forever to repeat itself, in exactly the same
manner in which self-consciousness repeats itself in de Manic
irony. Verbal confession is again divorced from history; it may
have a repetitive temporality, but, as a repetition in the mode of
identity, it has no historical dimension. In terms of representation,
this case is exactly parallel to that of irony: all representation,
being representation of the Same and an act of strict repetition, is
self-representation; the text re-presents itself. In 'Lyric and Modernity', de Man opposes the simplistic notion that 'modernity' in
literature is antipathetic to representation, arguing for a trace of
representation even in Mallarmé's difficult and seemingly resistant texts. But in 'Lyric and Modernity', the representational text

represents merely itself or, rather, those aspects of itself which are already present in other, prior, texts. It is in this essay that de Man anticipates Bloom's theory of revisionism, as Lentricchia has already noted, and here that he attempts to circumvent history once more by 'reconciling' it with modernity:

the crisis of the self and of representation in lyric poetry of the nineteenth and twentieth centuries should be interpreted as a gradual process. Baudelaire continues trends implicitly present in Diderot; Mallarmé (as he himself said) felt he had to begin where Baudelaire had ended; Rimbaud takes an even further step in opening up the experimentation of the surrealists — in short, the modernity of poetry occurs as a continuous historical movement. . . . The son understands the father and takes his work a step further, becoming in turn the father, the source of future offspring. . . . as far as the idea of modernity is concerned, it remains an optimistic story. Jupiter and his kin may have their share of guilt and sorrow about the fate of Saturn, but they nevertheless are modern men as well as historical figures, linked to a past that they carry within themselves.[12]

Representation here has become a process removed from empirical history and displaced onto verbal or textual history, located in an endless process of the repetition of the Same, in the mythic or linguistic level of a family romance in which the agonistic conflict has become a 'surface conflict'; it masks a deep affiliation and the real eternal substantiality of the Law of the Godfather, a singularly appropriate term, punningly understood, for the work of de Man's own 'son' or affiliate in this story, Harold Bloom. But the historicity of representation, in textual practice, cannot so easily be overcome or circumvented, as the case of the narrativity of *For the Union Dead* helps show.

For the Union Dead, like its predecessors *Life Studies* and *Imitations*, is organised according to what might be called the 'logic of the labyrinth', for there is a 'clew', a yarn being spun which links the various poems together in a defining configuration. The collection operates on the same model as a collection such as Herbert's *The Temple*, where:

This verse marks that, and both do make a motion
  Unto a third, that ten leaves off doth lie:
  Then as dispersed herbs do watch a potion,

These three make up some Christians destinie.[13]

Lowell, of course, was not at this time writing 'The H. Scriptures', for he had recently come to give up the Catholic faith which nonetheless continued to offer him materials for his metaphors and symbols. The principle that the narrative of a life can be told in this 'Herbertian' fragmentary fashion remains. Tropes, symbols, images, words and even parts of words recur in repetitions which invite the reader to actuate or 'motivate' a narrative which links them; and the result of this is that the lyric poems are infused with an impetus of narrativity which gives them a historical dimension. They do not record an 'instant of consciousness' as marker of 'identity', but rather stress the historical differences, the *heterogeneity*, informing that consciousness as a consciousness *in history*. Intertextual cross-referentiality as such a dominant force implies that the meaning of any poem is never 'present to itself' in the collection; it has to be threaded through the other clews in order to construct a safe passage to the centre of the labyrinth which is always, as Daedalus knew, decentred, elsewhere, an *alibi*. Here, I shall show not just the alibi of Lowell's collection, but also the various aliases under which he goes, in order to open out the question of the historicity of representation and of self-representation in this so-called poetry of confession.

The allusion to Herbert serves here also to raise the question of modernity once more; for Herbert's problem, writing in a late Renaissance moment which considered itself 'modern', was precisely an anxiety of anteriority. The problem was the stark one of how to write, how to assume authority in a situation where, as Herbert believed, the Great Book had been written and authoritatively translated into the English idiom in such a way that it could not, in principle at least, be improved upon. On what ground could Herbert's authority, as a writer, possibly rest? Lowell, at the time of writing the poems in *For the Union Dead*, may have given up on Catholicism as a faith but not as material for poetry; he was still interested in the Catholic Church and in the power of Rome which he understood, in a neat tropic turn, as the power of ancient Roman imperialism.

In one of the poems which makes explicit allusion to religion, 'Jonathan Edwardes', there is an invitation to the reader to cast a net slightly wider to include another 'modernist' figure in this authorial constellation. The modern and sincere Herbert is joined

by the Swift of *The Battle of the Books*. In that text, Swift had
written an allegory couched in the terms of fable, the fable of the
spider and the bee. The modern spider, it will be recalled, weaves
his texts from the inner lights of his own subjectivity and spirit, a
spirit satirised and materialised by Swift, of course, as a mode of
writing in one's own excrement. The bee, on the other hand,
provides a simple correspondence, it has always been assumed,
with the philosophy of the Enlightenment, here specifically in
relation to its commitment to serious study and learning and to
the knowledge of the ancient texts which have now been brought
to light. The bee, a proto-Arnoldian, claims to fly from flower to
flower (but we now know of the inherent dangers of the violent
rhetorics of flowers), from text to text, finding the materials in
these efflorescences of language for the production of honey and
wax, sweetness and light in the wax-candle. We thus have the bee
as 'sweet reason', which has come to us in the twentieth century
— after Arnold — as 'common sense' or the tyranny of the
terroristic ideology of 'the natural'. But it is of the essence of
Swift's radical irony that his text makes any simple valorisation
which prioritises bee over spider *or vice versa* strictly undecidable. The question of modernity, in the form of a question of
authority — the question of what is the authoritative reading, or
true reading of the text — is inscribed in this ironic text, as much
as it was in Herbert and, later, in Lowell.[14]

Spiders, in fact, play an enormous role in *For the Union Dead*,
for they figure among those intertextual references and figures
which narrativise the collection. With such recurring images and
tropes as the knot, the severed head, the alchemy of water and
fire, fish, oil and so on, there is a kind of modern bestiary
including a number of animals and insects organising this collection. I attend here to two such figures: spider and bull. In these
texts, it looks at times as if Lowell is locating himself firmly in the
position and identity of the 'modern' spider. But he is also aware
that this is a dangerous position, for in autumn 1961 with the
intensification of the Cold War, the Berlin crisis and the Bay of
Pigs episode, the spider spins under the approach of impending
apocalypse, crying meanwhile 'without tears', as Lowell puts it in
a striking image.

One crucial appearance of the spider figure is in 'Dropping South: Brazil', a poem written originally for John Crowe Ransom, in which, after the opening allusion to Yeats's apocalyptic 'The Second Coming', we have the reiterated 'coming' of the spider from Swift's *Battle of the Books*:

Walking and walking in a mothy robe,
one finger pushing through the pocket-hole
I crossed the reading room and met my soul,
hunched, spinning downward on the colored globe.[15]

The Yeatsian allusion here invokes a 'spectral echo' of 'turning', articulated as 'spinning'. One previous such 'spinner' in a reading-room is, of course, Swift's spider, the spider who, as Lowell's soul, now turns and thereby weaves a web on this globe. In Swift's *Battle*, the spider opposes the bee; in this poem, the spider opposes the 'Wasp', the white ango-saxon protestant who fears the 'communism' which creeps like a march of red ants, from Southern America into the USA of the North. The old civil war of north and south is re-lived here, with new boundaries. The poem was written at the time of Lowell's trip to Latin America, funded by the 'Congress for Cultural Freedom' — actually, and unknown by Lowell at the time, the CIA. It is against the dominant ideology of the 'Wasp' that the political stance of the collection — and of the title poem itself — is made. For instance the stone statues of abstract union soldiers 'grow slimmer and younger each year — / wasp-wasted' [sic].[16] But the fabular opposition of spider and wasp, and their political correspondences, is itself under threat in these poems from a more dangerous beast in the labyrinthine web of the text. This beast is in fact so dangerous that it is not specifically named within the collection as a whole — though its most dangerous appendage most certainly is.

The spider is an apt figure for Lowell to adopt for the obvious reason that the collection is organised like a labyrinthine yarn, spun like a spider's web, woven from the 'self' which confesses itself and to which all the peripheral tropes return for their meaning. The web, further, is like those various nooses which not only preserve but also threaten Lowell's identity. The poetry suggests that his life is, literally, hanging by a thread woven by himself but under constant threat from the *moira*. As a threatening mode of writing, then, a mode of writing which, far from preserving the self (as most confessional poetry is thought to do), actually threatens that self, this text approximates to what Leiris called the proper operation of confessional writing.

Leiris inaugurated his own poetic theme of the bull-fight in *Tauromachies* of 1937, at roughly the same time when the bull became an important figure for Picasso and Hemingway. Writing just after the war, he developed it with the proposition that real confessional writing must involve exactly the same danger of the horn which the bull-fighter confronts. Leiris, who was of the generation which just missed active involvement in the First World War, wrote in *L'Age d'homme* that the passage into the Second World War would be his 'blooding' into manhood. When confronted by the unmistakable reality of the historical destruction of a city like Le Havre, a writer — a confessional writer — must be assured of the comparable seriousness of her or his enterprise; consequently, for Leiris, there must be some real — not just metaphorical — danger involved in writing the confessional text. The writer must face the deadly horn of the bull, like the torero in the bull-ring. It is this which Lowell takes over here, for the web of the spider becomes analogous to the terrain of the bull or the arena in which Caligula, Lowell's namesake, placed his fattened animals for slaughter. Lowell, as the modern spider at the centre of the web is like a 'bull's eye', a sitting target under surveillance from the horn of the dangerous bull. This requires illustration and further explication.

The collation of spinner/spider and bull in the figure of the web suggests another source-narrative ghosting the collection. That story is Ovid's narrative of Theseus and Ariadne (and it is important to note that Ovid appears and disappears in the text, especially in the various revisions of 'Beyond the Alps'). The story alluded to involves the making of something very like a spider's web, made or spun in an effort not only to kill the bullish Minotaur, but also to enable Theseus to find a way home, to find a way out of the maze or 'a-maze-ment'. This is exactly akin to the movement out of the 'mazes of a weir' in 'Water'; and, very importantly, it is also a movement away from the 'maize', significantly an 'Indian maize' which occupies a central position in 'The Old Flame'. It is as if the activity of narrating, spinning a

yarn, offers the possibility not only of facing the horn at the centre
of the labyrinth, but also of escaping it. The centre of the web has
a triple figuration identifying three elements: spider; horned bull;
and Lowell himself as author spinning the web. In short, it
becomes clear that one central figure ghosting the text in antonomasia is not the self and name of Lowell but rather Tatanka
Iyotake, Sitting Bull, Chief of the nomadic Sioux who fought the
famous struggle against the colonialist and imperialist American
oppressors — specifically Custer — at the Little Big Horn river in
1876.

A number of alias figures begin to appear in this confessional
text. There is a breaking of the bounds of the identity of Lowell,
whose ethical condition gives way to a political history as Lowell
names himself as Iyotake, Caligula, Swift, Yeats and so on. That is
to say, there begins to appear a textual weaving of names and
identities such that a concern for ethos cedes place to a concern
for the narrative relation among a series of proper names: a history
of the polis. Insofar as Lowell's 'self' is also identified with
modern America, insofar as he is the 'representative' of America,
the series of aliases makes it clear that what is of major interest
here is the relation between the present politics of America and
the prior politics of other imperialist figures.

Just as he was writing these poems, Lowell had read Wilson's
Patriotic Gore, on the literature of the American civil war.
Wilson's text makes explicit comparisons between contemporary
America and other geographical areas where imperialism has
taken root. Interestingly, too, in the introduction to the text (to
which Lowell makes explicit allusion in a letter agreeing with
Wilson's sentiments), Wilson offers a 'bestial' comparison of
imperialism with zoology:

I think that it is a serious deficiency on the part of historians and political
writers that they so rarely interest themselves in biological and zoological
phenomena. In a recent Walt Disney film showing life at the bottom of the sea,
a primitive organism called a sea slug is seen gobbling up smaller organisms
through a large orifice at one end of its body; confronted with another sea slug
of an only slightly lesser size, it ingurgitates that, too. Now, the wars fought by
human beings are stimulated as a rule primarily by the same instincts as the
voracity of the sea slug.[17]

The 'bestiary' model here is apparent in Wilson's commentary on
Julia Ward Howe's words for 'The Battle Hymn of the Republic',
according to which the Unionist Hero operates as God's Hero to
crush the Confederate serpent underfoot with the heel. The song
also has what is, to Wilson, a mysterious reference to 'lilies in the
beauty of which Jesus is supposed to have been born'. Wilson
confesses that the only place in the Gospels (the intertext for
much of the 'Battle Hymn') where lilies are mentioned is in the
parable where 'they toil not, neither do they spin', and hence
where they appear as non-spiders. Wilson's anti-imperialist (and
to a large extent overtly anti-American) text is also a major
influence shaping the politics of *For the Union Dead*, poems
written in the centenary of the civil war. Wilson wrote that the
centennial was absurd, and that 'a day of mourning would be
more appropriate'; and it is worth considering Lowell's text as the
work of a mourning.

At the time of writing *For the Union Dead*, Lowell was also
pursuing his other writings as translator or 'imitator'; and the
main project which engaged him at the time was his translation of
Racine's *Phèdre*. Here too Theseus would figure, and when Lowell
presented this work in the *Partisan Review*, he offered a 'Back-
ground to the action' which dealt with the story of the Minotaur.
In his translation of II, v, Phèdre compares herself with Ariadne,
and Hippolytus with Theseus:

I would have reached the final corridor
a lap before you, and killed the Minotaur

and Phèdre goes on:

Prince, the gods corrupt
us; though I never suffered their abrupt
seductions, shattering advances, I
too bear their sensual lightnings in my thigh.
I too am dying. I have felt the heat
that drove my mother through the fields of Crete
the bride of Minos, dying for the full
magnetic April thunders of the bull . . .
plowing my body with its horny thrust.[18]

The deadly horn of the bull is clearly present here, and in ways
which are not at all as apparent in Racine's French text. But if

Theseus can be regarded as the proto-bullfighter ghosting the terrain of Lowell's arena, precursor of Leiris and Hemingway, then it might be apposite to explore the location of the bull's deadly horns, that threat to the self which is the very founding condition of Leirisian confessional poetry.

There is no shortage of horns in *For the Union Dead*; it is indeed a cornucopia. The horns take many forms, often not as a horn as such but as its cognate, the 'corn'. In these terms, we have for instance 'Alfred Corning Clark', where the horn/corn appears in the very centre of Clark's name. We also have a site for the horns which Clark lacked. The poem makes it clear that Clark was not 'horned', not a cuckold, though married several times; there were 'pale concavities of your forehead',[19] a site for horns which were not there. Similar corns/horns appear throughout the collection. For example, in 'The Drinker', there are corns flaking like dead skin, and 'milk turns to junket in the cornflakes bowl'.[20] The bowl becomes an arena in miniature for the thoughts on suicide and the murder of time, the 'killing time', which goes on in the poem. As in the corridor or *corrida*, at least as described by Hemingway in *Death in the Afternoon*, there are even horsemen in this arena, the space where time is at a premium, for the fighter has but fifteen minutes for the completion of the gladiatorial ritual. Here, the horsemen are police, and are 'yellow-skinned' for reasons that will be apparent later.

Clark's concavities in the temple recur in 'Caligula' where, following Suetonius's description of the emperor, Lowell gives him 'eyes hollow, hollow temples' and describes his legs as 'spindly', like a spider's. There are a number of sites for horns, targets, as it were, where the horn is to be placed. But the trope of the horn as corn takes on a different significance when it is interwoven with another sense of 'corn', the corn produced on the foot by shoes that pinch. In 'Buenos Aires', another of Lowell's South American poems, Lowell listens to the bulls and cattle lowing outside his hotel room:

I heard
the bulky, beefy breathing of the herds[21]

These herds of cattle provide the materials in which Lowell is dressed:

Cattle furnished my new clothes;
my coat of limp, chestnut-colored suede,
my sharp shoes
that hurt my toes

producing, as Webster's dictionary tells us, the callosities we call
'corns'. Lowell here features himself as an uncanny prefiguration
of the comic Woody Allen character, Zelig; for he has begun to
assume the precise shape of his hosts — here the bulls in Brazil.
This is precisely what does happen, for towards the close of the
poem an Ovidian metamorphosis occurs, signifying not only
Lowell's siding politically with the oppressed of Buenos Aires,
but also signifying an absurdist situation where, like Béranger in
Ionesco's *Rhinoceros* (first performed just prior to the writing of
this poem) Lowell actually starts to become a bull. The beefy
breathing of the herds which opens the poem is transmuted by the
end into Lowell's own breath (or spirit), now the breath of a bull
or man in bull's clothing — leather — which, as the joke here
suggests, is discomfiting:

I was the worse for wear,
and my breath whitened the winter air
next morning, when Buenos Aires filled
with frowning, starch-collared crowds.

In the course of this 'cultural mission' to South America, it is as if
Lowell becomes precisely the bull at the centre of his own
labyrinth; Lowell as Minotaur threatened by the very Theseus of
whose traducing he will write in his translation of *Phèdre*. Having
adopted the skin of the bull as well as its horns/corns, Lowell here
comes close to finding his Theseus — who in this text, goes under
the alias of General George Custer — in 'Hawthorne', another man
with a 'horn' at the very centre of his identity.

When the CIA sent Lowell on this South American trip, they
were concerned, as ever, with the threat from the 'reds', and
specifically from Neruda, to whom Lowell was supposed to
operate as a kind of cultural counter-agent. But the Union had, of
course, fought against 'reds' before. The civil war, resolving a geo-
political confrontation of North and South, allowed the other axis,
East/West, to swing into place. There was a constant pushing back

of the western frontier, an activity which relocated the 'red' Indians on reservations, deterritorialising them in the rush for land and gold: de-*racin*-ating them, as it were. Lowell was involved in a modern moment of deracination: imitating Racine, but complaining that Dryden and Pope should have attended to this near neighbour rather than to the less accessible Homer.

At this point, the implicit political dimension of *For the Union Dead* begins to come clear. It is certainly not just a re-presentation of Lowell's own consciousness; nor is it just about that battle between North and South, Unionists and Confederates as represented by Lowell and Tate; nor is it just about the symbolic equation of emancipation with North, slavery with South; nor is it just about communism in modern America. It is about the historical relations among Lowell's various aliases. It is about the historical relation of the civil war on its North/South axis to the moment of the American deterritorialisation of an indigenous population of Indians, the East/West axis. It is about the historical relation of the configuration formed by these moments to the moment of Lowell's writing. At that moment, the early 1960s, the North/South axis is being re-figured around the Bay of Pigs where a Northern USA faces a Southern American communism; and the East/West axis is reactivated around the focus of Berlin with the building of the Berlin Wall. The North/South divide is construed historically in these texts as a confrontation, across time, of at least two empires: the Spanish/Portuguese on the one hand (the Latin component), and the American on the other. These are both compared with the earlier empire of Rome and the Caesars. The East/West axis, focussed in Berlin, raises the spectre of Europe (as does the presence of Spain and Portugal). Bearing in mind the presence of Ovid in these texts, this also introduces the personage of Europa who, in *Metamorphoses* 2, p. 836ff., is taken by Jupiter, disguised as a bull, to Crete: this is the rape of Europe. It is to this that Lowell is relating the Berlin crisis which informs the poetry of this collection most overtly. Jupiter, like Lowell in 'Buenos Aires', assumes the shape of a bull:

His hide was white as untrodden snow, snow not yet melted by the rainy South wind. The muscles stood out on his neck, and deep folds of skin hung along his flanks. His horns were small, it is true, but so beautifully made that you would swear they were the work of an artist, more polished and shining than any jewel. There was no menace in the set of his head or in his eyes; he looked completely placid. . . . Now he frolicked and played on the green turf, now lay down, all snowy white on the yellow sand. Gradually the princess lost her fear, and with her innocent hands she stroked his breast when he offered it for her caress, and hung fresh garlands on his horns: till finally she even ventured to mount the bull, little knowing on whose back she was resting. Then the god drew away from the shore by easy stages, first planting the hooves that were part of his disguise in the surf at the water's edge, and then proceeding farther out to sea, till he bore his booty away over the wide stretches of mid ocean. The girl was sorely frightened, and looked back at the sands behind her, from which she had been carried away. Her right hand grasped the bull's horn, the other rested on his back, and her fluttering garments floated in the breeze.[22]

The rape of Europa involves a literal deterritorialisation of Europe, as she is, so to speak, given a *cornada* by the bull/Jupiter, and hoisted off the earth itself, put into flight. For Lowell, this is what the horn of the bull threatens: the rape of Europe in the name of a 'bullish' and imperialist USA.

The issue of the imperialist rape of Europe, the 'struggle for Europe', takes a number of forms in Lowell's writings of 1959–1965. It culminates in his opposition to the American presence not so much in Europe as in Asia, in his opposition to the war in Vietnam in 1967. The march on the Pentagon in which he took part, alongside Mailer, was to involve — at least as media event — the literal deterritorialisation of the Pentagon; Abbie Hoffman announced that the Pentagon would rise into the air and all the bad vibes would fall out.[23] The march led to the single most famous photograph of the anti-war demonstrations, in which a student is seen placing flowers in the barrels of the guns of the US National Guard. The language of flowers directly confronts violence.

Lowell's lifelong alias, of course, was 'Cal', the abbreviation of the name of Caligula, terroristic Roman emperor. Caligula plays an important part in the labyrinth traced by these poems. Caligula's was a European empire, neither American nor Soviet. When Lowell was writing *For the Union Dead*, the real arena of political engagement was organised in a crux between, on the one hand, the East/West confrontation in Berlin and, on the other, a North/ South confrontation in America (domestically, in terms of Civil Rights; internationally, in terms of Northern USA facing Latin

American communism in the Bay of Pigs). In both axes here, what is at issue is precisely time and history: the geopolitical assumes its fully chrono-political dimension. This is for the simple reason that the weapons which could be deployed in these confrontations were nuclear; and the single most significant point about these, as Virilio indicates, is not just their massive destructive power, but, strategically, their *speed*.[24]

Time, clearly, is an important recurring trope in *For the Union Dead*. It operates on both micro- and macro-levels: Lowell marks time all through the collection, insistently referring to counting down, to the various clocks which punctuate the text; simultaneously, he traces the historical relations between contemporary imperialism and the imperialisms of other regimes and times such as that of ancient Rome. Vitally, here, the imperialism figures in his namesake, Caligula. The implication is that imperialism exists within the self as well as within the state. In the many revisions of 'Caligula', there is one most significant change, involving a negation. The first attempt at a 'Caligula' poem is in *Imitations*, where Lowell works on the model of Baudelaire's 'Spleen (1)'; this re-appears as 'Caligula (1)' in *History*. The version in *For the Union Dead*, however, is not an imitation, though it is clearly influenced by Suetonius and by Wilson's occasionally allegorical 'Introduction' to *Patriotic Gore*. Lowell describes Caligula in terms which make him appear like a spider:

You hear your household panting on all fours,
and itemize your features — sleep's old aide!
Item: your body hairy, badly made,
head hairless, smoother than your marble head;
Item: eyes hollow, hollow temples, red
cheeks rough with rouge, legs spindly, hands that leave
a clammy snail's trail on your soggy sleeve . . .[25]

Vitally, this version of the poem ends on a hopefully positive note, after the deification of Caligula. Lowell alludes to the gladiatorial contests (the Roman equivalent of bullfights) which Caligula organised, and then to the suffering of Caligula's own death:

      Animals
fattened for your arena suffered less
than you in dying — yours the lawlessness

of something simple that has lost its law,
my namesake, and the last Caligula.

This is a leave-taking, then, of the name, identity or alias of 'Cal',
a farewell to the tyrant. There is a poem explicitly called 'Law' in
this collection (and hence Lowell has not 'lost' his 'law', though it
appears in an odd textual configuration with 'The F*law*'). Further,
if Caligula was the 'last' of the name, then Lowell has been
operating under a false alias, a misnomer. He has been 'anachronistic' and misplaced, his time being the twentieth century (and not
AD 12–48), his place America (and not Rome). However, the
revisions of the poem betray this as a false optimism, as if Lowell
had failed in the attempt to exorcise his famous manic admiration
of tyrants and power. In the revisions which appear in *Notebook*
and *History*, the final line has the addition of a negative (a
common manoeuvre in Lowell's revisions). In both cases, the final
line is 'my namesake, not the last Caligula'. And in the later
revision, in *History*, the opening of the poem makes a clear
allusion to Caligula as Lowell's alias, his own name. It is as if
Lowell tried, but failed, to exorcise his own imperialism, construed at the personal or ethical level, in *For the Union Dead*, by
making his alias a complete anachronism. At the larger political
level, the implication is that the imperialist tendency which
provokes the crucial political confrontations of North and South,
East and West, determinant of *For the Union Dead*, is also
anachronistic, somehow 'out of time', 'untimely'.

The problem, of course, is that time is of the essence in the
nuclear confrontation. As Virilio repeatedly points out, the
Second World War did not end, but continued under other means
(his parody of Clausewitz, of course) in the guise of the 'balance of
terror' and the subsequent supposed 'peace' (another misnomer).[26]
In the nuclear age, war is no longer a mere matter of space, of the
demaractions of boundaries; this is now complicated by — even
transmuted into — questions of time. Writing of SALT 1, Virilio
states:

En réalité, ce qui est en cause actuellement avec les accords sur la limitation
des armements stratégiques (S.A.L.T. 1) ce n'est plus l'explosif mais le vecteur,

le vecteur de délivrance nucléaire ou plus exactement encore ses performances. La raison en est simple: là où les déflagrations de l'explosif (molléc-
laire ou nucléaire) contribuaient à rendre l'espace impropre à l'existence, ce
sont soudain celles de l'implosif (véhicules vecteurs) qui réduisent à rien le
temps d'agir et politiquement celui de décider. S'il y a plus de trente ans
l'explosif nucléaire parachevait le cycle des *guerres de l'espace*, en cette fin de
siècle l'implosif (au-delà les territoires envahis politiquement et économique-
ment) inaugure *la guerre du temps*.[27]

This shift, from space to time, from phenomenology to historicity,
from outside (explosive) to inside (implosive) came to a head
specifically for the USA at the time of the Cuban missile crisis,
when, as Virilio points out, there was a drastic foreshortening of
range in the time required for a nuclear exchange. In 1962:

le délai de préavis de guerre est encore de *15 minutes* pour les deux Super-
grands. L'implantation de fusées russes dans les îles de Castro risquait de faire
tomber ce délai a *30 secondes* pour les Américains, ce qui était inacceptable
pour le président Kennedy quel que soit le risque de son refus catégorique.[28]

It is in the light of this, and of his comment that American bombs
should not be used at all, that Lowell marks time so insistently in
For the Union Dead. The police on horseback in 'The Drinker',
where the question is whether the persona is 'killing time',
suddenly assume the guise of horsemen of the apocalypse; their
skins are yellow, tinged with glowing radiation. The clocks which
mark time, further, are the kind that glow in the dark by emitting
radioactivity, as seen in 'Myopia: A Night' or 'Hawthorne'. The
'wasp-wasted' soldier has already appeared in another figure, in
'Those Before Us', where 'Sands drop from the hour-glass waist'.
In 'Mouth of the Hudson', 'The ice ticks seaward like a clock'; and
so on through many other examples.[29]

   But there are two extremely important temporal effects in these
figures, apart from their theme of the final countdown. First, there
is the fact that the dominant time-piece here is the grandfather
clock, marking time by its pendulous balance, by its swinging
back and forth in balanced movement: a balance of terror when it
is recalled that the time being passed, for Lowell, is the final thirty
seconds. Secondly, there is the relation established in 'Fall, 1961',
between time and the voice, through a pun on 'tock': 'tock, tock,
tock . . . we have talked our extinction to death'.[30] It becomes clear

that, for Lowell, the most terrifying figure is that of the clock itself, time and its insistent death-watch counting down to the apocalyptic visions of the title poem at the end of the collection. In this poem, the old South Boston Aquarium — that fish-bowl behind which Lowell had earlier swum like a minnow — is empty and destroyed.[31] The poem makes an explicit comparison between the internal civil war in America and the events of contemporary politics, those confrontations over Berlin and Cuba (the first a result of Yalta; the second a consequence, according to Wilson in *Patriotic Gore*, of America's victimisation of the Castro regime after Castro overthrew the cruel rule of Batista, a rule which had been US-supported). The monument to Shaw and his Negro regiment:

sticks like a fishbone
in the city's throat.
Its Colonel is as lean
as a compass-needle.[32]

This monument stands, though unwanted by Shaw's father, who:

wanted no monument
except the ditch,
where his son's body was thrown
and lost with his 'niggers'.

The ditch is nearer.

The fact that it stands offers a contrast with the Second World War, for which there are no statues. But two important themes are introduced in the comparison here: first, photography appears again; secondly, spatial contraction, the elimination of space, is stressed:

The ditch is nearer.
There are no statues for the last war here;
on Boyleston Street, a commercial photograph
shows Hiroshima boiling

over a Mosler Safe, the 'Rock of Ages'
that survived the blast. Space is nearer.

In the poem, the elimination of space is of the essence; but it runs concurrently with the elimination of time. Not only has the elimination of space brought the United States and the Soviet Union closer, around the Bay of Pigs, but also fifteen minutes is thus reduced to thirty seconds. Extending this principle, Lowell is able to conflate the civil war with his contemporary position.

The notion of the 'balance of terror' is usually referred to as a strategy of 'deterrence'. In fact, it is a continuation of war through a terror of balance, the necessary continued equal preparation for war, as Virilio has indicated.[33] The increased speed with which missiles can move, due to technology, is approaching ultimate speed, the speed of light (in the laser). This has the effect of collapsing space entirely, tantamount to making space disappear in fact. The 'terrain of the bull' has shrunk to nothing: the horn touches the poet/torero. Custer has, as it were, met Sitting Bull.

What is at issue here, then, is not simply geo-political representation, in which Lowell becomes a representative of the space or identity of 'America', or in which his personal identity is entwined 'democratically' with the identity of America in the world. There is a chrono-politics here, in which Lowell has to adopt a series of aliases, personae from other times. He is, as it were, *anachronistic* with respect to America, searching for or constructing another time (the alias) of America. In short, he constructs America not as a geography but as a history; and in this, there is a historical relation between for instance, Caligula and Tatanka Iyotake, and between them and Swift, Swift and Jupiter and so on in a series of significant geographies.

This historicity — anachronicity — informs the geo-politics of America, in those confusions of the North/South axes with the varying East/West axes. Further, this anachronicity is, paradoxically, both 'untimely' and 'timely'. It is untimely in the sense that Lowell is clearly not simply representing a present-day contemporary America, but is rather constructing a narrative history where things and subjects are out of their proper time or moment. It is timely in the sense that, first, Lowell is here obsessed by time, and secondly, the poetry is uttering a warning about the relation of time to 'tock/talk', time to poetry. In short, if poetry is heard, history continues. History has become dependent upon poetry itself which is now, therefore, always upto-the-minute, and therefore seemingly 'modern'. But, insofar as this poetry is anachronistic and proleptic, it has become fully *postmodern*: not prophetic, but rather anachronistic, a mode of representation which has fully entered the historical, accepting its own historicity (its future anteriority) as representation.

De Man's argument, then, that 'It is a historical fact that irony becomes increasingly conscious of itself in the course of demonstrating *the impossibility of our being historical*',[34] is severely limited, and is effectively disproved by an ethics of postmodernism in which the problem of representation is addressed, in fully *historical* terms, as a chrono-political issue. It is not at all the case that our being historical is impossible. Such an argument depends upon a retreat to a Cartesian or 'modern' view in which there is a radical and profound split between subject and object (or, as it is mediated in Romanticism and since, between Humanity and Nature, or between Self and Other). For this argument to be sustained, either representation as an issue has to be ignored, or it has to be treated in purely spatial, geo-political — phenomenological — terms. The postmodern condition not only attends to representation, but also indicates that the movement of history itself is nothing other than a series of engagements between and among representations. Postmodernism shows that the self which, in de Man, is divorced from historicity, can itself be enacted only in the form of representations.

The important aspect of this, however, as my analysis of Lowell bears out, is that this representation operates not as representation in the mode of identity but rather as representation in the historical mode of alterity. That is, it is perhaps better considered not as 'representation' but, to coin a neologism, as *aliation*: an anachronistic historical enactment of the Self through the figures or alias of the Other. This postmodern aliation proposes the *inevitability* of our being historical, an inevitability which an entire modernist project has tried to circumvent. But historicity is thus inevitable only when the self is figured or represented through the Other, not as an identity but rather as a heterogeneity: a self whose condition is always to differ from itself. The bourgeois individualism proposed by the de Manic position leads only and inevitably to the evasion of history. Individualism is itself resistant to historicity, largely becuse it is based on an ethics of identity which is founded on a phenomenological geo-politics merely. A postmodern politics of heterogeneity is, by dint of its inclination to aliation, always fully historical, anachronistic, circumventing the 'end of time' through its status as aliation.

IV

Aural Labyrinth

Listening

Poisons in the Ear

6.1 DANCING IN THE LABYRINTH: ENCHANTMENT AND AMAZEMENT

It is obvious that something goes awry with the function and understanding of representation in the postmodern condition. Fundamentally, my argument in preceding pages has been an elaboration, in very different terms, of Irigaray's attack upon the 'specularity' of Western thought at least since the time of Descartes, that self-reflexive specularity which eventuates in the characterisation of the subject as masculinist.[1] It might be worth considering the modernist project, from Descartes to the Frankfurt School, as one which holds a particular tendency towards masculinism, with its prioritisation of specularity in the various metaphorical tropes of 'introspection' (Descartes), 'vision' (the Romantics), or 'Enlightenment' (the *philosophes* and their progeny all the way to Habermas who thinks modernity as 'an unfinished project').[2] The postmodern, consequently, might productively be thought as that which questions the very modes of thought, knowledge and representation of the social formation or ideology of masculinism as such; and it does this by questioning the specular (even as it clearly plays with it), by becoming uneasy with what I have referred to as a dominant *photological imagination* of modernism itself.

This is to say, of course, that there is some relation between, on one hand, the heterogeneity characteristic of eclectic postmodernity, and, on the other, 'thinking otherwise', a thinking characterised by alterity which organises much feminist politics. If masculinism is dependent upon the primacy of a particular kind of modernist geopolitics of representation (typically, a modernist bourgeois democracy lends a vote only to men in the first instance: property, held by men, is the passport to a vote, to representation of the voice), then postmodernism marks the readiness of the moment for a feminisation of culture, a turn away from the eye and from what Baudrillared refers to as the 'ob-scene' towards a different sensuality, a different (non-visionary) imagination: an imagination without the tyranny of the iconic image. Such an iconoclasm, of course, is itself a dominant part of the postmodern.[3]

Such iconoclasm leaves a 'heap of broken images', and it is obvious that any such fragmented art-form organises itself not as a spatial whole, not in terms of a geo-political integrity, but rather in terms of *time*, in terms of the time taken to construct the narrative of its perception. Representation, then, has not ended, but has simply shifted from a geo- to a chrono-political modality; and the postmodern can be characterised as, among other things, that moment when the historicity of representation becomes apparent in all its temporality.

Temporality, however, as aestheticians at least since G.E. Lessing have always known, is perceived not so much by the iconic eye as by the narrative ear. A modernist cultural theory found its politics by suggesting that all readers 'participate', finding their individualist and quasi-democratic voice in a modern Babel (all readers become quasi-writers and shape the text; or, in structuralism, the world becomes a scene of writing, and so on). Postmodernism discovers the necessity for, or organises itself around, the primacy of the ear, of listening as a vital part of this babbling democracy. But this, as it stands, is too passivist: listening itself has an active component and becomes fully itself only when it enters the stage which Attali has characterised as 'composition'.[4]

It might appear that my argument here flies directly in the face of a leading theorist of postmodernity, Jean-François Lyotard, who argues in an early text, *Discours, figure*, for the primacy of the eye, for the primacy of perception over language, of line over letter as he puts it:

La position de l'art est un démenti à la position du discours. La position de l'art indique une fonction de la figure, qui n'est pas signifiée, et cette fonction autour et jusque dans le discours. Elle indique que la transcendance du symbole est la figure, c'est-à-dire une manifestation spatiale que l'espace linguistique ne peut pas incorporer sans être ébranlé, une extériorité qu'il ne peut pas intérioriser en *signification*. L'art est posé dans l'altérité en tant que plasticité et désir, étendue courbe, face à l'invariabilité et à la raison, espace diacritique. L'art veut la figure, la 'beauté' est figurale, non-liée, rythmique. Le vrai symbole donne à penser, mais d'abord il se donne à 'voir'. Et l'étonnant n'est pas qu'il donne à penser si tant est qu'une fois le langage existant, tout objet est à signifier, à mettre dans un discours, tombe dans le trémis ou la pensée remue et trie tout, l'énigme est qu'il reste à 'voir', qu'il se maintienne incessament sensible, qu'il y ait un mode qui soit une réserve de 'vues', ou un entremonde qui soit une réserve de 'visions', et que tout discours s'épuise avant d'en venir à bout.[5]

Lyotard's prioritisation — here, at least — of the visual, even in writing, seems to be reinstating the very mode of specularity of which, according to my argument, postmodernism marks the decline. But his phenomenological point here is simply to prioritise some level of historical representation in the mode of 'experience', literally *avant la lettre*, a level of experience which is always in place prior to its symbolisation. Although he argues that '*L'oeil, c'est la force*', Lyotard also indicates a similar effect in terms of the aural:

Ce qui parle est quelque chose qui doit être en dehors de la langue et ne pas cesser de s'y tenir même quand il parle. Le silence est le contraire du discours, il est la violence en même temps que la beauté; mais il en est la condition puisqu'il est du côté des choses *dont* il y a à parler et *qu'il* faut exprimer. Pas de discours sans cette opacité à tenter de défaire et de restituer, cette épaisseur intarissable. Le silence résulte du déchirement à partir duquel un discours et son objet se placent en vis-à-vis, et commence le travail de signifier; et il résulte du déchirement incorporé à la parole, ou le travail d'exprimer s'effectue.[6]

The perception of which Lyotard writes here, then, may be aural every bit as much as visual. His crucial point is not the prioritisation of one sense over the other but rather the historicity of perception and representation as such. Much of *Discours, figure* attends precisely to matters of the operation of verbalised language or discourse, considered eventually in the paradigmatic form of the *rébus*. When Lyotard indicates the predominance of the perceptual as the condition of the conceptual-linguistic, he invokes Klee:

Le tableau n'est pas à lire, comme le disent les sémiologues d'aujourd'hui, Klee disait qu'il est à *brouter*, il fait voir, il s'offre à l'oeil comme une chose exemplaire, comme une nature naturante, disait encore Klee, puisqu'il fait voir ce qu'est voir. Or il faut voir que voir est une danse. Regarder le tableau c'est y tracer des chemins, du moins, puisqu'en le faisant le peintre a ménagé impérieusement (encore que latéralement) des chemins à suivre, et que son oeuvre est ce bougé consigné entre quatre bois, qu'un oeil va remettre en mouvement, en vie.[7]

According to this, all painting should be considered in the terms of 'Action Painting', where one traces the lines followed by, say, Pollock, de Kooning or late Hoffman as they moved or 'danced' over the canvas; such painting becomes the temporal narrative of an act of painting. And, as with paint, so with discourse which now is considered in terms very close to those elaborated by Valéry in his delineation of the differences between prose and verse. Writing too becomes a dance, a movement whose condition is historical: 'l'oeuvre poétique ... peut être caractérisée sommairement comme constitutée d'un texte travaillé par la figure', as Lyotard puts it.[8]

This figural historicity — which becomes the narrative or temporal condition of textuality according to this — makes it difficult, if not impossible, for a text to advance propositions which have any serious theoretical or systematic truth-claims whatsoever. This holds insofar as we consider truth to be, by definition, totalising, a truth which is true for all time and for all places. Truth, as the quarry of art, is here replaced by the enactment of desire. In giving up the ghost of a systematising theorised truth, Lyotard's postmodern converges with the thinking of another intellectual, Julia Kristeva, who became disillusioned with Marxism in the wake of 1968. Kristeva replaces a totalising linguistic theory with the prioritisation of the historical speaking subject, the *sujet-en-procès*, to whom Kristeva, as psychoanalyst, learns to *listen*. For Lyotard, all art-works are *en-procès* like this; their postmodernity lies precisely in their historicity, their orientation towards a future, or in my own preferred terms, their anachronicity or aliation.

One can thus relate closely Lyotard's prioritisation of the visual in these terms (i.e., as historical activity, as the work *en-procès* or as aliation) both to the Kristevan speaking psychoanalytic subject (and the ear which listens to that voice), and, more widely or abstractly, to Jacques Attali's comment, that:

For twenty-five centuries, Western knowledge has tried to look upon the world. It has failed to understand that the world is not for the beholding. It is for hearing. It is not legible, but audible . . . Nothing essential happens in the absence of noise.

Today our sight has dimmed; it no longer sees our future, having constructed a present made of abstraction, nonsense, and silence. Now we must learn to judge a society more by its sounds . . .[9]

Postmodernism adjures us to learn to *listen* though not as a passivity; this listening is highly active; we should hear, as it were, the noise of art as well as the Art of Noise. As at the opening of what might be considered one of the first postmodern plays, Ibsen's *Ghosts*, we must listen hard, for Regine is keeping her voice low, complaining at the quasi-Oedipal Engstrand to 'Stop clumping about with that foot, man!'[10] Or, as in the poem which itself inspired much contemporary music, Mallarmé's 'L'après-midi d'un faune', we must not only see but also hear inspiration:

> le seul vent
> Hors des deux tuyaux prompt à s'exhaler avant
> Qu'il disperse le son dans une pluie aride,
> C'est, à l'horizon remué d'une ride,
> Le visible et serein souffle artificiel
> De l'inspiration qui regagne le ciel.[11]

While it would be Vaslav Nijinsky who allowed us to see this inspiration, in his choreographed leaps which '*regagnent le ciel*', it was of course Debussy who made this breathy inspiration *audible* in his 'Prélude a l'après-midi d'un faune' in 1894, some 18 years before Nijinsky danced it. But that figural dance is itself latent in the art of this noise itself, both Debussy's and Mallarmé's. Nijinsky's dance is, as it were, the composition which figures the active listening to the noise of this art, its historicity. It is a dance whose primary characteristic is, literally, *flight* or deterritorialisation. Nijinsky's leaps are the dominant trope in his figures.

Listening, is, of course, shaped by a labyrinth, the labyrinth of the ear itself. Daedalus, maker of labyrinths, knew that the best way to avoid the threat of labyrinthine 'a-maze-ment' — or enchantment — is through flight, through what Joyce's Daedalus might have thought as a 'flee in your ear'. Modernist demystification — the tendency to disillusion or 'disenchantment', an attempt to escape magic which characterises the modernist project — produced one dominant understanding of flight: as exile. But exile itself implies a stable territorialised home. Postmodernism is able to sustain the possibility of enchantment — known conventionally as the 'postmodern sublime' — and will take the risk of enchantment in listening, the risk of self-amazement; as a result, the flights which it has privileged are those which have no root and no landing: a state of exile without territory.

As with the Futurists, it is this tendency to flight — and also to speed — which is the Lyotardian 'figure' working itself out across or through the textual 'discourse'. Diaghilev's dancers, Mallarmé's verse, Debussy's music, Futurist proto-happenings are all usually considered as founding components of the modernist movement; but this is a rather parochial understanding of the modernist project. In their tendency to a historical labyrinthine figuring, in their ability to risk enchantment or incantatory magic, in their noisy temporality, in their fully deterritorialised flights, their fully *postmodern* impetus is to be discovered.

In the present argument, I shall outline a tension between a modernism which territorialises and a postmodern characterised by deterritorialisation and the eradication of 'roots' and 'rootedness'. Developing the arguments advanced in earlier chapters of this book, I shall show that modernism claims America and colonises the imagination of Europe from that position; the postmodern is de-colonialist, anti-imperialist, deterritorialising and fully internationalist. There are three components constituting the 'figure' 'danced' by my text. First, I attend to a configuration of texts in which problems of hearing predominate. The difficulty of hearing, I argue, is precisely the difficulty of hearing/ understanding a womanly voice from within a masculinist problematic of modernist ideology. Secondly, I examine in more detail the tension between, on the one hand, modernist territorialisation (with its attendant problems of nationalism, and the prioritisation of the earthy metaphor of 'culture' in all its forms), and, on the other, postmodern deterritorialisation with its consequent prioritisations of exile and flight. The third part of this argument is a brief outline of a sociology of postmodern music or noise.

6.2 INVIOLABLE VOICE

According to Virginia Woolf, T.S. Eliot did not merely recite 'The Waste Land' at her house, he 'chanted it, sang, it rhythmed it',[12] as if it were rather music than poetry; and, as Ackroyd indicates, following what is by and large accepted opinion, the poem, especially in its final section (largely unchanged by Pound), marks a return to 'the music which he had otherwise suppressed or tightened into strict and undeviating shapes'.[13] But the composition of the poem, as is well known, was anything but straightforward. Eliot had enormous difficulty in articulating his vengeful 'grouse against life' in this 'piece of rhythmical grumbling'.[14] Moreover, as the manuscripts show, Pound was performing his savage 'Caesarean' operations, ostensibly violating Eliot's new voice even as it originated in the attempt to found a new poetry.[15]

My point here is not simply that Eliot had difficulties in formulating the poem, but rather that those difficulties in speaking are a major part of the substance of the poem itself: the text is *about* the difficulty of writing 'The Waste Land', indeed and more importantly, about the difficulty of writing, speaking, 'composing' at all. Almost every character who figures in the text experiences a difficulty with her or his voice; and this difficulty often goes hand in hand with a difficulty of visual representation, a difficulty of seeing. From the earliest moments in the text, speakers are having problems with language, veering off into 'foreign' tongues or simply enduring pains with their voice. One of Pound's first annotations was to underline the four words early in the text, 'I could not/Speak' (lines 38–9). The impossibility of speaking here is immediately followed by 'and my eyes failed'; and the alignment of failing speech and failing vision is developed in the subsequent lines on Mme Sosostris, who 'Had a bad cold'; there seems to be no other reason for this other than that it affects the way one speaks: bad colds block noses, and tongues. Further, this 'famous clairvoyante' is 'forbidden to see' certain things, and cannot find — or see — the Hanged Man in her Tarot cards. What she does see are figures who themselves have something wrong with their vision, as in the reference to *The Tempest*, '(Those are pearls that were his eyes. Look!)', or to 'the one-eyed merchant' and so on. The theme of enforced silences continues in 'A Game of Chess', where one figure asks another to 'Speak to me. Why do you never speak. Speak', and where the replies to this appeal are themselves thought but unspoken. Whenever language does seem to have any success in this text it is always in a seemingly corrupt form, as for example in 'demotic French', or the demotic English of the discussion in the pub which closes 'A Game of Chess', where 'I didn't mince my words'. The speaker in 'The Fire Sermon' speaks 'not loud or long'; and even the thunder in 'What the Thunder Said' seems to have a stutter, stammering out only the beginnings of what it has to say, 'Da', for 'Datta, Dayadhvam, Damyata'. The poem seems at many points to be organised around this difficulty of finding a 'proper' voice, if not around the difficulty of speaking as such.

One figure has a major and profound difficulty with her voice in the text: Philomel. In Ovid's version of her tale, Tereus rapes his sister-in-law, Philomela, and she, outraged, threatens to 'fill the forests with my voice', proclaiming the crime of Tereus:

Her words roused the fierce tyrant to anger, and to fear no less. Goaded on by both these passions, he snatched his sword out of its scabbard where it hung at his waist, and seizing his victim by the hair, twisted her arms behind her back, and bound them fast. Philomela, filled with hopes of death when she saw the sword, offered him her throat. But even as she poured out her scorn, still calling upon her father, and struggling to speak, he grasped her tongue with a pair of forceps, and cut it out with his cruel sword. The remaining stump still quivered in her throat, while the tongue itself lay pulsing and murmuring incoherently to the dark earth.[16]

Having eventually revenged themselves on Tereus by making him eat his own son, Philomela and her sister, Procne, are turned into nightingales, and Tereus is transformed into a hoopoe. When Philomel is 'by the barbarous king/So rudely forced', she has to discover a 'barbarous' or foreign way of communicating the fact. Like Lavinia in *Titus Andronicus*, she must use 'texts'; Philomel weaves her story in the form of a representation made on 'a barbarian loom'. The entire situation here bears some telling resemblances to Eliot's concerns in his grousing 'revenge' text made up, like a tapestry, of so many disparate fragments asking to be woven into a coherent narrative. This 'barbarous' language, then, must in some sense become euphemistic, a 'language of flowers', if Eliot is to discover an 'inviolable voice' even after the mutilation of the womanly tongue. Perhaps the first place to look for this would be in the passage concerning the woman whose floral name, 'Lil', is itself an abbreviation, a cutting-short, of the name of the flower associated with purity and inviolability.

In this passage, we have a speaker who ostensibly has no verbal hang-ups: 'I didn't mince my words'. The usual reading of the passage frames itself according to whether or not the reader believes that Eliot is snobbishly mocking a working-class speech and life. But this is restricted, no matter how important, and misses much of the point of the ironic allusion to Ophelia's language made as the passage closes. Of more pressing import than the issue of class here is the issue of the womanly voice, for here we have one of the 'set-piece' monologues which organise the text as a whole. The crucial lines for the present argument are the closing ones:

Goonight Bill. Goonight Lou. Goonight May. Goonight.
Ta ta. Goonight. Goonight.
Good night, ladies, good night, sweet ladies, good night,
                    good night.

In these lines, we have an ironic counterpoint of what criticism usually unproblematically construes as a sweet and refined language of Ophelia with a supposedly low, vulgar, demotic or debased English. But it is important to recall at this point that Ophelia too speaks a language of flowers in her 'madness', and that the passage closed by her 'Good night' is thoroughly bawdy, and thus exactly akin to the speech of this woman in the pub in its lack of 'decorum'. The supposed irony of the counterpointing begins to dissipate. The passage, however, with its music-hall bawdiness, looks forward to the songs of the Rhine-maidens in 'The Fire Sermon', and in particular to the refrain 'Weialala leia/ Wallala leialala', a refrain which, after some bawdy verses, collapses into an exhausted 'la la'. Now, however, the organisation of this 'looming' texture begins to become apparent. The 'Ta ta', echoed in this 'la la', looks forward to what the thunder said, the equally banal noise, 'Da da da'. The structural organisation of the poem can be reduced to these three fundamental noises or sounds and to the movement between them: 'Ta ta . . . la la . . . da da da'; it is as if the poem itself becomes akin to the very music-hall songs which Eliot used, then cancelled, in his drafts of the first section of the poem.[17] The various kinds of 'music' in this text must be addressed.

There are basically three kinds of music here, which organise themselves around one fundamental opposition. First, there is the music of Wagner, that wailing 'la la' from *Götterdämmerung*. This harmonic form of 'high art', opera, *seems* to work in opposition to the second form of music, the 'working-class' form of the music-hall ballad, 'O O O O that Shakespeherian rag', 'O the moon shone bright on Mrs. Porter', in which 'high art' is supposedly vulgar-ised. This second type may also include the music which the typist plays, when, after seemingly uninspiring sex, she 'puts a record on the gramophone'; the 'vulgarity' of the sex, one might think, leads us to expect this music to be equally 'vulgar'. But it could equally be 'high art', for immediately the record is on, there is an allusion to *The Tempest* in a line which also permits a cross-reference to Wagner's rhine-maidens: '"This music crept by me upon the waters"'. So the seeming opposition of high art to vulgar, of opera to music hall, collapses: both are based upon *harmony*, especially upon a sexual harmony. The third kind of music is that of *discord*. It is the jarring birdsong of the nightingale's 'Jug jug' or 'Twit twit', the hermit-thrush's 'Drip drop drip drop drop drop drop', the cock's 'Co co rico co co rico'. To these basic noises of unharmonised sounds, one must add, of course, those three basic noises which, I argue, organise the text in a movement from 'Ta' to 'Da' by way of 'la'.

Three musics offer one basic opposition. On the one hand, there is harmony, and on the other, noise; on the one hand, rhyme and rhythm, on the other a 'jarring' (or jugging) fundamental noise in this 'grouse' against life. Further, it seems immediately apparent that the text, in its interior fragmentation, must clearly be on the side of the jumble of sound rather than on that of the harmonic whole. 'The Waste Land' is, as it were, precisely a model of birdsong, of the song of the nightingale. But where other versions of this Ovidian story depend upon a tongue being cut out, this one operates according to an aesthetic of glottophagia — 'O swallow swallow'. It is the obstetrician Pound who must cut out or bring out this Eliotic swallowed tongue. That, of course, places Pound in the position of Tereus, Eliot in that of Philomel; harmony on the side of force and rape or murder, birdsong or discord on that of the oppressed womanly voice. The poem thus construed demonstrates the impossibility of hearing or of listening to a womanly voice; for such a voice is thought as 'discord', heard as 'Jug jug', or as the most indecorous reminder of the sacrificial origins of song (and thus also of poetry).[18] In 'The Waste Land', women speak a language of flowers which is either unheard or misunderstood; they sing in incoherent birdsong, and this is a scandal which modernist poetry — and more especially modernist criticism — cannot bear. As Maud Ellmann has indicated, it is somewhat difficult to see the waste land for all the reconstruction that 'criticism' has been building around it; criticism has always striven to discover a principle of harmony or unification in this text, trying to hear harmony where there is only birdsong: ta . . . la . . . da.[19]

Criticism has suggested that the poem gains a mode of coherence from its trajectory, from its shape as a pilgrimage with various obstacles or deaths to be overcome. In this respect, it is thought as a simple re-writing of Chaucer, starting the pilgrimage from the common discourse of the pub like Chaucer's pilgrims, and moving towards some portentous closure, at Canterbury. There is, of course, one major difficulty with this: the poem takes a wrong turning somewhere, ending up not at Canterbury but rather somewhere east of the Ganges, some foreign place where a 'barbarous' tongue is spoken, and where one is never at home in language. The mapping of the pilgrimage, like a modern European package-tour where one struggles across Europe while one's luggage is always somewhere else, has gone wrong; and one discovers not a set of Roman Christian commandments, but rather a banal noise, 'Da', translated immediately (as if by a helpful tour-guide) into the three commandments 'Datta, Dayadhvam, Damyata'. But the single most important thing about this portentous announcement, the announcement which informs us of the end of

the journey and of our limited success in negotiating the pilgrimage (and thus in making coherent teleological sense of the text,
'reconstructing' it), is quite simply that if we are attuned to the
noise made by this poem, if we learn to listen to it properly, we
realise that we have indeed heard the message before, right at the
start of the supposed pilgrimage.

The thunder, it seems, stammers in Sanskrit. In Sanskrit, this
initial sound, 'Da', is made with the tongue not swallowed as in
English, but rather at the front of the mouth; it thus sounds more
like 'dtsa', or, putting it bluntly, 'ta'. The poem hovers between the
two sounds, 'ta' and 'da', with now an utterly minimal difference
(though still a difference) between them. 'The Waste Land' *is* a
pilgrimage; but a pilgrimage in which the only thing to move is
the tongue. The tongue moves slightly forward, thus attempting to
counter the poem's own aesthetic (or Eliot's aesthetic) of glottophagia; trying to bring to speech rather than swallowing one's
tongue. While he bore his grouse against life, listening to the birds
singing in Margate, one could certainly say to Old Possum,
'Whassa matter? Cat gotchya tongue?'

This poetic arrangement of 'The Waste Land' depends upon a
mode of listening, a mode of hearing the noise made by this
labyrinthine poem, as it slips gently from 'ta' to 'da', from west to
east, from glottophagia and the difficulty of speech to actual
utterance. It is further important that it is a working-class woman,
and a woman like Ophelia, who has already uttered the vital
phrase or noise, 'Ta ta' (or 'Da da'). That bawdy womanly voice is,
as it were, advanced in the mode of discord in the poem; it is a
voice, like the jarring jugging birdsong which cannot be heard, at
least by western ears attuned to a western harmonic and masculinist noise, a noise whose message is clear: 'HURRY UP PLEASE ITS
TIME', a noise which, in articulate speech, silences (or like Tereus,
rapes and murders) the womanly voice.

There is, however, a further complication. There exists another
figure in the poem who has difficulty speaking, Hieronymo from
Kyd's revenge-play, *The Spanish Tragedy*. Eliot considered this
play in some detail, writing about it in a number of essays.
Perhaps the comments most relevant to my argument come in the
essay on 'Seneca in Elizabethan Translation' where, first, Eliot
remarks on the importance of *hearing* Seneca: 'Seneca's plays

might, in fact, be practical models for the modern "broadcasted drama"'; and secondly goes on to disengage Kyd from the direct Senecan influence, especially given the concern for *plot* in *The Spanish Tragedy* which is unlike anything in Seneca.[20] Interestingly, the one specific element of Kyd's play on which Eliot directly comments is the episode in which Hieronymo bites off his own tongue, the bloody violence of which is aligned with that in *Titus Andronicus* with its similar concerns:

in *Titus Andronicus* ... there is nothing really Senecan at all. There is a wantonness, an irrelevance, about the crimes of which Seneca would never have been guilty. Seneca's Oedipus has the traditional justification for blinding himself; and the blinding itself is far less offensive than that in *Lear*. In *Titus*, the hero cuts off his own hand in view of the audience, who can also testify to the mutilation of the hands and tongue of Lavinia. In *The Spanish Tragedy*, Hieronymo bites off his own tongue. There is nothing like this in Seneca.[21]

The Spanish Tragedy is indeed organised around a complex plot, which turns violently upon a hanged man, Horatio, and which unravels when Hieronymo's dumb-show at the beginning is matched by the play-within-the-play at the end. This latter play eventually confuses its own status as sub-text and becomes the play which enacts the final violences in the main text. Like 'The Waste Land', Hieronymo's little play is enacted in 'unknown languages', and veers into silence when Hieronymo refuses to speak and bites out his tongue, ending up 'violate' like Philomel and like Eliot himself. It is important that the fragment from the play which Eliot directly quotes, 'Why then Ile fit you', is followed in the play by the phrase 'Say no more', for this text too is largely about discordant silences and jarring or jugging tongues.

Apart from the obvious correspondences between Kyd's play and Eliot's poem, including direct quotations and especially the King's demand, 'Speak, traitor; damned, bloody murderer, speak!', 'Why speak'st thou not', which are picked up in 'A Game of Chess', there are two extremely pertinent allusive links between the texts. The first concerns the doomed tryst between Bel-Imperia and Horatio, that tryst which will provide this text's 'Hanged Man'. Arranging this meeting, Bel-Imperia says:

Then be thy father's pleasant bower the field,
Where first we vowed a mutual amity:
The court were dangerous, that place is safe.

And at this point, the echoes which Eliot uses begin to appear, as Bel-Imperia describes the 'violet' hour, an hour which will become one of violation:

Our hour shall be when Vesper gins to rise,
That summons home distressful travellers.
There none shall hear us but the harmless birds:
Happily the gentle nightingale
Shall carol us asleep ere we be ware,
And singing with the prickle at her breast,
Tell our delight and mirthful dalliance.[22]

Sexuality here is marked, as in Eliot, by the song of the nightingale; but the important thing is that the gentle nightingale does not get the chance to sing them to rest. Its song remains unheard as Horatio becomes the hanged man in 2,iv, murdered by Lorenzo and Balthazar, who is jealous of Horatio's sexual success with Bel-Imperia. This nightingale, like Philomel and like the womanly tongue in general in 'The Waste Land', goes unheard. It is the fact that its song goes unheard — because sex is replaced by murder — which causes Hieronyno to go mad, having seen (unlike Mme Sosostris) a hanged man, his son.

The second point of contact between Kyd and Eliot relevant here comes later in *The Spanish Tragedy* when Hieronymo, by this time acting somewhat like Hamlet, meets and judges the case of an old man, Bazulto, whose son has also been murdered. At this moment, Hieronymo sees himself, so to speak; but this self-reflection, this echo of himself in Bazulto, is unharmonious:

Ay, now I know thee, now thou nam'st thy son;
Thou art the lively image of my grief:
Within thy face my sorrows I may see.
Thy eyes are gummed with tears, thy cheeks are wan,
Thy forehead troubled, and thy muttering lips
Murmur sad words abruptly broken off
By force of windy sighs thy spirit breathes;
And all this sorrow rises for thy son:
And selfsame sorrow feel I for my son.

Come in old man, thou shalt to Isabel;
Lean on my arm: I thee, thou me shalt stay,
And thou, and I, and she, will sing a song,
Three parts in one, but all of discords framed —
Talk not of cords, but let us now be gone,
For with a cord Horatio was slain.[23]

Here, as Hieronymo puns on the consonance of 'cord' with
'chord', there is an alignment of harmony ('chord') with murder
('cord' and hanged man). It is as if discord were necessary for the
maintenance of life itself, as if life depended upon hearing (as
indeed it does) the song of the nightingale, the birdsong which in
Eliot's text becomes explicitly discordant in its sexual associa-
tions, a jugging, jarring song.

There are at least two ways in which the song of the nightingale
has been mediated. The first of these, subscribed to by such as
Keats and Hans Christian Andersen, is that the song is charming,
harmonious, beautiful even if tinged with a plaintive note. The
second, alluded to by Lyly and, I suggest, by Eliot, is that the song
is discordant, unharmonious, a reminder of pain rather than a
balm for it. These two ways of hearing the nightingale's song are
perfectly recapitulated in Stravinsky's *Le rossignol*. Due, it is
usually agreed, to the accidental interruption of Diaghilev's
commission of *The Firebird* — and the further intrusion of
Stravinsky's composition of *Le sacré du printemps* — *Le rossignol*
was composed at two different times. The result of this is that the
first passage, composed in 1908-9, was written in recognisably
'harmonic' mode; but the later passages bore all the marks of the
more 'pagan' and discordant music which Stravinsky later came
to write. *Le rossignol*, then, is — as a whole — discordant,
clashing between its first section on one hand and its second and
third on the other. It is precisely the kind of discordant nightingale song which Eliot has difficulty not only in articulating but
also in hearing.

What, however, is this nightingale song? What is it that is being
oppressed in the use of the nightingale? What is the music that
these texts are trying (failing) to listen to? To find an answer to
these questions, we must turn to the verse of the poet who, in one
text at least, wanted to be the nightingale himself: the poet who
sang the bird's song, Keats.

The 'Ode to a Nightingale' is a somewhat problematic text, for the simple reason that the difficulty of hearing — a difficulty of hearing the poem — is structurally written into it. But it is difficult at a more banal level, too. There are, for instance, a number of odd moves in the poem, the first of which comes at the end of the first line: 'My heart aches and a drowsy *numbness pains/* My sense'.[24] The intrusive word here is 'pains', especially in its collocation alongside 'numbness'. Many critics rationalise this away by refusing to hear 'pains', replacing it with 'impedes'. But if we hear 'pains', then we are faced with this odd oxymoronic notion that numbness, usually precisely an *an*aesthetic, something which dulls the perception of pain, is here the *cause* of pain. 'Numbness', then, is operating oddly here. Alerted to this, it is odd to hear the word 'numb' recur as an echo in this first stanza, as Keats hears the bird singing 'In some melodious plot/Of beechen green, and shadows *numb*erless'. The stanza is organised between these two echoing sounds, 'numb' and 'number'. The substance of the stanza relates precisely to the poet's inability to sing, especially in comparison with the bird who sings 'in full-throated ease'. Heard in this way, 'numb' becomes, as it were, a stuttered version of 'number': the poet, literally, cannot get his 'numbers', his poetry, out; he is himself 'numberless', unlike the bird. Something is stuck in the poet's throat, unlike the bird's, making it difficult for him to get out the noise, '-er', which constitutes the satisfactory completion of his song, his 'number'. The problem is rapidly addressed in the second stanza, where the poet asks for a drink, a cool drink (presumably, of course, to clear his throat):

O, for a draught of vintage! that hath been
  Cool'd a long age in the deep-delved earth,
Tasting of Flora and the country-green,
  Dance, and Provencal song, and sunburnt mirth!
O for a beaker full of the warm South . . .

At this point, the poem again starts to go wrong. The opening request for a cool drink has become, in the couple of lines required for its articulation, a request for a 'beaker full of the warm South', a hot drink. Further, the word 'beaker', though taken

from the scientific discourses known to 'Dr' Keats, glares somewhat here, especially if we remove the two letters which had
caused the poet's stammering throaty difficulty in the first stanza,
leaving him surreptitiously asking for a 'beak' — which is, of
course, extremely pertinent given his envy of the bird's unselfcon-
scious singing. This 'beak', however, is to be warm, or even
warmer:

> O for a beaker full of the warm South,
>> Full of the true, the blushful Hippocrene,
>>> With beaded bubbles winking at the brim,
>>>> And purple-stained mouth . . .

The scenario at this point comes clear, and the blockage in the
throat which afflicts the poet and his numbers begins to be
identifiable. The poet takes his cool draught, but it immediately
returns in his 'beak', not simply warm, but positively bubbling
and leaving a purple stain on the mouth. He is, in his vocal
difficulty, enacting the tubercular spitting of blood, and it is the
clot of blood in his throat which makes singing difficult.

This has all been structured around a graded repetition: from
'numb' to 'numb-er' to an implied but unstated 'numb-est' in the
request, after all this chill, for a cool drink. But, as Eliot might
later put it,

>> Other echoes
> Inhabit the garden. Shall we follow?
> Quick, said the bird, find them, find them . . .[25]

The request to 'fade away', for example, moves into 'Fade far
away' and on into 'Away! Away!'; 'Forlorn' draws explicit attention to its own verbal repetition; 'soul' returns as 'sole'; 'Adieu'
returns thrice; '*murmur*ous . . . sum*mer*' offers further inwoven
repetition; and so on. Some of these repetitions are particularly
important for the present argument. In the fourth stanza, for
instance, we have a movement from the two initial cries, two
'aways', to the final word, 'ways' in the phrase 'winding mossy
ways', a phrase which suggests some kind of maze or, more
properly, a labyrinth. If we take this in relation to another
repetition, the function of the text's verbal echoes begins to

become more apparent. Just prior to the 'a-ways', we have a stanza governed by its initial phrase, 'Fade far away'; and this stanza is one which contains a fairly precise echo of another literary melancholic voice, one which complains that the present world is one 'Where Beauty cannot keep her lustrous eyes'. This 'lustrous' is echoed in the fourth stanza when Keats flies off with the bird:

> Already with thee! tender is the night,
>> And haply the Queen-Moon is on her throne,
>>> Cluster'd around by all her starry fays . . .

Interestingly, when the sound of 'lust' returns, it returns with the addition of the difficult suffix, '-er'. But, as I indicated above, many of these repetitions are graded and, at least implicitly, tripartite. It is thus as if Keats here is surreptitiously repeating a phrase which would proceed along the lines of 'Lust, lust . . . O lust'. And, of course, this has been heard before, in its form as 'List, list, O list' when the Ghost speaks in *Hamlet*. The difficulty here, of course, is that the poet is having some bother in 'lust-ing' or 'list-ing' (in the senses of pleasing or desiring, listening or hearing); and the poem begins to be expressly about some kind of erotics of the ear, with its own labyrinth, but a labyrinth which is 'mossy', as blocked indeed as was the poet's throat. Stanza five moves from a difficulty of vision, 'I cannot see what flowers are at my feet', towards a kind of 'darkness of hearing' through the repetitive 'mur' in 'murmurous haunt of flies on summer eves'. Then there is the third repetition of 'lust', one which converts it explicitly to its cognate, 'list': 'Darkling I listen', as Keats goes off into a kind of parody of the voice of Hamlet, which is the voice we have already heard in the figure of the melancholic speaker of stanza three. This is also the voice which we will again hear as a kind of keynote speaker in Eliot's 'The Waste Land', when the Sybil speaks in the epigraph to the poem, 'I want to die'.

These allusions to *Hamlet* in Keats's poem affect the noise or music of the nightingale and how we hear it. The song of the bird is precisely a poison being poured into the porches of Keats's ears, for it is the cause of the poet's pain, the cause of the very poisoning or disease which started the poem in the first place. But the song is also, paradoxically, the cure: the more he hears the bird, the more he is cured; but the more well he becomes, the more diseased he actually is in acknowledging his own relative poetic inability, and so on. The text is, as it were, a re-writing of the Ghost's demand for a revenge in *Hamlet*; and Keats's difficulty in avenging a familial death (perhaps that of Tom, perhaps his own impending death from the 'clots' or 'clusters/clysters' of blood which block his throat) is that he cannot properly hear what the nightingale sings. Making utterly explicit the debt to the night-singer, the Ghost, in *Hamlet*, Keats cannot hear the deceptive song of the bird:

Adieu! the fancy cannot cheat so well
  As she is fam'd to do, deceiving elf.
Adieu! Adieu! thy plaintive anthem fades . . .
  Fled is that music . . .

Heard melodies may indeed be sweet, but those unheard dominate this text just as much as they dominate that other Ode, on the 'Grecian Urn'. To hear the night-singer, the nightingale, is to commune with the voices of the dead, and to accept the call for a murderous revenge. There is a clear and explicit link, once more, between the song of the bird and some kind of call to revenge, a call to murder. That murder is sexual.

Effectively, what is being murdered is a disharmonic language, a birdsong which is indecorous and whose music has to be rendered harmonious if it is to be heard at all. The murder is committed through an act of effective silencing, according to which an alien noise, — an 'Other voice' as it were — goes unheard precisely because of its alterity. The dominant discourse of a particular music or noise (say, a discourse of masculinism) which thinks itself as a decorous harmony can only hear itself, can only accommodate sounds which it recognises as its own, sounds which it deems to be harmonious and in accord with itself. It hears only itself, and when the voice of alterity (say, that of a woman) speaks, it does one of two things: it either 'mishears' discord as harmony through an act of ideological translation (as in the nightingale's song mediated by Keats) ; or it simply ignores it (as happens to the voice of Ophelia in *Hamlet*) In both cases, silencing is equivalent to a kind of murder, according to which alterity has to be sacrificed in order for a homogeneous, unified, decorous dominant ideology to legitimise itself.

The case of Ophelia is particularly instructive. As Eliot must have noted, the songs she sings prior to uttering 'Good night' are bawdy. These songs, further, are silenced, thus forming a precise counterpart to the text's perverse 'bedroom-scene' in which Hamlet shows Gertrude's image to herself in literally specular fashion, and in which Gertrude insistently requests that Hamlet be silent, that he stop murdering her through the ear:

> O Hamlet, speak no more.
> Thou turn'st mine eyes into my very soul,
> And there I see such black and grained spots
> As will not leave their tinct . . .
> O speak to me no more.
> These words like daggers enter in my ears.
> No more, sweet Hamlet . . .[26]

This scene, of course, offers the text's literal *hamartia*, its 'missing of the mark' in which Hamlet hears a 'rat', perhaps indeed the same rat which rattles in rats' alley in 'The Waste Land', and murders it, mistaking it for the king. The rat, of course, is Polonius whose function in the play is precisely to be an ear, to listen and to do no more, to 'Give every man thine ear, but few thy tongue',[27] as he himself puts it.

When this 'ear-piece', Polonius, is murdered, there follows a great difficulty of hearing in the text,[28] focussed most pointedly on Ophelia who simply goes unheard from this moment on. When she enters in the wake of Polonius's death, she sings her 'Valentine' song, but not before we have been explicitly told that she will lack an attentive audience: Gertrude 'will not speak with her', and the Gentleman explains that her listeners simply hear what they themselves want to hear or to derive from her words:

> Her speech is nothing,
> Yet the unshaped use of it doth move
> The hearers to collection; they yawn at it,
> And botch the words up fit to their own thoughts . . .[29]

Her bawdy song gets precious little response: 'Nay, but Ophelia — '; 'How do you, pretty lady?'; 'Conceit upon her father' (addressed not to Ophelia, of course); 'Pretty Ophelia'; and, finally, 'Follow her close; give her good watch', instead of a good hearing. The company here simply cannot accommodate her scandalous song, her bawdy, discordant or indecorous 'Jug, jug'. It is as if the entire social formation represented here recapitulates Hamlet's own clear difficulties in accommodating the difference of the womanly sexed body. She has been, in fact, a kind of 'hearing-aid' to Polonius and Claudius, and it is vital that when this hearing-aid begins to pour forth another kind of voice, a leperous distillment or poison into the ears of her manipulators, they are in a hurry to silence it, to switch it off. But it is the silencing of Ophelia which constitutes what is effectively her murder.

In her next appearance, Ophelia tries another method of speaking: the coded language of flowers. She is immediately considered to be mad, and even though Laertes finds some 'method' in her madness, she is still ignored. The simple fact of thinking this to be a 'mad' discourse, no matter how methodical, delegitimises it. Her death comes when, trying again to find a language, having picked some flowers, she literally 'posts' her letter, her coronet of flowers, hanging it, as a 'hanged letter' upon a tree; and falls into the water below, undergoing her own 'Death by Water' as a result:

There is a willow grows aslant the brook,
That shows his hoar leaves in the glassy stream:
Therewith fantastic garlands did she make
Of crowflowers, nettles, daisies, and long purples,
That liberal shepherds give a grosser name,
But our cold maids do dead men's fingers call them.
There on the pendent boughs her crownet weeds
Clamb'ring to hang, an envious sliver broke,
When down her weedy trophies and herself
Fell in the weeping brook.[30]

'"This music crept by me upon the waters"'. That reference to *The Tempest* exists now in a complex intertextual relation with the song of Ophelia, a song or music which the social formation of Denmark could not accommodate. She dies trying to speak — or, more properly, trying to be heard. It is the fact that her song, her music, is rationalised away rather than heard which causes her desperate death. A womanly voice, an explicitly sexual womanly voice, simply cannot be accommodated in this ideology, except as a 'scandal' whose function it is to regenerate the ideology in its own assumption of its own values.

When Eliot was writing 'The Waste Land', the British ideology was faced with precisely this scandal, the scandal of the voice — or vote, its cognate — of women. The British ideology had begun to face what it saw, in the suffragette struggle, as the scandal of woman representing herself in and through her own separate voice, speaking with her own tongue in her mouth. The notion of a vocal representation for woman is, at one level, what 'The Waste Land' is about. It is vital here to recall the metaphor which Pound used to decribe the poem's appearance in his letter of 24 December 1921 to Eliot:

These are the poems of Eliot
By the Uranian Muse begot;
A Man their Mother was,
A Muse their Sire.

How did the printed Infancies result
From Nuptials thus doubly difficult?
If you must needs enquire
Know diligent Reader
That on each Occasion
Ezra performed the caesarean Operation . . .[31]

The Eliotic 'inviolable voice' is, at one level, what the poem is after; while at another level, the inviolable voice is precisely the womanly voice which is to be silenced. In its form as nightingale's song, it is to be delegitimised through going unheard, to be 'murdered'.

The scandal of the womanly voice/vote which haunts the poem constitutes what might be thought of as its Orphic moment: it wants to hear a music, but this music is a noise it cannot bear. In Ovid, Orpheus occupies a position very close to that of the 'Fisher-King' so crucial to Eliot. Having effectively murdered Eurydice in his backward glance, Orpheus returns alone from the underworld, and 'For seven days, unkempt and neglected, he sat on the river bank, without tasting food'.[32] After some three years of despair, he turns away from women completely, preferring the company of boys. Like Eliot, he too sings of a 'hyacinth girl', only in his version, Hyacinthus is a boy, killed by the flying discus of his friend Phoebus. At his death, Hyacinthus undergoes his metamorphosis, being changed into a flower, 'a new kind of flower' which 'will show markings that imitate my sobs. Further, a time will come when the bravest of heroes will be connected with this flower, and his name will be read on these same petals'.[33] This new flower is, quite literally, a 'violet-ed' lily. As Orpheus sings it:

While Apollo, who cannot lie, was uttering these words, the blood which had flowed to the ground, and stained the grass, ceased to be blood, and a flower brighter than Tyrian purple grew up and took on the shape of a lily: but it was purple in colour, where lilies are silvery white. Phoebus was responsible for so honouring Hyacinthus, by changing him into a flower; not content with that, he himself inscribed his own grief upon the petals, and the hyacinth bears the mournful letters AI AI marked upon it.[34]

In 'The Waste Land', then, it is more appropriate to say that the subject of the poem is, as it were, the violation of a lily: the violating of purity, at least in the sense that the poem looks for a womanly voice (the birdsong), but does so only in order to violate it, to cut out its tongue, to render it 'harmonious' ideologically with the tradition of male voices, masculinist discourse.

In its cryptic invocations of the language of Ophelia, in its call for a womanly language of flowers, the text runs into a problem. For the single most important thing about Ophelia in her language of flowers passage is that she is, literally, 'inviolate': 'I would give you some violets, but they withered all when my father died'[35] — she has no violets. Eliot's difficulty is the difficulty of bringing a purely womanly speech to audience. In this, he is in exactly the same position as Hieronymo at the close of *The Spanish Tragedy*, whose final speech denies himself any further possibility of speech:

Thou may'st torment me . . .
But never shalt thou force me to reveal
The thing which I have vowed inviolate . . .
            [*He bites out his tongue*][36]

Eliot will not, cannot, reveal the language of the inviolate, the language, as it were, of Ophelianism: his text cannot bear the scandal of the womanly voice.

But at this moment, one begins to realise that the main issue here is not simply the issue of gender, important though that is. Rather, Eliot's concern seems to be rather for the notion of a purity of voice as such, an 'inviolable voice'. Women, here, operate as an allegory of alterity as such; for Eliot's own voice to be 'pure', it has to be contaminated by alterity, it has to be simply a voice speaking the words of others, the words of the great dead poets. His concern is for the purity of himself as a *medium*, mediating the language of other poets in a pure mode, thus rendering his own voice silent (and thus inviolable), and their voices trancendent (and thus, equally, inviolable). Hartman has drawn attention to 'the return of the dead' in 'Tradition and the Individual Talent', a return which is understood in a different sense from the Bloomian apophrades with which Hartman compares it.[37] Commenting on part of Eliot's use of the metaphor in 'The Waste Land', referring to the corpses that sprout and speak, Hartman writes that this is 'quite close to the madness of hearing inner voices, of being "impersonalised" this way, but the voices, or ghosts, are kept within the locus of the poem, shut up there as in a daemonic wood'.[38] But there is more to be considered here. Writing of the modern poet, Eliot asserts that 'we shall often find that not only the best, but the most individual parts of his work may be those in which the dead poets, his ancestors, assert their immortality most vigorously'.[39] Taken together with the comment, in the same essay, that 'the poet has, not "personality" to express, but a particular medium, which is only a medium and not a personality, in which impressions and experiences combine in peculiar and unexpected ways',[40] there emerges a notion of the poet as hallucinating medium or Orphic musician, allowing other voices to speak in and through the body of the poet. This is further corroborated by the notion that the modern poet loses consciousness in the process of composition or writing: 'What happens is a continual surrender of himself as he is at the moment to something which is more valuable. The progress of an artist is a continual self-sacrifice, a continual extinction of personality'.[41] This poet sings rather like Orpheus, after he has been torn to pieces by the outraged Maenads, and his head floats down the river, still singing before he is finally reunited with Eurydice: '"This music crept by me upon the waters"'.

Moreover, it is interesting to note that Eliot calls the revered dead poets 'ancestors'; there is the construction or adoption of a genealogical tradition or lineage here, conceived in terms of familial generation. Such notions of generation and genealogy seem to 'ghost' many of Eliot's critical writings, most often in allusions to maturity or to degrees of consciousness in the poet. But there are some more specific references pertinent to the present argument. Apart from viewing dead poets as ancestors, biologically linked to the modern poet in a blood-lineage, Eliot remarks that the tradition thus acquired is not a matter of straightforward inheritance: tradition 'cannot be inherited'.[42] Some years after writing this essay, Eliot introduced his Norton lectures, on *The Use of Poetry and the Use of Criticism*, with a suggestion for criticism:

I wish that we might dispose more attention to the correctness of expression, to the clarity or obscurity, to the grammatical precision or inaccuracy, to the choice of words whether just or improper, exalted or vulgar, of our verse: in short to the good or bad breeding of our poets.[43]

Here again is the concern for a purity: Augustan notions of propriety or notions of what is ideologically decorous — i.e. audible — have become a question of the purity of the familial genealogy of the poet, expressly conceived here as 'breeding'. The suppressed sexuality which many critics have noted as a dominant 'absence' in Eliot's verse does seem to appear in his criticism. We might add to these notions of the breeding of poets another comment from the same Introductory lecture:

The experience of poetry, as it develops in the conscious and mature person, is not merely the sum of the experiences of good poems. Education in poetry requires an organisation of these experiences. There is not one of us who is born with, or who acquires at puberty or later, an infallible discrimination and taste. The person whose experience is limited is always liable to be taken in by the sham and adulterate article; and we see generation after generation of untrained readers being taken in by the sham and the adulterate in its own time — indeed preferring them, for they are more easily assimilable than the genuine article.[44]

The kind of 'experience' discussed here undergoes a subtle but significant shift half-way through my citation. At the start there is the clear issue of the experience of poetry. But what might 'puberty' have to do with increased awareness or discrimination and taste in this department? The onset of puberty marks a moment of organisation of other experience, the sexual. Further, the person whose 'experience' is 'limited' might be taken in by 'sham' and 'adulterate' articles. The very repetition, the insistence on those words 'sham and adulterate', ought to draw critical attention to them. They are contrasted with the 'genuine', with something generically purer. As the passage goes on, it becomes more and more easy to describe this gestation and growth of the poetic critic, this literal 'culture' of the critic, as a kind of sexual — or more precisely, marital — odyssey:

Yet a very large number of people, I believe, have the native capacity for enjoying *some* good poetry . . . It is only the exceptional reader, certainly, who in the course of time comes to classify and compare his experiences, to see one in the light of others; and who, as his poetic experiences multiply, will be able to understand each more accurately. The element of enjoyment is enlarged into appreciation, which brings a more intellectual addition to the original intensity of feeling. It is a second stage in our understanding of poetry, when we no longer merely select and reject, but organise. We may even speak of a third stage, one of reorganisation; a stage at which a person already educated in poetry meets with something new in his own time, and finds a new pattern of poetry arranging itself in consequence.[45]

Here, the 'enjoyment' has become thoroughly ambiguous, and could be understood as a muted or displaced sexual enjoyment which settles down, as it were, into a well-balanced or regulated appreciation (perhaps of the sexual partner, in this case a wife who is not an 'adulterate article' but a 'genuine' wife); thus the original 'intensity of feeling' (appearing here for the first time in the essay) takes on a new sense. Selection and rejection, those two important factors in sexual awakening and orientation at puberty and after, become 'organisation', or perhaps the arrangement of the selected entities into convenient marital groupings. Then, there might be a third stage, the meeting with something (or someone?) new which stimulates a re-organisation, perhaps divorce and re-marriage or some other arrangement. The lecture discussed here was delivered on November 4th, 1932, and published in this form in 1933. One of the reasons why Eliot was actually giving the lectures in America at this moment was to be away from his first wife, Vivienne Haigh-Wood, whom he formally left in 1933. The essays reveal Eliot's discomfort with the notion that the purity of his own identity be contaminated by the womanly, which he began, conveniently, to think of as the mad: Ophelia once more.

The 'tradition', which Eliot hoped to mediate appears to be masculinist, thought of in terms of familial 'heritage'. But, of course, he wrote that tradition 'cannot be inherited, and if you want it you must obtain it by great labour'. It involves the historical sense, and 'the historical sense compels a man to write with his own generation in his bones'.[46] This male poet seems to be in some sense responsible for his own generation, for his own birth, a birth attained through 'great labour'. In a muted sense, again, the male poet here occupies or is preoccupied by some feminine constellation; moreover, the tradition is given birth by the now labouring poet, rather then the more expected converse where the poet is the product of a tradition. Eliot situates himself as poet in precisely the position he would later describe as that of the 'adulterate article', the woman who gives birth to the other voices which come to generation, come to 'presence' through her own toils of reproduction and *representation*, voicing. But this womanly voicing is, for Eliot, the locus of impurity, adulteration. By 1948, Eliot was explicitly writing that such impurity was of the essence of poetry. In his lecture, 'From Poe to Valéry', he argued that:

The process of increasing self-consciousness — or, we may say, of increasing consciousness of language — has as its theoretical goal what we may call *la poésie pure*. I believe it to be a goal that can never be reached, because I think that poetry is only poetry so long as it preserves some 'impurity'.[47]

Poetry is only poetry so long as it is the discordant music of the nightingale's song, the discordant music of the Ghost in *Hamlet* calling Hamlet to a task which is fundamentally displaced (Hamlet's own desire is for revenge upon Gertrude, not upon Claudius), the discord of *Le rossignol*.

This Eliotic 'adulteration' involves a reversal of historical chronology: the present author gives birth to the voices of the past and generates the tradition which legitimises the contemporary writer. In one respect at least, such a reversal of chronology is

frequent in the writings of modernism. Much of the writing of
Eliot, together with that of Joyce, Proust, Mann and others is a
response to prior texts. Joyce's *Ulysses* is a critical response to
Homer; de Man shows how Proust's text is a kind of 'pre-response'
to itself, an allegory of its own reading; Mann re-works the Bible
and the Faustus myth from Goethe and others; and Eliot's 'Waste
Land' is a response to the texts which constitute 'the tradition',
and to the letters and comments which Pound wrote during its
gestation. In fact, 'The Waste Land' is largely composed of prior
writings, becoming an allusive *criticism* (almost a 'critical edition'
or anthology) of them through its juxtapository and comparativist
mode. This is important: it is by hard work that the poet acquires
the tradition, allowing the ghostly voices of the past to be
mediated by a poet who is merely a catalyst, aiding in the
production of a text which is, literally, a 'com-Pound', a text
which includes its own criticism in Pound's editions and which is
written in collaboration with Pound.

The influence of tradition works in two directions, however.
The new work exists as a criticism of the past; but it is already an
aspect of that past, of that tradition, having already been inserted
into it; it thus exists in a critical relation to the other works which
comment critically upon it, as another work in the tradition itself,
juxtaposed and compared with those it invokes. The Eliotic poem
contains, in this modernist enterprise, its own criticism within
itself. 'The Waste Land' is not simply a critical response to, or
reading of, the writings of its anterior tradition: it is also a
response to the tradition which has been adulterated by its own
presence, a response to the tradition which *includes* 'The Waste
Land'. The tradition or genealogy, of course, does not exist
without 'The Waste Land' in the first place, for it is invented by
that poem's referential range. But this is to say that 'The Waste
Land', as a poem or exercise in writing, is a response to its own
reading, a criticism of itself *before* it has actually been written, or
at the very least coterminous with the period of its own writing/
reading. The poem exists not simply as poem-in-itself, as modernist formal verbal icon, nor simply as a critical edition of an
anterior body of writing; it is also a critical edition of itself. Its
explicit editor, of course, if not Eliot himself, is *il miglior fabbro*,
Pound. The poem, then, is a response to itself, a criticism of itself,

before it can be written, a response to its own reading; and this criticism is thus prior to the 'creative' writing of the poem itself. It is this which makes the poem not a modernist poem at all in the final analysis, but rather a postmodern poem. It works without rules in order to formulate the rules of what will have been done once the poem is written. But the thing about 'The Waste Land' is that it is, according to this argument, in a crucial sense still *unwritten*: it is always read before it can be written, and is thus always 'about-to-be-written', never properly formulated.

In other words, this poem is exactly akin to the discordant nightingale's song: its discords have still not been heard, as criticism has always struggled to harmonise it, to find an acceptable mode for its noise. Criticism has tried thus to render it a modernist poem — *understandable* — which means that its alterity, its suppressed womanly voices, still remain unheard by criticism. The present critical establishment can still not accept the discord promised by the intrusion of the nightingale song, the womanly voice, into a masculinist club called 'poetry' or 'The Atheneum'. In the words of Elizabeth Bishop, we are still 'In the Waiting Room':

> Outside,
> in Worcester, Massachussetts,
> were night and slush and cold,
> and it was still the fifth
> of February, 1918.[48]

We are, as it were, still waiting to hear the articulation of the nightingale's song, still waiting to hear or even to listen to the womanly voice. In this respect, we are still waiting for the political change which the women's suffrage movement promised. But the womanly voice or vote has been rendered harmonious by the dominant ideology: there is still no place from which the womanly voice can speak and be 'legitimate'. More importantly such a place will not be available until the dominant ideology finds a place from which it could be heard or listened to in any case. What happens here is that the womanly voice is heard only as an echo of the male, only insofar as it conforms to masculinist notions of democracy. For that ideology to hear the womanly voice would mean its own internal rupture and the production of a discord. We have not yet found a real politics of *representation*, and are thus still organising ourselves according to what Benjamin thought of as a fascist mode:

The growing proletarianization of modern man and the increasing formation of masses are two aspects of the same process. Fascism attempts to organize the newly created proletarian masses without affecting the property structure which the masses strive to eliminate. Fascism sees its salvation in giving these masses not their right, but instead a chance to express themselves. The masses have a right to change property relations; Fascism seeks to give them an expression while preserving property. The logical result of Fascism is the introduction of aesthetics into political life. The violation of the masses, whom Fascism, with its Führer cult, forces to their knees, has its counterpart in the violation of an apparatus which is pressed into the production of ritual values.[49]

The masses of women, for instance, are given a chance to express themselves — as long as that expression is decorous, harmonious and in accordance with the existing political structures. Sing as nightingales, and women go unheard.

My introduction of Benjamin here indicates that this is not simply a matter of feminist politics, of gender relations or of the importance of listening to a women's poetry. The issue becomes the entire question of 'translation', of hearing the voice of alterity without endlessly reducing that Otherness into the Same, the re-cognisable, the knowable, understandable, 'genuine'. The issue is that of listening in the mode of aliation: hearing an 'illegitimate' alterity without reducing it to a 'genuine' identity.

This appears, then, as a call to dialectical thinking, seemingly a neo-Hegelianism, or a call to what Descombes indicates as a practice of philosophy which has been discredited since, roughly, 1968.[50] What makes it dialectical, of course, is simply the orientation towards alterity:

Non-dialectical thinking would hold to the opposition between the rational and the irrational, but any thinking which aspires to be dialectical must, by definition, induce in reason a movement towards what is entirely foreign to it, towards *the other*. The whole issue now rests upon whether *the other* has been returned to *the same* in the course of this movement, or whether (so as to embrace rational and irrational, the *same* and the *other*, at once) reason will have had to transform itself, losing its initial identity, *ceasing to be the same* and *becoming other with the other*. For the other of reason is unreason, or madness. Thus the problem is raised of the passage of reason through *madness* or aberration, a passage which would precede all access to an authentic *wisdom*.[51]

But my argument complicates this by its appeal to a *historicity* of this dialectical thinking. That is, the object is not to attain a knowledge or a wisdom, but to transform reason in historical practice. As it is elaborated here, the dialectical position is simply not dialectical enough: the pretended orientation to alterity rests on a counter-movement which sees that alterity quite simply as a transformed Same, the Other as a metaphor of the Same. It is exactly akin to the change promised in political terms by women's suffrage, a transformation which produces no fundamental change other than the expression of an-Other voice permitted to say only exactly the same as the Same voice.

The claims upon an authenticity of wisdom here (in a position which Descombes rightly ascribes to Kojève) reduces the dialectical thinking to the point of eradicating totally its dialecticity. What happens is that in the orientation towards the Other, the embrace of the Other, there is a final collapsing of that Other into a new identity (the classical synthesis). But this is not enough: I submit that that Other must itself be thought in the mode of aliation. Descombes can again be of help in articulating this. In thinking the issue of another of the 'three H's', as he calls Hegel, Husserl and Heidegger, Descombes articulates the problematic of identity and difference:

there is identity not only, as formal logic would have it, between identity and identity, but between difference and difference; there is a certain *being* in *not-being*. Now, is there the slightest difference between the identity of identity with identity, and the identity of difference with difference? Certainly not. For there is no more *identity* between identity and identity than there is between difference and difference. And there is no more *difference* between difference and difference than there is between identity and identity. And yet identity and difference are clearly different types of relation. Yes, certainly. So the *identity* between, on the one hand, the identity of identity and identity, and on the other, the identity of difference and difference, is the very factor of *difference* between identity and difference.[52]

Here, the result is that in the orientation towards the Other in classical dialectical thinking, we must add a further move, in the realisation that that Other is not identical with itself, but is, as it were, other than itself, different from itself rather than self-identical. Once we make the dialectical shift towards alterity, we have to discover that the orientation towards aliation is never-ending. In listening for the voice of alterity, one hears only that that voice is never identical with itself, but always 'aliating' itself, always finding yet another displaced locus from which to come.

The passage cited here from Descombes is, clearly, somewhat baroque; and a similar issue is addressed by Buci-Glucksmann in her *La Raison Baroque*, where she makes a vital distinction between baroque allegory and modern allegory: '*seul le statut du féminin comme corps à la fois réel et fictif permet de différencier l'allégorie moderne de l'allégorie baroque*'.[53] Baudelaire and Benjamin, according to Buci-Glucksmann, address in their writings the redistribution of gender-valuations in the nineteenth century. Women are inserted into the industry of the big cities, thereby losing their 'natural' or 'poetic' qualities: the sociological demythologisation of women. In aesthetic terms, this is reiterated in the new figuring of the woman's body, after the androgynous impulse of Baudelaire, as delineated by his reader, Benjamin:

Baudelaire pris dans toutes les ambivalences qu'analyse Benjamin (historique, psychique, poétique), decouvrant sa propre 'androgynéité' s'identifiera tour à tour à la prostituée — image de la modernité.— et à la lesbienne, protestation heroique contre cette modernité.[54]

Baudelaire, here, makes the dialectical orientation towards alterity, in what Buci-Glucksmann herself will later term precisely an *esthétique de l'altérité*. He identifies himself with his Other, the prostitute; and then with the Other of that Other, the lesbian. However, there still remains here a residue of identity, the identification which Benjamin notes of Baudelaire with these others, and these others with themselves. In short, this is not a fully historical dialectic. Buci-Glucksmann goes on to indicate the effect of the presence of the prostitute in the nineteenth-century city:

le développement de la prostitution dans les grandes villes comme phénomènes de masse donnant lieu aux législations, la massification visible des corps féminins traduisent une mutation historique beaucoup plus général du milieu du XXe siècle: la crise du regard. . . . Plus que tout autre, le corps féminin est le support de 'cette archéologie du regard' dont parlait Foucault.[55]

But it is, of course, *le regard*, the primacy of the notion of the visible and the primacy of the force of ocularity, the force of the eye, which allows the arrest of the dialectic, for '*le désir masculin vise à immobiliser, à* pétrifier *le corps féminin*'.[56] Here, there is a tendency towards immobilisation, petrifaction, or, in the terms I prefer here, towards a territorialisation (literally a *terror*) of the Other/Woman. The otherness of alterity is, finally, reduced to the Same as long as the primacy of the eye, of *le regard* and its associated modes of representation, are given sway. What is needed is to give credence to the priority of that figure so beloved of Benjamin, the labyrinth; but to understand this as the labyrinth of the ear, and, thus, to construe our way through these labyrinths according to the logic of Ariadne and her womanly thread, the womanly voice which works its way through to the monstrous, masculinist Minotaur at the centre of the ear/labyrinth — and murders it.

This means, of course, that the postmodern depends upon (*inter alia*) two factors: the struggle to hear the voice of the Other; and a movement away from terror or territorialisation. The postmodern is characterised by *flight* and by the discordant song of alterity, the harsh heterogeneity of the nightingale's 'Jug jug', which is a *poison* in the masculinist ear.[57]

Deterritorialisation

Ending Culture

Philly: Supposing a man's digging spuds in that field with a long spade, and supposing he flings up the two halves of that skull, what'll be said then in the papers and the courts of law?

Jimmy: They'd say it was an old Dane, maybe, was drowned in the flood.
(Synge, *The Playboy of the Western World*)

A prime figure in my characterisation of postmodernism, and one who enters into a configuration with the 'scandalous' characters of Ophelia or Yorick in *Hamlet* (scandalous in their respective languages, of flowers and of clowning), is Vaslav Nijinsky, the dancer whose figures involve flights or deterritorialisation in his remarkable leaps. Those leaps made him akin to the flighty nightingale, and if we are to hear the song of this bird, the noise of alterity and discord, then it might be advisable to attend to the importance of flight, especially in its aspect as deterritorialisation, in postmodern culture. Benjamin, of course, was fully aware of the Futurist tendency to aestheticise politics in a glorification of the machines of flight and the wars which those aeroplanes fought at high speeds; but to fly towards alterity, to fly as Keats proposes to do in order to hear the voice of the nightingale, to fly as Nijinsky does in order to hear the music of Stravinsky and Debussy in all their 'barbarism' or difference, comprises a different orientation from that advanced by Marinetti and his Futurist cohorts. This kind of flight is one which will not murder or destroy the Other by reducing it to the principles of the Same or to identity; the aim, rather, is to fly away from the earth in order to lose one's roots, to leave one's rooted and terrifying identity or self-Sameness. The task here is akin to that proposed by Derrida in 'Tympan', when he addresses the difficulty of transgressing the margins identifying 'philosophy':

> But indefatigably at issue is the ear, the distinct, differentiated, articulated organ that produces the effect of proximity, of absolute properness, the idealizing erasure of organic difference. It is an organ whose structure (and the suture that holds it to the throat) produces the pacifying lure of organic indifference. To forget it — and in so doing to take shelter in the most familial of dwellings — is to cry out for the end of organs, of others.[1]

The hearing of alterity which I am proposing here is one which transgresses the boundaries of dialectical thinking. Dialectics operates on a simulated scandal of hearing the antithesis to every thesis; but this is nothing other than an 'operational negativity' producing a 'scenario of deterrence', as Baudrillard terms it, in which everything is actually proved and validated by a scandalous entertainment of its opposite. Watergate, for instance, simulates a scandal in the interests of regenerating the moribund principle of the honesty of the Office of the President of the USA — which means, in effect, that after Nixon, it becomes possible to elect to the presidency a man whose actual *profession* is that of acting a role, or of misleading people. Similarly, psychiatry is proved by anti-psychiatry, art by anti-art, capitalism by revolution, exploitation by the strike, masculinism by feminism, and so on.[2] What is required, clearly is a way of going 'beyond' dialectics in order to discover an alterity, a difference, which cannot so easily be recuperated by the synthesising principle of identity. Criticism must attempt to get beyond the 'modern', a modern which defines itself by its dialecticity.

Modernism, broadly, territorialises, and tends towards a cultural imperialism based upon an ethics of 'enlightenment'; postmodernism, by contrast, deterritorialises, and tends towards an internationalist pluralism. In literary terms, modernism is about the discovery of a tradition or of a national voice which one can claim as one's own; in the postmodern condition, one speaks always with the tongues of others in one's ear/throat.

In articulating this argument, I attend here to a poetry which is clearly concerned with the land, and with the relation of poetry to culture in its literal Georgic sense of 'tilling the soil'. In elaborating the distinction between modernism and postmodernism, between the impulse to territorialise and the counter-impulse of flight, a specific poetry of decolonisation proposes itself as the obvious material on which to work. It is at the moment of political decolonisation that a consciousness of the land and of a specific and identifiable national cultural identity becomes most punctual. It is, for instance, in twentieth-century Irish poetry that one can discern the issue of geographical or territorial boundaries which have been erased from the most immediate surface of American poetry, that poetry which has learned how to re-draw national boundaries at will in its poets such as Lowell, Bishop and, later, Ginsberg.

In the Virgilian or Georgic obsession with the land which is everywhere evident in the mainstream tradition of twentieth-century Irish poetry, it is a paradoxical fact that the land is not construed as the site of political or historical struggle, despite the equally salient fact that the poetry is often overtly political. But this poetry constructs a geography in which the secularity of history is collapsed into the identity of 'tradition' or 'heritage'; and historical *difference*, that '(non-)principle of heterogeneity' which constitutes historicity as such, has been denied, fairly consistently, since Yeats.

Since Yeats, the task seems to have been to construct and identify (to homogenise, even) a tradition rather than to delineate one's own present historicity. The result is what might be termed a 'poetry of archaeology', in which the poet is concerned to dig for and to lay bare a tradition for which she or he invokes a degree of nostalgia and the desire for return. More precisely, this would be a desire for a reconstructed continuity in a tradition which is everywhere fractured by colonialism and British intervention. The political concern over land and its divisions, no matter how dominant this may be as a theme or content of the verse, is subverted by the aesthetic impulse in which the modernist poet sees herself or himself as a 'representation' of the dead generations of poets and of the ghosts of the past. The potential for political revolution, indeed even for historical difference, is subsumed in the demand for aesthetic representation of the past and for the reiteration of the Same, a reiteration which, it is thought, might repair the damage done to the continuity of an Irish tradition by cultural imperialism.

Marx offered what might productively be used as a gloss on such a situation when arguing that people make their own history, but only 'under circumstances directly encountered and inherited from the past'. His text goes on in terms which are specifically relevant to what I am describing here as the collapsing of history into mere tradition or heritage in some contemporary modernist poetry:

The tradition of all the generations of the dead weighs like a nightmare on the brain of the living. And just when they seem involved in revolutionizing themselves and things, in creating something that has never before existed, it is precisely in such periods of revolutionary crisis that they anxiously conjure up the spirits of the past to their service and borrow names, battle cries and costumes from them in order to act out the new scene of world history in this time-honoured disguise and this borrowed language.[3]

My contention here is that it is the *modernist* impetus which is characterised by the collapsing of history into tradition or heritage, while the postmodern runs counter to this, allowing entry into a fully historical condition. The tradition produced through modernism, further, is one constructed in accordance with a dominant principle of homogeneous identity, in which the present re-enacts the past in the mode of the Same, in the guise of 'representation' of the past. Postmodern historicity, by contrast, is fully oriented towards heterogeneity, even though the historicity in question here might be condemned forever to the status of *repetition*. Such repetition, however, is always farcical, parodic, and is thus based on a (non-)principle of heterogeneity — or, if you will, upon an *ethics of aliation*. Marx, indeed, opened the second edition of the *Eighteenth Brumaire* with the famous comment that historical repetition devolves the tragic into the farcical. In the specifically Irish context delineated here, one might add to this Blumenberg's contention in *The Legitimacy of the Modern Age* that, strictly speaking, 'History knows no repetitions of the same; "renaissances" are its contradiction'.[4] This is

thoroughly in accordance with my own argument here, an argument figured on the Deleuzian insight that repetition is a privileged site of difference, the locus of an almost imperceptible but
undeniable heterogeneity.[5]

The autochthonous impulse informing Irish poetry produces a
geography or tradition of the 'catastrophic land', a modernist
version or representation of Thebes. Seamus Deane, for instance,
finds that in Heaney's poetry, 'his Ireland becomes a tragic terrain';
and in this regard Heaney is but one typical figure who powerfully
articulates certain themes found equally in Kavanagh, Montague
and others. But in Deane's reading of Heaney, there is a specific
'tragedy of identity' being acted out on this modern Theban
terrain, the site of the 'revival' or 'renaissance' (a counter to
'history'). Deane discovers a family romance in Heaney's Ireland:
'Maternity is of the earth, paternity belongs to those who build on
it or cultivate it'. Though he argues that there is a politics to this,
Deane rapidly provides the machinery whereby it becomes easily
translated into the representation of a tragic story known before —
and elsewhere:

Heaney's fascination with the soil, for which he has so many words, all of
them indicating a deliquescence of the solid ground into a state of yielding and
acquiescence — mould, slime, clabber, muck, mush and so on — ends always
in his arousal of it to a sexual life. Quickened by penetration, it responds.[6]

Here, quite simply, is Heaney as Oedipus with the earth as
mother/Jocasta; it is no wonder that Deane finds a tragic terrain
here. Heaney takes his place in the series of 'Celtic *Revivals*'
which Deane carefully charts; but this revival, this quickening of
Oedipus to life in the figure of Heaney, drains the terrain of
historicity and consequently of political import, even at the very
moment in which the poetry seems to be dealing most overtly
with the political questions of the divisions of land. In the
identification of a tradition here, in the revival of Heaney's
heritage deriving from Oedipus, whose catastrophe enacts itself in
a land ravaged by plague and famine, Deane's reading collapses
his own 'History Lessons' into a kind of geo-political 'Field Work',
a Georgic devoid of politics.[7].

In these terms, Heaney's 'dead father', the Laius-figure in the
narrative, is represented by Yeats; for if Heaney is in some sense a

poet of the contemporary land-division, the poet of the border-question, then Yeats is clearly the poet of a similar division, that between the Republic and the UK earlier in the century, a land division which is the ground or foundation of Heaney's particular problem.

Yeats too is a 'poet of archaeology' rather than of historicity: his concern is with the origins of the past, that 'past of the past' as Descombes calls it.[8] This is perhaps nowhere more evident than in a text such as 'No Second Troy':

Why should I blame her that she filled my days
With misery, or that she would of late
Have taught to ignorant men most violent ways,
Or hurled the little streets upon the great,
Had they but courage equal to desire?
What could have made her peaceful with a mind
That nobleness made simple as a fire,
With beauty like a tightened bow, a kind
That is not natural in an age like this,
Being high and solitary and most stern?
Why, what could she have done, being what she is?
Was there another Troy for her to burn?[9]

In proposing a reading of this poem, I aim to demonstrate its modernist impulse to reject historicity in favour of an antiquarianism. Yeats, I argue, thinks his own historicity 'back-to-front'. He sees the present as a model for understanding the past; and as a result, the alterity of the past becomes reduced to conformity and identity with the present. The past becomes immediately knowable and recognisable, just as the present is supposed to be. His desire to have such knowledge of the past lies in his need for a specific identity or 'root'. The poetry takes the temporal flow of historicity and reverses it, turns back to the archaeological origin and locates the present, Yeats himself, in relation to that originary moment. 'No Second Troy' is explicitly a poem of the nostalgic desire to return to one's earthy or territorial roots. Hoewever, I shall also indicate a tension in this text between its modernist territorialising impulse and a postmodern orientation towards flight. In its *post*modernity, the text will be shown to be thoroughly historical, not in the sense of being oriented towards a past, but rather in providing a flight from the past, from the earth, and becoming proleptic of Yeats's later verse, specifically the 'Byzantium' poems.

The poem's title suggests immediately the importance of repetition and originality. The thing we all immediately know about Troy, the thing which caused the 'first' Troy to be in need of repetition, was fire: Troy was burnt. The poem closes on the word which explicitly recalls this. But that closing line of the text immediately sends a reader backwards, towards the title of the poem, for it poses a question that has already been answered in that title. Two things should be noted here. First, it is as if the poem, in some sense, needs to be read *back to front*: the title is an answer to the question posed in the closing line of the text. There is, then, not so much a simple repetition demanded here, but rather some kind of 're-versal' or *re-versing*, the versing of another poem. Secondly, the poem clearly brings epistemology into play; for it is composed entirely of questions, questions to which the title seems always already to have provided the answer. This assumes, of course, that we can know what the title means; yet I shall argue here that we do not know this, indeed that we cannot know it — yet.

The text, these *verses demanding reversing*, is comprised entirely of questions, but these are odd questions. They are rhetorical, and do not immediately demand epistemological information, information already provided by the title. It might be worth considering the notion of the rhetorical question with regard to the text as a whole. A distinction should be drawn between rhetoric and violence, for example. This is especially pertinent because it speaks directly to the conditions of the relations between Yeats and Maud Gonne with respect not only to the political situation but also to the state of their interpersonal relations at the time when the poem was written in December 1908. The big and essential difference between them with respect to Ireland's political situation was precisely the difference between rhetoric and violence. Gonne was prepared for direct and, if necessary, violent revolution; Yeats wanted to effect change by rhetorical and indirect suasion in the form of his verse. The opposition of rhetoric to violence is that between poet and Gonne, and the poem explicitly addresses this opposition.

The first of the four rhetorical questions occupies the first five lines, and relates to violence, asking (perhaps violently, and certainly in firm prosodic form) why Yeats should blame Gonne for teaching 'to ignorant men most violent ways'. The question is itself tentatively answered: 'tentatively' for the reason that the answer comes in the form of the third rhetorical *question*, 'what could she have done, being what she is?' Again, two crucial points emerge. First, this is itself a rather strong, even violent poem; it is as if Yeats himself is one of the 'ignorant' men to whom Gonne has taught the 'violent ways', as he now writes a poem more strident than any prior to this date. Secondly, the issue of epistemology and the function of the questions is important.

On one hand, there is a text composed of four questions; it would seem to have been cast therefore from a position of ignorance, of not knowing (and would thus cohere with the idea that Yeats himself is in some fashion ignorant). On the other hand, these are rhetorical questions, not seriously functioning in the normal epistemological manner. But the violence of the questions lies in the fact that they are also, in some measure, ironic. The normal rhetorical form would operate on the principle that the question 'Why should I blame?' implies 'I do not blame'; but here, it is evident that Yeats is indeed apportioning blame. The insistent repetition of questions in this vein means that we as readers are left in a position of some ignorance as to what is the genuine impetus of the poem: is it a blessing or a cursing, so to speak? Further, it is worth addressing that issue from the stance of the text itself: does the text 'know' what it means or is it not, like all ironic statements, duplicitous and at odds with itself? It could be thought as a crisis-poem, a self-crossing poem; but a poem whose crisis is fully temporal in the sense that it is anachronistic with respect to itself in terms of its irony. It is as if the poem is itself merely an 'original' or 'archaic' and 'archaeological' starting-point for us to compose its 'Second' version, its *reversing* in a second Troy to combat the negative epistemology of 'No Second Troy'. To put this simply, the text demands its own reversing by the reader, like all irony, which demands that the hearer reverse the propositions advanced by the ironic speaker.

Consequently, we can now suggest that in an ironic proposition, the speaker deliberately makes her or his statement anachronistic, 'archaeological', and demands two things. First, the speaker requires that the hearer of the statement complete it. This move complicates the phenomenology of authorisation for the statement's truth-claims or propositional status. Secondly, the meaning of the statement must be not merely displaced (geo-politically) but also anachronistic (chrono-politically), for the speaker looks back in time while attending to the future or proleptic fulfillment of her or his statement in the other voice/ears of the listener.

In 'No Second Troy', the problem enunciated here opens another opposition around which the poem is organised, an opposition of *ignis* and *gnosis*, fire and knowledge. Fire is clearly an important element in the text; and as an alchemical element it is, as Yeats rightly implies, 'simple'. The mind that is made 'simple as a fire' here is that of Gonne; and it is a mind made simple by 'nobleness', a word often taken as an opposite of 'ignorant' when this latter is construed as 'vulgar'. But 'nobleness' is itself an interesting word. It usually suggests ideas of aristocracy, of being 'illustrious by rank or birth', as the dictionary has it. In chemical terms, a 'noble' gas is one which, by virtue of its 'nobility', does not mix with other elements: it remains pure and uncontaminated. It is thus unamenable to the historicity or temporalities of *irony*. 'Nobles' allow for no contamination of their stable identity as authoritative phenomenological subjects of their enunciations. 'Nobility' is incapable of hearing alterity; it refuses to have its verbal or vocal identity or authority contaminated by the voice of the Other, the 'vulgar'; it cannot survive the possibility of discovering itself speaking in a foreign tongue. Nobility, in these terms, is a full transliteration of the metaphysics of presence; the noble are those who believe themselves to be fully present to their own consciousness, unamenable to irony, and thus also unamenable to historicity and to the heterogeneity which constitutes it. The word 'noble' can be traced to the Latin root '(g)nobilis', itself deriving from '*gno-', a root meaning 'know'; and 'nobilis' in Latin means 'which can be known, knowable', or acknowledgeable, identifiable, recognisable.

There are now two modes of knowledge at work and apparent in the text. On one hand, Yeats poses rhetorical questions, feigning ignorance so that he may demonstrate his superior knowledge of the true state of affairs; on the other hand, we have that know-ledgeable educator of ignorant men, Gonne, whose mode of knowledge comes from a mind that is simple as fire. The opposi-tion, then, is between *gnosis* and *ignis*, knowledge and fire. The text 'focusses' on this binarism between, on one hand, a meta-physics of presence (a 'noble' self-knowledge) which is radically unamenable to historicity; and, on the other, an irony which demonstrates that one's own voice can never know its own propositions fully, that one's voice depends upon a historical *hearing* in the ear of an Other or upon a radical reversing in the ear/voice of an Other, for the production of any knowledge at all. This latter mode of knowledge can never be located in one consciousness, for it demonstrates the inability of a consciousness to know itself or to be self-present. In its ironic status, it opens the consciousness to the unconscious, and to a proleptic historicity of that unconscious. In other words, this unconscious is unFreudian in that it does not contain memories of a past which is con-stitutive of the repertoire of a sure and stable identity or self-sameness; rather, it looks forward proleptically to a future, a future based upon heterogeneity and difference.

The text's four questions culminate in 'Was there another Troy for her to burn?' *If* this is answered by the title, '*No* Second Troy', then the questions become redundant, already answered. That is, it is as if the poem consumes itself, burns or destroys itself like a Fishian selfconsuming artifact. The production of knowledge, *gnosis*, as found in the title, depends upon the poem's consump-tion by fire, upon *ignis*. But since we do actually have a poem before us, an extant 'No Second Troy', it follows that the title must after all be no answer; and the text is concerned to preserve itself not by the production of knowledge but rather by the production of ignorance. It moves, so to speak, from *ignis* to ignorance. It wants to remain not a 'noble' poem at all, not one that can be known; on the contrary, it remains ignoble, confused or complex, mixed with alien elements, contaminated by other texts and voices. It is thus necessarily unaware of its own being or meaning. The text produces its own historicity and its own unconscious.

Undoubtedly, this makes it a most complex poem, one which enters into 'All complexities of mire or blood', as Yeats put it in 'Byzantium'. It also demands that we re-examine those rhetorical questions. The first is, as I mentioned, answered by the third (and the second); but this third question is itself answered by the fourth and final one. The third proposes an identity of *being* with *doing*, 'what could she have done, being what she is'. But it is this very modernist identity, based upon a metaphysics of presence, which the text is calling into question in its postmodern orientation towards the production of an unconscious which proposes a wedge between one's being and one's doing, a wedge between agency and the knowledge one has of such agency or intention. Sure enough, at this point in the text, we do *not* know who this 'she' is.

If the final line is supposed to identify her, then it does so by the circumlocutionary trope of antonomasia, the evasion of proper names. I take it that we are to infer that 'she' is, in some sense, Helen, for it was Helen who indirectly caused the sack of Troy according to the legend. But there is another sense in which we know that 'she' is clearly not Helen at all, but rather Gonne. What she is, then, turns out to be what she is not: her 'identity' is not 'simple as a fire', but is rather complex, contaminated by impurity and difference, in a promiscuous mingling of Helen with Gonne. Her mind is itself 'ignoble', in the sense of being unabale to know itself, unable to be fully present to itself. We have a text, then, which proposes itself as the site of a knowledge and nobility, the site of a modernist metaphysics of presence on one hand; but which, on the other, re-verses itself such that it becomes the site for the production of ignorance, unknowability and the unconscious. The text hovers uncertainly between these two modes, and if it is to avoid its own consumption or burning in the flames that sack Troy, then it must produce not the knowledge of identity but rather the ignorance of itself which characterises its historicity and its unconscious. Even while proposing that it is the site of such self-knowledge, it dramatises the impossibility of a consciousness being present to itself, of a subject being 'nobly' present to its own intentionality: it demonstrates the logical impossibility of nobility. To produce any kind of 'meaning' for this text, one must, as it were 'listen towards the future' or wait for a *re-versing* (even perhaps for a *revolving*, a revolution) of the text in the voice or ear of alterity. We must wait until it can be 'heard', but in a fully foreign mode, in the mode of difference or alterity, rather than according to an identifiable meaning, a recognisable meaning, one based upon the self-sameness of the metaphysics of presence.

The text enacts not the crisis of a poet's personal or artistic 'development', but rather a general crisis with respect to its own status; it hovers between a modernist principle of identity (in its desire for nobility) and a postmodern dispersal of any archaeological origin which is supposed to define the meaning of a self (the logical impossibility of Yeats's heart's desire for the validity of an aristocracy). For example, the trope of antonomasia is a form of euphemism, 'well-speaking'; yet the poem opens by posing a question of 'bad-mouthing', cacophemism, in the phrase 'Why should I *blame*', for 'to blame' is 'to blaspheme' or to speak badly. The text hovers between euphemism and euphony on the one hand, and its disturbance by the discords of blasphemy and cacophony on the other. It is the site of a euphemism, but a euphemism which is instrumental in bad-mouthing Gonne. There is a discrepancy between what the poem is and what it does: it is a euphemism, it does blaspheme, and its prosodic tightness becomes contaminated by the cacophony of bad sounds. It is proper that we should attend to some of these cacophonous interruptions to the 'nobility' of the poem, proper that we reveal its vulgar historicity.

The idea of 'hurling little streets upon the great' is an odd one, and the phrase 'little streets' is a reminiscent re-versing echo or repetition of another poem. 'No Second Troy' is complicated or rendered ignoble by the intrusion here of another text, Keats's 'Ode on a Grecian Urn':

And little town, thy streets for evermore
Will silent be, and not a soul to tell
Why thou art desolate, can e'er return.[10]

In making this rhetorical detour through Keats, it is entirely appropriate that we turn to this particular Ode, for Troy, of course, was not burnt by Helen at all, but was rather burnt by the Greeks; and this Grecian urn begins to haunt Yeats's poem. Keats described that urn as a 'still unravished bride of quietness', terms which, Yeats lamented, were no more applicable to Maud Gonne. To 'ravish' is, among other things, 'to fill with delight'; if Yeats is 'filled with misery', then we might well describe his days as 'unravished', and hence as a re-versing of Keats. But while Yeats's days — and nights — are 'unravished' at this moment in 1908, the same could not be said for Gonne. For Gonne was no longer who she was. A few years prior to the writing of this poem, in February 1903, Gonne had indeed been 'brided', marrying Major John MacBride in — of all places — Paris, that geographical name so easily confused, when heard, with the name of Helen's ravisher in the Trojan myth. Yeats wrote virtually no poetry in the years between hearing of this marriage when he was in America in 1903 until 1908, that is, until he wrote 'No Second Troy'. The poem is, as it were, a response to the ravishment of the bride of quietness and slow time. But the poem also takes a particular geographical turn as well here; in re-versing Keats, it turns from Troy and looks instead to Greece, in the Grecian urn.

That urn was used to contain ashes, and was most frequently a burial urn. Again this seems apt, for we have in 'No Second Troy' a text which hovers uncertainly over its own ashes, reposing on the site where it has consumed or burnt itself. As such, Yeats's poem *is* the Grecian urn itself, in a curious reversal of chronology. This reversal is itself constitutive of that particular understanding of history which collapses history into tradition or heritage, through the search for archaeological origination, and in which the past is seen as a recognisable version of the present, as a representation. At a simpler level, Yeats is offering a repetition of the poem by Keats, but one which attends to the content of the urn rather than the art which is 'wrought', written or inscribed upon its surface. Yeats's text, as ashes, becomes the text which fills, completes or 'ravishes' Keats's poem in a movement which allows these two texts to 'brede' together, or to 'over-write' each other in a complex weave or wroughting.

While Keats looked to Greek art to effect an opposition between secularity and the eternality of art, Yeats, in looking at the auguries of the ashes in Keats's urn, turns to an even earlier culture to address a similar opposition. In September 1926 he wrote, seemingly, of his abandonment of Ireland, his flight from that troubled land, as he set sail for 'Byzantium' where he was to be consumed by fire and turned into a bird, a singing prophet extremely like the bird which so fascinated Stravinsky in Andersen's tale:

Once out of nature I shall never take
My bodily form from any natural thing,
But such a form as grecian goldsmiths make
Of hammered gold and gold enamelling
To keep a drowsy Emperor awake;
Or set upon a golden bough to sing
To lords and ladies of Byzantium
Of what is past, or passing, or to come.[11]

In asking for the sages to 'Come from the holy fire, perne in a gyre,/And be the singing-masters of my soul', Yeats asks for his own burning and 'wroughting' into the form of a bird on a bough: he himself asks, as it were, to become a 'second Troy' of sorts. 'No Second Troy' becomes prefigurative of the poem written in 1926, 'Sailing to Byzantium', as if this latter poem performs precisely the re-versing that the former had demanded. Once more, the meaning of 'No Second Troy' looks, historically, both ways: in its modernism, it looks to an archaeological root in Keats; in its postmodernity, it looks forward to a meaning which is, at the moment of its writing, deferred and which will, of course, change the meaning of 'No Second Troy' itself, whose meaning cannot therefore be known — yet. 'No Second Troy' is rather a first attempt at the writing of a Byzantine poem. The dichotomy here is between, on one hand, a desire for rooted identity, for a tradition into which Yeats can locate himself as a descendant of Keats and, on the other hand, a flight from any such territorialisation, a flight away from the earth or at least from this land which has given Yeats his name.

The goldsmith upon whom Yeats calls for his 'breding' is Grecian, and so the configuration of Greece with Troy remains important, and deserves further comment. Yeats was in London between 1867 and 1880. During these childhood and teenage years, there appeared a series of articles in the newspapers (*The Times* and *The Daily Telegraph*) from Heinrich Schliemann, whom some have called the first of the modern archaeologists. Schliemann was excavating the site of Troy in these years, in his attempt to locate the Troy sung by Homer.

Yeats would certainly have known of Schliemann's findings; and the leading articles in *The Times* would have made interesting reading for his circle, as they frequently made more or less explicit comparison between what was happening in general terms in Asia Minor with what was happening in specific terms in Ireland during these decades. In both areas, there were problems related to what *The Times* termed 'religious inequality'; but for the leader-writer in this newspaper, events in the east were prefigurative of events to come in the west: 'our world has begun to die in Asia Minor' where there is a 'bitter rivalry of religion and race'.[12] Reports of Schliemann's excavations appear alongside articles debating the 'burial question' and the 'Land Question' in Ireland. In Galway, for instance, the local Bishop reduced the already tiny portion of land available for Protestant burial in the cemeteries from one-and-a-half acres to one acre, while six acres were set aside for Catholic burial. Here is the 'land question' in its most direct and brute form. To bury one's dead here is to make a claim on the land such that the land itself acquires a tradition or identity, a heritage which tries to be pure by being unhistorical. Burial — the Grecian funereal urn and its ashes — becomes the site of a struggle for land and for a national (as well as personal) identity.

But if Yeats was, as seems inevitable, aware of Schliemann, then he was also aware of the fact that there was indeed a 'second' Troy; for Schliemann — controversially — had discovered some *nine* levels on which the ancient city had been built, destroyed, and re-built. Perhaps the single most significant factor in Schliemann's excavations — for present purposes at least — was his discovery of traces and remains of a civilisation anterior to those which the west had assumed to be 'original' or archaic; and he dated the earliest ruins of the city of Troy to the Early Bronze Age, around 3,000 BC. This would have been of some interest to the later Yeats who wanted a 'Vision' which could encompass precisely all such ancient civilisations in one synchronic scheme, one 'wroughting' or 'breding'.

Like the Bishop of Galway, Yeats in this poem makes a claim upon land, and uses that claim to make a heritage or tradition within which his own specifically Irish writing can be located and identified. But the land here is not simply that of Ireland, nor of

Dublin burning, nor indeed even of Troy. It becomes more and more clear that 'No Second Troy' has little to do with Troy or Dublin as such, and rather more to do with the archaeological notion of a return to origins and to the origins of those origins. The land being claimed here is a symbolic land; or, rather, Yeats's claim upon it is a symbolic claim. It is like the claim made upon Hamlet's attention by the skull of Yorick or the body of the dead Ophelia in her grave; or like that made upon the people of 'the western world' (Mayo and America) by the cracked skull of Christy Mahon's father in Synge's *Playboy of the Western World*. In each case, a claim upon land is related to a burial of sorts followed by a flight: Hamlet's exile to England, Christy Mahon's flight from the police as well as his Nijinskian 'lepping' at the races (a flight from earth). In Yeats this same motif is reiterated, through the allusions to the burial urn and through the text's prolepsis of the 'Byzantine' poems of flight written later.

As the poem is not about Troy, nor about Ireland, then it has made some geographical errors, especially if, as I suggested, it is proleptic of the later successful attempt to 'reach' Byzantium in 1930 after 'Sailing' there in 1926. Geographically, Troy and Byzantium/Istanbul are broadly in the same area, near the Sea of Marmara and on the border of east and west, Asia and Europe. But to get to Byzantium by boat (sailing there), one would have to pass Troy and to proceed up the fierce current of the Hellespont or Straits of Dardanelles. This journey had been made before. It was made by Xerxes, who built a bridge of boats to cross in his invasion of Greece in 480 BC, after engaging in the battle of 'the hot gates', Thermopylae.[13] It was also a journey made by a lover, Leander. According to the story of Hero and Leander (told by Musaeus, Ovid, Marlowe, Byron and others), when Leander saw Hero at a festival they immediately fell in love; their only problem was that they lived at opposite ends of the Hellespont. Allegorical parallels between this story and that lived out by Yeats and Gonne offer themselves here. For love, Leander would every night swim against the mighty current of the Hellespont to visit Hero, guided by the light from her Tower. This lasts until a violent storm extinguishes the light, Leander drowns and Hero drowns herself in despair. 'No Second Troy', seen in these terms, becomes Yeats's own Thermopylae, his battle with the fiery gates on his way to

Byzantium. The poem is, of course, a 'hot' poem, full of the imagery of fire; and it is a 'crisis' or crossing-poem. It sits, so to speak, between the concerns of Grecian Troy (via Keats) and the Byzantium to which Yeats himself wanted to 'sail' in 1926 and which he 'reached' in 1930.

Yeats's claim upon an Irish 'territory', his cultural claim upon land, operates here in a tension with the flight from that land. Through odd-sounding words, 'No Second Troy' in fact provides Yeats with a craft for sailing away. Gonne's beauty is, like that of Keats's urn, 'not natural':

With beauty like a tightened bow, a kind
That is not natural in an age like this,
Being high and solitary and most stern . . .

These lines are puzzling, especially in that odd simile for beauty, 'like a tightened bow'. But we might hear the word 'bow' as 'bough', and thus hear it as that golden bough on which Yeats, like a Keatsian nightingale, will sit; or, indeed, we may hear it as the *Golden Bough* which James Frazer wrote and published in 1890, a text which influenced Yeats as much as it did Eliot. The beauty here is not natural, being 'high and solitary and most stern'; by implication, the opposite of these terms would be 'natural'. To be a natural beauty would imply some 'vulgarity', for it would be to be 'low, gregarious, and . . .' Here is a problematic term, for the opposite of 'stern' is not immediately obvious. Perhaps 'pliable' suggests itself, pliable like the string of a bow or like that bough on which Yeats will later sit and sing. But recalling the pronunciation of 'bow' as 'bough', we do have an opposite of 'stern' within the text itself: the 'bow' as the bow and stern of a ship. Gonne's aritificial beauty, then, is cast between the terms 'bow' and 'stern'. Provided we can *hear differently*, or can hear these 'unheard melodies' in this complicated text — melodies unheard until Yeats would later sing them like a bird in Byzantium some 20 years later — we can discern Yeats's building of the vessel of Gonne's beauty which will not root him but will rather allow his flight from the land. She *is* his escape, not something which ties or tightens him to the land of Ireland. This poem, then, looking back to an archaeology, also looks forward to a flight from the earth or from Yeats's land and origins. It is a celebration of his flight from

Gonne. 'What could she have done, being what she is?': Gonne is gone, like romantic Ireland, like O'Leary.

How, then, to make a sense for this text? When Schliemann went digging, he exposed the false *arche* or origin of knowledge for civilisation. Among other things, he discovered evidence of Phoenician culture in Troy. This is important. 'No Second Troy' organises itself around two basic elements of fire and water: the burning, and the waters of the Hellespont; and the poem drama-tises the alchemical struggle between these elements, between male fire and female water, between a ritual funereal burning which returns to roots and a naval escape or flight from the land. This again is the crux of the modernist/postmodern nexus. Returning to the earlier suggestion about the relation of fire to knowledge, we have a conflict of two epistemologies. One episte-mology here is based on the re-cognition of an early culture in which the world can never surprise, and, indeed, can never change; this epistemology operates to reduce all alterity to a recognisable Sameness. The other is an epistemology based on *hearing otherwise*, fleeing every recognisability in the attempt to discover new knowledges and different worlds, or to strive to avoid the tyranny of the unhistorical Same by making the Same into the Other or, simply, making things different.

The poem itself seems to demand its own burning, but also demands its own repetition or development in the Byzantine poems; it has, as it were, its own 'second coming'. At a banal level, its rhetorical nature (answer followed by question) makes it recursive. But just as it is a repetition or re-versing of Keats, so too the text looks forward to its own re-versing. This makes the text into an archetypal model of the great symbol of the Irish literary renaissance, the phoenix rising from its own ashes. It is, thus, a 'phoenixian' text. Schliemann's discovery of a Phoenician culture in Troy, of course, was the discovery of the culture which invented the first alphabet, an alphabet of twenty-two letters which read from right to left or — to the ears of the culture of the west, that Greco-Roman culture — *backwards*, like this poem itself.

Here, however, is the political rub. That Phoenix which stands in Phoenix Park in Dublin and which appears as the recurrent symbol of the Irish cultural renaissance, is built upon an interesting linguistic slippage or upon a *mishearing* of Gaelic. 'Phoenix' in this context is an anglicisation of the Gaelic 'Fionn Uisge', which means 'the waters of Finn', 'the waters of the clear one' ('Finn' itself meaning 'fair' or 'clear'). The basic opposition around which this text is constructed then, finally, is the cultural opposition of Phoenix with Phoenician, the Gaelic language (misheard and misunderstood) with the Greco-Roman Germanic (heard and understood) which Yeats speaks. He is speaking a foreign tongue, speaking with the tongue of the Byzantine or with the tongue of the nightingale in his mouth (and is thus, in marxian terms, taking his poetry from the future). But as yet, the song towards which 'No Second Troy' proleptically signals cannot be heard: it demands a *hearing otherwise* which is unavailable to Yeats at the time of writing the text.

Further, in terms of the cultural mapping of land, as Friel demonstrates in *Translations*,[14] the question of *hearing otherwise* is crucially and politically important. In the case under present discussion, the Anglo-Irish cannot hear the Gaelic *Fionn Uisge* but collapses that incomprehensible, unheard alterity into something recognisable, something grounded in the always already known of their own culture and language. Yeats's poem operates on the crux between that modernist impetus to reduce alterity to sameness (its 'Anglo-'impulse; its search for archaeological roots) on the one hand; and, on the other, the postmodern impetus to flee the land and to flee 'culture' as such (the 'Irish' search for a different hearing, for a new epistemology, a new mode of representing or mapping the world and thus a new mode of inhabiting it). This opposition is that between culture or tradition on one hand and flight or history on the other.

It is interesting to note the recurrence of these concerns in Heaney. 'Digging', for instance, re-works the trope of Yeats's 'tightened bow' in the arched back of the father who digs not only in space but also, archaeologically, across time:

Between my finger and my thumb
the squat pen rests; snug as a gun.

Under my window, a clean rasping sound
When the spade sinks into gravelly ground:
My father, digging. I look down

Till his straining rump among the flowerbeds
Bends low, comes up twenty years away . . .[15]

Poised as a sniper here, the poet again makes an opposition of
rhetoric to violence, pen to gun, for the poem ends where it began,
with Heaney deciding to 'dig' with his pen. The text, like Yeats's
above, reads back-to-front; indeed, the obtrusive phrase, 'snug as a
gun' is itself almost precisely a palindrome, allowing Heaney the
Georgic trope of constructing his writing as a form of farming, that
kind of writing known as *boustrophedon*, where alternate lines
are read in opposite directions. The concern with digging in
precisely the archaeological manner explored by Yeats continues
into *Wintering Out*. Many poems in this collection reveal Heaney
searching the earth for skulls of some 'old Danes' found in Viking
Dublin and using those dead bodies to make his claims upon the
land of Ireland, that 'tragic terrain' which Deane notes in his work.
But in *North*, there is the beginning of a turn from this modernist
(and, in the final analysis, reactionary) position to a more radical
postmodern figuring of the verse. For here, although Heaney still
dabbles in the earth and with digging, the text stages the defeat of
his strategy of attempting to root himself in a tradition. It may be
slightly more accurate to suggest that in this collection, Heaney's
attitude to tradition changes slightly: from now on, tradition is
nothing if it is not alive and continuing; he gives up on an older,
'easier' notion of tradition as a heritage which is fixed, stable, in
place and dead. At one level, this is clear in that the collection
opens with 'Antaeus', the poem about the figure who, like the
early Heaney, gained his strength and power from contact with the
earth itself. But Part 1 of the collection stages the defeat of
Antaeus in the poem 'Hercules and Antaeus', where the poetry
finally frees itself from the Georgic commitment to the earth. This
emancipation opens the way into the second part of the collection, especially the long poem-series 'Singing School', where the
poet aligns himself with Wordsworth: 'Much favoured in my
birthplace, and no less/In that beloved Vale to which, erelong,/I
was transplanted'.[16] Heaney's subsequent work then involves the
more explicit turning away from the earth (perhaps related, if
Deane's thesis is correct, to the death of his own mother), and a
movement towards flight, as he eventually becomes the figure or

'voicing' of the mad King Sweeney, turned into a bird and exiled to the trees by the curse of St Ronan towards the end of *Station Island*. After this, *The Haw Lantern* opens with 'Alphabets' in which there is a suggestion that Heaney, having explored various 'rooted' alphabets, alphabets where the letters are rooted in images of the earthy world he knows, is moving towards a different writing, a different and fully deterritorialised script. The closing image of the poem compares his own sight of a plasterer writing the family name on a gable at home with the astronaut who sees the earth as the letter 'O', 'this wooden O':

> As from his small window
> The astronaut sees all he has sprung from,
> The risen, aqueous, singular, lucent O
> Like a magnified and buoyant ovum —
>
> Or like my own wide pre-reflective stare
> All agog at the plasterer on his ladder
> Skimming our gable and writing our name there
> With his trowel point, letter by strange letter.[17]

What Heaney begins to hear in this is an alphabet based not on the violence of writing/digging (the alphabet of the earthy Modernist father, Yeats), but rather an alphabet based on the 'magnified and buoyant ovum', a womanly writing, perhaps. It is certainly a writing which, although still very concerned with the politics of land in Ireland, does not think that problem in easy 'rooted' or modernist terms. The answer here, as Edward Said has indicated with respect to the similar issues in the Middle East, does not lie in any easy parcelling-out of lands specifically assigned to various races or tribal groupings. In fact it is the very notion of a tradition or *culture* which, by verbal definition and by ideology, *grows* from and in an earth claimed as racial or national or private property, claimed as the burial place of one's dead and hence of one's 'history' (actually, of course, merely one's 'heritage'), which has caused the political problem in the first place.

The postmodern impetus towards an explicit deterritorialisation and the subsequent abandonment of (at least the metaphor of) culture offers a genuine and historical way of advancing political solutions to such issues. This postmodern, like those flights of

Nijinsky at the turn of the century, promises the possibility of a *hearing otherwise*, of a mode of hearing/understanding which involves the orientation towards alterity rather than the constant modernist reduction of all alterity to the ideology of the non-historical Same, in a principle of identity which leads only to nationalism, racism or imperialism. The postmodern epistemology is one which acknowledges the difficulty of understanding.

Understanding as such may be difficult for the simple reason that in order to understand something which is, by definition, Other than the Self, something which is not already known and re-cognisable, involves a danger to the identity of the Self as such: the danger of the Self's becoming historical, becoming different, becoming oriented towards alterity. Such a difficulty is manifest in, for instance, reactions to the new music of the twentieth century, for which we might require new ears or a different mode of hearing. Otherwise, we end up as the ineffectual modernist Prufrock who has heard the mermaids signing, but cannot heed them for they do not sing to him. Modernist 'hearing' is a mode of silencing the Other by ignoring anything in the Other's discourse which disturbs the principle of identity or which disturbs one's own identity or territorial rootedness. The postmodern question is not whether one *has heard* the voice of alterity here, but rather whether one *will hear* such a voice, whether one will take one's poetry from the future.

'List, list, O list . . .'

'Any new composition must contain at least one new chord.'
(Franz Liszt)

In a self-portrait painted in 1967–8, *Interior with Plant, reflection listening*, Lucian Freud produced an image of the artist in a posture of listening, as if the labyrinth of the ear cupped in the hand was almost as important to him as the visual reflection. This would, of course, run counter to premises taken for granted at least since the eighteenth century when Lessing articulated a distinction between temporal and spatial forms of art. In this aesthetic, music, as an art of listening in time, belongs to the former category, and painting, as an art of looking across space, belongs firmly to the latter. Much twentieth-century art has questioned the simplicity and decided stability of such an opposition. In Abstract Expressionism, for instance, it is important that the perceiver follows and articulates the 'dance', both physical and psychological, which a painter made in the construction of the painting. Pollock, de Kooning, Hoffman, Tobey and others all made the painting-area itself into the arena for their dance; and Kline, for one, painted Nijinsky in figures which became less and less representational, and which more and more bore the traces of Kline's own movements. In these paintings, the eye follows lines and movements, and, as in the dance itself, the art becomes a temporal configuration.

One seemingly banal but actually important factor here is scale: many of these paintings are simply too big to be encompassed

fully in one self-present instance of perception. That phenomenology in which the subject of the act of perception forms and
figures herself through a relation to a stable Object in a configuration which grants the subject an assured, stable and self-present
identity is questioned. The subject now exists in time and is thus
opened to the possibility of *difference*, of differing from herself in
the very construction of a supposed 'identity', an identity which
is no longer definable, namable. The stability of the Object, the
painting, whose function it was in such a phenomenology to grant
the subject a stable point of reference from which to define herself
has been abandoned.

Such undecidable instabilities in the twentieth-century art-
Object are rife. The sculptures of Tinguely self-destruct, and since
they take time to do so, become fully historical (and thus more
than merely temporal) because they cannot strictly be repeated. In
this respect they are like much conceptual art which exists as
record only in *documentations* of the art-happening itself. They
are also like the wrappings and 'revelations' of Christo whose
basic manoeuvre is a continuation of the Formalist *ostranenie*,
returning a defamiliarised world to us, but returning it to us —
after it is unwrapped — as something less than recognisable, as
something *different* from what it used to be. Bridget Riley's so-
called 'Op-Art' produced paintings which seem literally to move,
refusing to stay still under one's gaze. Such a figuration finds its
logical culmination in Yaacov Agam's *Double Metamorphosis II* of
1964, where the painting actually *changes* as the perceiver moves
in front of it. Agam has employed a trope of reversing Renaissance
perspective here, reversing that perspective which, according to
Berger and others, is partly responsible for the construction of the
subject of the gaze as 'the Individual'.[1] We have not one painting
here, but the site in which a number of paintings are constructed,
depending on the position of the spectator whose act of perception is thus rendered historical, and whose phenomenological
subjectivity is temporalised, forced to base itself upon self-
difference rather than self-identity or self-sameness. These conditions obtain even in Rothko who, working within an extended
tradition of landscape, in his sheer stress on horizontality, produced paintings which question the prioritisation of space. In his
work in the colour-field 'rectangles', what one discovers is not the

stability of line in painting but rather its eradication as such. The colours work by 'reflecting' upon each other, composing each other as it were, thereby losing their stability as definite colours with a definite demarcation-line between them. The horizons in this landscape disappear. These paintings, like Riley's or Agam's, 'change' during the perception of them. This is not an optical illusion, but is rather a condition of the temporality of painting itself: what begins as stable difference marked by a separating line begins to shift and the difference between the colours becomes more important than the colours in themselves. This is most evident in the series of 'Black on Black' paintings which Rothko made towards the end of his life, where the difference between the repeated blacks takes time to be perceived and can only be perceived in time.

In postmodern architecture, one finds a similar effect of prioritising time in what had been thought of as a spatial scenario. The typical postmodern building makes a shift away from phenomenology in architectural theory, away from the notion of architecture as a lived space devoid of a temporality.[2] In place of lived space, one finds the emergence of lived time, as the building is formed from an eclectic *mélange* of styles and parodies from different historical moments, such that the movement through the building becomes not so much an occupation of space but rather an occupation of time. An interesting problem-case here would be the Getty Museum in Malibu, where one moves through a perfect replica of the Villa dei Papiri, which stood in the ancient city of Herculaneum until it was buried under the volcanic eruption of Vesuvius. As Baudrillard has noted, in his meditation on *Amérique*, this re-make of the Villa is, in a sense, awaiting its own destruction in the expected earthquake on the San Andreas fault in California. When buried by this earthquake, it will become even more 'genuinely' the replica of its model: there will be no fundamental difference, Baudrillard suggests, between the ruins near Naples and the ruins in Malibu.[3] This is not so much a building which exposes historicity as a building whose function it is to collapse history itself, to eradicate the difference between the ancient world and the contemporary. It is 'traditional', a mark of heritage rather than of history. Its supposed postmodernity (in its parodic mode) is thus questioned by its own internal stability, in the sense that it is all consistently, on the inside as the outside, extremely like the Villa dei Papiri; no other conflict of style questions the illusion of similarity. More truly postmodern would be those buildings (typically shopping-malls in the USA) where there is a *mélange* of various styles from different historical moments, where one moves from Egyptian motifs to English Georgian overlooking Venetian roofs and so on.[4]

In music, the converse of this shift in the plastic arts also holds. The 'temporality' of music is called into some doubt when, for instance, Rainer Wehinger can make an 'aural score' for the works of Ligeti, producing a score which bears a remarkable visual resemblance to some twentieth-century paintings, especially to the work of painters such as Klee, Matisse and Kandinsky.

Michel Serres indicates, rightly, that music is a 'dialectical confrontation with the course of time'; but what should be added to this is the relation of music to space and to the occupation of, or flight from, territory. Attali makes this relation clear when he writes of one 'origin' of music in birdsong:

> More than colours or forms, it is sounds and their arrangements that fashion societies. With noise is born disorder and its opposite: subversion . . . Among birds a tool for marking territorial boundaries, noise is inscribed from the start within the panoply of power. Equivalent to the articulation of a space, it indicates the limits of a territory and the way to make oneself heard within it, how to survive by drawing one's sustenance from it.[5]

Messiaen, influential composer of the *Catalogue d'oiseaux*, knows fully the claims made upon territory by birdsong; but he is also the composer of the *Quattuor pour la fin du temps*, that apocalyptic piece written at what may have seemed an end of time, in the concentration camp Stalag-8 when the possibility of flight was denied. My present argument is that in what I term 'active listening', one approaches the condition which Attali calls 'composition'; and that such listening can become a paradigm for the epistemology of art at the end of culture, in the postmodern mode of a flight-oriented deterritorialised art.

Attali's thesis is that music is political through and through, and that 'Nothing essential happens in the absence of noise'.[6]

Noise itself is violence, he argues, on the grounds that it constitutes a disturbance: 'To make a noise is to interrupt a transmission, to disconnect, to kill',[7] and it is thus a simulacrum of the
ritual murder which is at the basis of social organisation as such.
Noise produces disorder but also its opposite: the world or
cosmos, order. The production of noise, as in birdsong, is closely
related to violence, to the violent act which stakes a claim either
upon territory or upon sexual partners, claims which will be
substantiated by violence and murder if necessary. Music, according to Attali, channels this noise. It effectively directs noise,
making it into a useful weapon or political tool. Music is thus a
simulacrum of noise, which is in turn a simulacrum of murder;
and hence music becomes 'a sublimation, an exacerbation of the
imaginary, at the same time as the creation of social order and
political integration'. Noise produces the world; music produces
the scenarios of power which organise or channel that world — as
well as providing the possibility of subversion in noises which
challenge the dominant social music. The theorists of totalitarianism

have all explained, indistinctly, that it is necessary to ban subversive noise
because it betokens demands for cultural autonomy, support for differences or
marginality: a concern for maintaining tonalism, the primacy of melody, a
distrust of new languages, codes, or instruments, a refusal of the abnormal —
these characteristics are common to all regimes of that nature.[8]

Attali's awareness of the politics of music, and of the possibility of
subversion through the new music, compares neatly with the
sociology of music outlined by Adorno earlier in the century,
though there are also some differences in their respective positions, especially with regard to their acceptance or rejection of the
music of mass-culture.[9]

Further, for Attali, music is prophetic and in advance of the
politics of a society which will only later become 'visible'. This
can be explained by outlining his 'mapping' of the historical
zones of music. He postulates three already occupied or realised
zones: of *forgetting, believing,* and *silencing,* as well as one zone
yet to come to being, a zone of *composition.* Each such zone has
an appropriate 'power', and an appropriate 'musical form'. This

can be laid out schematically, with the addition of a fourth term to describe the political mode appropriate to each zone as follows:

ZONE	POWER	MUSICAL FORM	(POLITICS)
1. Forgetting	Ritual	Sacrifice	(Violence)
2. Belief	Representative	Representation	(Harmony)
3. Silence	Bureaucratic	Repetition	(Normality)

In the first of these zones, music is used to make people ignorant of the general violence in which they are involved and which music rationalises and makes bearable. In the second, music makes people believe in or subscribe to the 'harmony' of the world, a harmony which channels forces and violations in a way which pretends to be concord rather than discord; in this, people are encouraged to believe 'that there is order in exchange and legitimacy in commercial power'.[10] This stage, clearly, is that of the development of harmonics, especially in the eighteenth century, a harmonics which lies behind or gives the theoretical grounding of commodity capitalism and the capitalist modes of production and exchange. It is a 'music of the spheres', the harmonious repertoire of Baudelairean 'correspondences'. In the third stage, we have a music whose function is to silence people through the mass-production of repetitious and incantatory musics (as in some popular forms, but also in the minimalist music of composers such as Reich, Glass, Riley and Adams). Through repetition, this music proposes a normality against which any voiced criticism would be deemed 'abnormal', and would thereby be silenced. Attali suggests that:

Today, in embryonic form, beyond repetition, lies freedom: more than a new music, a fourth kind of musical practice. It heralds the arrival of new social relations. Music is becoming *composition*.

Representation against fear, repetition against harmony, composition against normality. It is this interplay of concepts that music invites us to enter.[11]

While being slightly more sceptical about the utopian promise of composition as advanced here by Attali, one can nonetheless retain much of the force of the argument; and one can certainly endorse the orientation towards emancipation explicit here.

To hear the new music would be akin to hearing the scandalous 'jug jug' of the nightingale. It would involve active listening or composition, in which one would be always *hearing otherwise*. This involves hearing a noise which disturbs the silence and which forbids the possibilities of representation and recognition. In listening to music, it involves the endorsement of disturbance as such, and the refusal to accommodate the sounds one hears in any predetermined format, or according to any expected thematics. In writing music (and often today there is little difference between listening and writing: that *is* the condition of 'composition') it would be to strive, as Liszt suggested, to include a new chord in every piece. Since the advent of electronic music and the development of aleatory methods both of writing and of performance, a 'composition' in which the music is forever new, forever strange, forever defying recognisability and accommodation within the already known musical forms or systematicities, has become dominant in much new music.

This postmodern music — 'composition' — might productively be dated from Debussy's *Prélude à l'après-midi d'un faune*, which established the idea that it is possible to compose in the absence of a stable *key*. The music becomes, in a sense akin to some twentieth-century plinth-less sculptures examined earlier, ungrounded or deterritorialised, like the scandalous dance of Nijinsky, whose movements suggested the erotic orientation towards an autonomous pleasure of the body implicit in such a deterritorialisation. But further, Debussy's music, both here and in a piece such as *La mer*, performs another important function later extended in twentieth-century music: the abandonment of an explicitly linear narrative progression. What we have here is a music which prefigures the developments in narrative of writers such as Joyce or Gide, or, more recently, the entire anti-linearity of the *nouveaux romanciers* (Robbe-Grillet, Sarraute, Butor, Sollers, Pinget), and the extremely important and innovative work of Wittig whose texts eschew linear narrative as a masculinist form.

With Debussy, of course, one might align Stravinsky and Schoenberg as innovators affording a glimpse of postmodernity. Stravinsky abandons key, replacing that ground with a more explicitly temporal 'grounding' in *rhythm* for a work such as *Le*

Sacré du printemps; and Schoenberg abandons (reluctantly, perhaps) the existing tonality and harmony. These are probably the
most important factors in the developments of the new music and
in the political orientation of such work. Attali argues that with
Schoenberg, Berg and Webern,

music forced a break with tonality before economic accumulation forced a
break with the laws of the economy of representation. Harmony — the
repressive principle of the real — after having created romanticism — the
utopian principle of the real, the exaltation of death in art — became the death
of art and destroyed the real. An excess of order (harmonic) entails pseudodis-
order (serial). Antiharmony is the rupture of combinatory growth, noise. At the
end of meaning, it sets in place the aleatory, the meaningless, that is to say . . .
repetition.[12]

For Attali — as indeed, one might suggest, for Lyotard,
Baudrillard, Agamben and other postmarxist thinkers — the
present society, foreshadowed by the music of repetition, is one in
which nothing happens, '*except for the artificially created
pseudoevents and chance violence that accompany the emplace-
ment of repetitive society*'.[13] The classic dramatic text here, of
course, is Beckett's *Waiting for Godot* in which silences are
punctuated by acts of violence, and the play suggests its own
endless self-repetition, a repetition which becomes explicit in
Beckett's later *Comédie*.

If one understands such repetition as the site of the production
of an ethics of normality, even of a law of normativity and of
conformity, as Attali suggests, then one might think it an entirely
regressive force in music. And yet in an active listening, this can
have a different effect, leading explicitly towards the emancipatory condition of composition. Paul Griffiths has rightly
indicated that the musical textures of a composer such as Reich,
or the heavily overloaded pieces of Ligeti (to whom one ought to
add Penderecki), make it difficult to hear the work at all as any
kind of *recognisable* event.[14] Rather, what happens in listening to
such works is that the ear cannot accommodate the sounds into
any easily recognisable mode (repetitions are irregular, or the ear
is simply receiving too much information at once), and it tends to
pick out more or less random sounds, or to prioritise different
elements of the music at each instant during performance. Thus

one finds that the music, although repeating itself, always includes or produces not *similarity* through this repetition, not normality at all, but rather a listening which is based on the production of *difference* and of abnormality. The same effect occurs in many aleatory works, obviously, which differ on subsequent hearings. But that production of abnormality happens even on an initial listening to a piece such as Reich's *Music for Eighteen Musicians* or Ligeti's *Artikulation*. One begins to 'compose', for in actively listening to such works, the ear begins to discern a music which is often not there at all, a music which certainly has not been scored or transcribed or even played. The ear itself in active listening produces a music which is, strictly, *unrecognisable*; it is a music which differs internally from itself and therefore denies the very possibility of recognition as such.

If one discusses twentieth-century music in relation to birdsong and to claims upon territory, however, one must mention Messiaen, who has consistently turned to birdsong as an elemental form of music. In the extensive *Catalogue d'oiseaux*, Messiaen thinks of birdsong as a kind of primary music, a music allowing access to an underlying sacred 'music of the spheres', a theological law of music available to those who have ears to hear it. In this respect, he is a last romantic, still straining to hear the song of the nightingale, but believing that song to be a harmonious balm rather than a subversive poison. His Catholicism, of course, suggests that Messiaen in hearing and transcribing the songs of birds is, as it were, hearing a fundamental *harmony*, a harmony or regulation guaranteed by the real underlying voice of God which speaks through nature and which Messiaen, as modern scribe or disciple, merely transcribes. Two further aspects of Messiaen's work, however, deserve mention in the present context. First, there is *Chronochromie*, in which he produces a music which, like Ligeti's, is capable, he believes, of bringing to light a range of colours or a painting of sorts. Here, one has discovered a visual from a prior aural art. Secondly, one might consider his *Quattuor pour la fin du temps*, which, although again explicitly religious, proposes an end of time and of timing in music. It becomes almost impossible, in listening to this piece, to ground oneself with respect to its rhythm and tempo. It is, as it were, temporally unrooted. Messiaen has argued that this, as in other pieces, is meant to propose the end of secularity and to allow an access to a theological or sacred time, as Eliade might call it.[15] But it might work equally well to do precisely the opposite, producing an extreme awareness of time and of the act of listening as a fully temporal activity. The general thrust of Messiaen's music, however, seems to tend towards territorialisation in music, a final 'landing', as it were, or final nesting for the song of the bird in Messiaen's theological perspective. This explains the tendency towards the spatial in his music, towards that attempt to spatialise time. In its theological impetus, it is developed even more fully and characteristically more spectacularly and flamboyantly by one of Messiaen's pupils, Stockhausen. Stockhausen's most recent work, *Licht*, though taking a full week to hear, marks a return to a biblical version of Enlightenment modernism.

The tendency towards rootedness and territorialisation, towards the situation where, as in Messiaen's conception of the meaning of birdsong, 'the Eagle has landed', as it were, is perhaps also apparent in the music of composers such as Ives and Bartok, who mark a return to 'traditional' or peasant forms of music. But if this was all that their music did, then it could not escape the merely modernist conception of tradition. It is important to note that the ethnicity of their music is not engaged in order to make a claim upon any specific territories: on the contrary, both composers here uproot their adopted traditional forms and transplant them into unexpected terrains. It is in this 'grafting', this lunatic flight which takes place before the eagle can land, so to speak, that they effect a breach in the walls of the modern and make the successful move into postmodernity, into its deterritorialising flights from rooted, organic culture.

Certain major distinctions can now be made between modernist and postmodern art. Modernism is an *art of the cliché*: its 'shock of the new'[16] is a 'shock' which is easily accommodated within an expanded framework of 'the old'; it thus becomes, in actual fact, a 'shock at the persistence of the old', the shock of *tradition*, as Eliot well understood. It is an art of *memoration*: its aim is the recuperation of a 'reality' which it assumes was always already known, but simply temporarily forgotten. Such a reality may be the 'reality' of race, nation, gender and so on, the reality of a 'history' (which is only ever a 'tradition' or 'heritage') supposedly

informing the identity of a Self in its present moment. Modernism's prioritisation of the specular, its introspections, makes it an
art of surveillance: it is an art which, like Bentham's Panopticon
as discussed by Foucault, attempts to discipline its terrain of
speculation, to parcel it out in neat, identifiable (examinable and
punishable) bounded areas called 'cultures'. Its aim in this function of 'the disciplining of cultures' is to understand; but such
'understanding' is only ever the tyrannous collapsing of alterity
into Sameness; it is an understanding which claims to know the
Other in all its difference from the Self, and which proves that
knowledge by imposing the language-game or discourse of the Self
upon the heterogeneous language-game or discourse of the Other.
It is thus not so much understanding as a 'soft' cultural imperialism, a *tort*, 'patronage' and punishment.[17]

The postmodern offers a kind of re-versal of these traits.
Postmodernism is that which can be heard in the dissonances
produced by experimental art, making thought as such possible,
even necessary, again. The 'shock' of postmodernism, with its
parodic deployment of already established styles, is one which
questions 'the old' or the already known by relocating it, dis-
cordantly, in an inappropriate context, making the known unrecognisable. It does not aim at the recuperation of a 'forgotten'
reality, but at the construction of an imaginary or of an imagination. Such an imagination, like the unconscious which postmodernism produces alongside it, is thoroughly historical, not
merely traditional. It is thus an imagination not based upon the
self's 'narcissistic' self-reflexivities, but rather an 'echo'-ing imagination based upon the production of difference and heterogeneity, a counter to identity. This imagination, however, is primarily
aural: postmodernism depends upon hearing what is not actually
there. It requires a mode of hearing, of *entendre*, which will not
allow for an easy slippage into 'understanding', into the recognisability of the always already known. On the contrary, it is that
which defies recognition as such, defies the reduction of thought
to cliché, for its form is never self-identical: it sounds different
and is made from different sounds.

A fine example of such a postmodern prioritisation of aural over
visual is the work of Miller Levy. In his 1988 exhibition at the
Pompidou Centre, Levy offered what could be termed 'aural

images'. Groups of people stared at magnetic tape which was stretched out in the shape of a race-track, while it played back the sounds of racing-cars screeching round bends, skidding, crashing and so on. The tape carried images of tiny racing-cars, but these were much less important than the sound of the work, which could be heard all over the Beaubourg building, a dissonance distracting spectators who were there to see Cy Twombly's paintings or, indeed, to see the building itself. The images on the tape could only be seen if one had a ring-side position. The speakers were so arranged that the sound of the car screeching round a corner was perfectly co-ordinated with the image of the car on the tape as it too circled the track. In this, and in all the other works in this exhibition, one was encouraged, as it were, to hear paintings, for all the works offered some image, but most of the 'image-making', most of the poetic imagination involved was dependent upon the primacy of the ear. For Levy, '*La bande magnetique est une surface mystérieuse. Elle imite la pensée*'. He suggests that in watching the tape, we can:

Lire la pensée des petits objets, des dessins; voila à quoi servent ces machines. A voir l'invisible: qui peut dire que là il n'y a rien? Dans des assemblages de renvois, poulies, retours et roues de métal, avec sa force infime, elle zigzague se frottant le dos et la face, pour accomplir le mécanisme de sa mémoire. Elle est la liaison la plus délicate entre la pensée et la transmission.[18]

Thought is once more possible.

In terms of the art-object as commodity, postmodernism *fails to produce*, even while it may still effectively 'seduce'.[19] The typical postmodern form is one which can never easily be reified into the condition of an object as such, and certainly never into a self-present object. If postmodernism does seem to offer objects, they are objects contaminated by a lack of stability, objects whose condition is that of historical mutability (and thus precisely unamenable to commodification or to representation). It is thus that postmodernism produces a mode of being approximating to Attali's condition of composition, for in composition there is emancipation from commodity capitalism and an entry into new social relations. For Attali, this new mode presaged by composition is one in which the body takes autonomous pleasure in itself. But for this to be fully postmodern in the terms outlined here, this body would have to be one whose form was never self-identical, a body which, like the bodies of characters in Wittig's fictions, is self-differing, self-modifying, interfused with the other bodies which shape the configurations of its history, lacking therefore any stable identifiable commodity-presence: a 'body politic'.

Attali writes that composition will produce a music which:

> would be performed for the musician's own enjoyment, as self-communication, with no other goal than his own pleasure, as something fundamentally outside all communication, as self-transcendence, a solitary, egotistical, noncommercial act. . . . At the extreme, music would no longer even be made to be heard, but to be seen, in order to prevent the composition from being limited by the interpretation — like Beethoven, brimming with every possible interpretation, reading the music he wrote but could no longer hear. Thus composition produces a radical social model, one in which the body is treated as capable not only of production and consumption, and even of entering into relations with others, but also of autonomous pleasure.[20]

In the silent labyrinth of Beethoven's ears, the horn — this time as hearing-piece — once more provides a danger. Here it is the danger of accepting only the audible as reality and refusing to entertain the possibility of imaginative change, of *hearing otherwise*. The postmodern *aural imagination* approaches the condition in which, like Beethoven, one hears every possibility, and hears them all equally in all their contradictory difference. In this, the music becomes, literally, a visual image, as in Wehinger's aural scores for Ligeti; and the ear enters the *ima*ginary, a seeming metaphorical impossibility. We have the beginnings, in postmodern music, of a pardigm for political change: the possibility of hearing what is not actually there, of hearing the poetry of the future, a future which remains unrecognisable.

If the future is to be comprehensible, or if it is to be *predictable* in the mode of, say, Marxism, then what we call 'history' has become nothing other than the scenario of the deterrence of history. The imagination has collapsed or reduced all potential fundamental difference into the already recognisable. Postmarxism would replace such unsecular 'prophecy' with a more fully historical notion of 'prolepsis'. As a result, 'understanding' may have become more difficult; indeed, it may even become part of the problem to be overcome. Certainly, critical understanding in the modernist manner of the demystification of ideologies, has failed in its ostensible political project of emancipation. 'Enlightenment' understanding is itself a mode of 'soft imperialism' which a postmarxism must question.

= V =

Conclusion: Going On

9

Postmarxism

Marxism has a vested interest in criticism, for it is involved in the necessary and continual production of crisis. However, what Marxism cannot admit, despite the theoretical necessity of auto-critique, is the possibility that it might itself be in crisis. This remains at least an empirical if not also a theoretical fact. Ever since Stalin, Marxist revolution has had no chance in the west; all revolutionary and leftist movements live haunted by the shadow of the camps. Since 1968, this has been more or less admitted by a number of erstwhile socialist or communist intellectuals who have abandoned Marxism as both theory and practice. There emerges a new confrontation between a revitalised or new 'New Right', concerned to re-instate old and often discredited rightist ideologies and discourses, and the postmarxists whose concern has been the radical questioning of Marxism not in the interests of the reinstatement of old-fashioned or centrist liberalisms but rather in the interests of a proper historicity and the possibility of emancipation from oppressions and from all forms of coercion including terror. In arguing for such an emancipation from terror, the postmarxist not only thinks that Marxism itself has become obsolete — or, one might say, *historical* — but also that it is time to rehabilitate the aspect of an ethical (and indeed, early Marxist) 'pity' in political thought.

The current postmodern condition is inimical to Marxism. Contemporary technology, for one thing, has constructed socio-political relations in the social formation to which classical Marxism has simply nothing to say. All 'classic' Marxisms rest fundamentally on a claim to demystification. They are based upon

243

the dichotomy of *appearance versus reality.* But this ideology-criticism, according to which Marxism claims a privileged ability to unmask ideologies in the name of revealing a truth or reality, is no longer applicable when reality itself has been thrown into question and when culture has entered the age of what Baudrillard calls 'simulation', the Debordian society of the spectacle, a society governed by representations with no prior presence or ground. There is, as it were, no 'material' reality in the sense in which Marxism has always understood that term, no uncontestable 'reality' which lies veiled behind ideology. As the 1984 exhibition mounted by Lyotard and Thierry Chaput demonstrated, the contemporary age is one of *Les immatériaux.*[1] It is an age in which, again thanks to the current state of technologies, it becomes difficult to 'root' oneself firmly in a defined social class, and hence the 'motor of history', class struggle, becomes somewhat more difficult to articulate. This is not to say that we have reached the much-vaunted 'end of ideology' discussed during the late 1950s and 1960s (much less the end of history advertised by Fukuyama in the 1980s), nor is it to say that 'class' or 'class struggle' do not exist. Rather, it simply suggests that these concepts are in crisis and that they require re-thinking. Postmarxism has realised that Marxism has itself now become part of the problem, not part of the supposed cure (a cure which, even Marxists agree, is a long time coming). The institutionalisation of Marxism within various critical and cultural practices has certainly worked as a kind of innoculation against change, against the 'disease' of revolutionary practices. Postmarxism addresses this impasse in critical thought and practice.

In these concluding comments, I shall outline some of the premises of the postmarxism which governs the critical procedures of the preceding pages. Two basic points should be made here. First, the rejection of Marxism here is not in any sense a recapitulation to a reactionary ideology; rather, this rejection arises from the realisation that Marxism has not in any sense been radical enough: Marxism itself, at least in the thoroughly institutionalised and 'comprehended' form in which it now exists, is itself a primary locus of reaction. Secondly, it is only in the rejection of Marxism (and, indeed, of 'theory' in the classic sense of the term), that thought becomes possible once more.[2]

Hegel remarks somewhere that 'It is by naming that we think'; postmarxism would reply to this that 'In naming, we construct a social formation which is eminently *re-cognisable*; and, in this re-cognisability, there lies a fundamental "identity principle" which is inimical to thinking as such: naming is the contradiction of thought'. This principle not only 'identifies' the world (as phenomenal Object), but also 'identifies' its thinker (as its stable and authoritative subject). In the resultant phenomenology, there is inscribed a resistance to historicity, a resistance to alterity, and there arises a production of that very bourgeois individualist identity-principle which has arrested radical thinking at least since the Enlightenment. Since the Enlightenment, thought has been rigorously policed or disciplined, 'conventionalised'. The discipline of thinking — the province of intellectual practice — has been established within rigorously conventionalised boundaries whose function is the legitimisation and, indeed, recuperation of all thought such that it is made to conform to the norms of 'Enlightenment'. The incipient radicalism of thinking as such, of a mode of thinking which escapes or questions dogma or ideology, becomes an impossibility: its status is that of 'illegitimate' thought, schizophrenia or madness.[3] All so-called 'thought' now takes place under the sign of a dominant schema or ideology — a 'logic'. As in mathematical logic, no real critical thinking is required; for, given the counters at work in any mathematical situation, it is the *system* of mathematical logic which does the thinking and which provides the answers. The subject has no thoughts or stakes in this matter. Postmarxism, like postmodernism, strives to make the possibility of thinking — of an unpoliced, undisciplined thought, or of thinking differently — available once more.

9.1 AFTER THEORY

When Habermas names a group of philosophers 'conservative' (old, young and neo), what he finds troubling in their thinking is their seeming rejection of Critical Theory, a rejection which previously was specific to right-wing ideologies which could not allow the underlying realities of their social formation to be too closely scrutinised. Habermas's concern is even more specifiable than this. In *The Postmodern Condition*, Lyotard rejected the 'grand metanarrative' proposed by Marxism; and, in their *Anti-Oedipus* and *A Thousand Plateaus*, Deleuze and Guattari rejected the similar grand metanarrative of Oedipus as proposed by Freud.[4] Once the theoretical grounding in Marx and Freud has been rejected in this manner, a critic is left in what appears to be a dangerously 'pragmatic' position, one where she or he has no *theoretical* reason to prefer one course of social action (say 'emancipation') over another (say 'oppression' or 'libertarianism'), and where any similar theoretical reason for understanding the 'political unconscious' of a social formation according to a 'therapeutic' or unrepressive guiding principle is lost. Habermas thinks that, in rejecting these theoretical grounds for their philosophical practice, these intellectuals are in danger of falling into a rejection of 'rational' discourse itself, for they are now, in principle at least, capable of behaving whimsically, irrationally, or merely pragmatically and expediently, not in accordance with any firm — predictable — social or political programme of rational enlightenment and emancipation.

Habermas, in this procedure, is hankering after a grand theory in the manner of Enlightenment science, a theory which should prove capable of explaining all phenomena and thereby of totalising experience in all its apparent heterogeneity. As Lyotard indicates:

What Habermas requires from the arts and the experiences they provide is, in short, to bridge the gap between cognitive, ethical, and political discourses, thus opening the way to a unity of experience.[5]

Habermasian theorising, then, is the attempt to 'identify' — even to homogenise — the heterogeneity of the disparate language-games which constitute historical experience. His quest for a governing theory or principle which underpins experience is founded in an 'identity principle'. But as Lyotard argues, such a procedure is in danger of committing *un tort*, of proceeding unjustly by thinking and adjudicating on one language-game according to the tenets of another. There is a danger of what he calls a 'soft imperialism' here. Lyotard prefers to respect the heterogeneity of language-games according to the logic of *le différend* which can be briefly stated:

Je dirais qu'il y a différend entre deux parties quand le 'reglement' du conflit qui les oppose se fait dans l'idiome de l'une d'elles alors que le tort dont l'autre souffre ne se signifie pas dans cet idiome.[6]

It is in collapsing one language-game under the idiom of another, in homogenising them according to an identity-principle, that there arises the possibility of imperialism, which, as I argued above, is imbricated in the Enlightenment project.

Baudrillard has argued that Marxism is caught up in precisely the reactionary forces it was meant to contest. Marx's critique of political economy depends fully upon the 'form production' and the 'form representation' of political economy, both of which reinscribe the critique fully within the bounds of political economy itself. As he writes in *The Mirror of Production*, in an argument which locates Marx's own critique firmly within the bourgeois mode of Enlightenment rationality it is supposed to challenge:

> Radical in its *logical* analysis of capital, Marxist theory nonetheless maintains an *anthropological* consensus with the options of Western rationalism in its definitive form acquired in eighteenth century bourgeois thought. Science, technique, progress, history — in these ideas we have an entire civilization that comprehends itself as producing its own development and takes its dialectical force toward completing humanity in terms of totality and happiness. Nor did Marx invent the concepts of genesis, development, and finality. He changed nothing basic: nothing regarding the *idea* of man *producing* himself in his infinite determination, and continually surpassing himself toward his own end.[7]

For Baudrillard, revolt against capitalism is already accomodated by capitalism itself, and Marxism has failed to escape the concepts of *production* and of *representation*: the determining instances not only of capital but also of Marxist revolt against capital.

Further, the very rationality which Habermas requires as an instrument in emancipation is revealed by Baudrillard (as also by Lyotard) to be itself terroristic. Baudrillard discusses the various forms of non-marxist revolt which are increasingly available as political options – such as the Black revolt, the feminist revolt, the revolt of youth-culture and of the unemployed and so on – and finds that these operate at a level much more radical than that of

mere economic exploitation. These revolts aim not at the economic at all, but rather at the very code which legitimises
economics, or at the very system which inscribes race, gender,
maturity and so on as a systematising force in the social formation. And he argues that:

> The more the system becomes concentrated, the more it expels whole social
> groups. The more it becomes hierarchized according to the law of value (sign
> or commodity) the more it excludes whoever resists this law. So it was that
> madness was confined (Michel Foucault) at the threshold of Western ration-
> ality. Today it is the same for all civil society, which has become a place of
> confinement where tranquillized man is closely watched. Everywhere behind
> the factory and the school, the suburb or the office, the museum or the
> hospital, it is the asylum and the ghetto that are profiled as the purest form of
> a truly rationalized society.[8]

Enlightenment rationality itself has contributed to the very
oppression which Habermas wants to challenge; but he wants to
challenge it by means of Enlightenment rationality in the project
of modernity. Logically, he is caught up in the very system of
oppression which he contests. Marxism, fully involved in the very
political economy it exists to challenge, is fundamentally unable
to make the break from the form production and the form
representation which govern it. Its revolt is thus always a revolt
which is operational within the system of capital itself; the best it
can hope for is the occasional 'scandal', the occasional seeming
threat to the system of capital. But capital simply uses such
scandal to innoculate itself against further attack.

It begins to appear in the logic of this argument that it is
precisely Habermas and the Marxists who are conservatives. What
they share in common with the political Right is the subscription
to a principle of identity, eventually recuperable as a metaphysical principle of self-presence. The Right subscribes to a code
or system which is basically that of capital itself, in which there is
a more or less dogmatic framing ideology within which local
modifications are possible, but only permissible when they contribute to the increased efficiency of the capitalist ideology itself.
Pragmatism is nothing more or less than the (un)acceptable face of
this Rightist ideology, for pragmatism in the manner espoused by
Rorty (or, in literary criticism by Hirsch, Benn Michaels, Fish and
others) merely reacts to the system's demands for modification in

order to 'keep the conversation going' as Rorty puts it — or, as might be more accurately stated, in order to maintain the efficient organisation of the system of conversation (capitalist exchange). Behind this there lies a metaphysical belief in a reality present to itself, a truth — even if that truth of reality is only 'what is better in the way of belief'. Habermas and his fellow Marxists (including structural and poststructuralist Marxists such as Althusser and Jameson) share this metaphysic. What they cannot abide — and what Marxism cannot abide — is the attack upon the very reality principle itself which has become a dominant feature of post-modernism.

Edward Said offers a slightly different position for criticism than that proposed by Marxism, though a position which still claims radical credentials. What worries him about conventional Marxism is its sheer institutionalisation in the Academy, together with its tendency to become dogma:

> on the important matter of a critical position, its relationship to Marxism, liberalism, even anarchism, it needs to be said that criticism modified in advance by labels like 'Marxism' or 'liberalism' is, in my view, an oxymoron. The history of thought, to say nothing of political movements, is extravagantly illustrative of how the dictum 'solidarity before criticism' means the end of criticism. I take criticism so seriously as to believe that, even in the very midst of a battle in which one is unmistakably on one side against another, there should be criticism, because there must be critical consciousness if there are to be issues, problems, values, even lives to be fought for.[9]

Said wants criticism to remain always 'oppositional', although never fully formulated into a single theoretical position. This way, he believes, criticism can come into its proper articulation as that which is 'life-enhancing and constitutively opposed to every form of tyranny, domination, and abuse'. This enables criticism to attain the goal of 'noncoercive knowledge produced in the interests of human freedom'.[10] Such 'oppositional criticism' is a position which has become much favoured in recent years. But there are problems with this for any criticism that would be radical.

Two points should be made. The first is the rather banal — if telling — observation that, logically, it becomes difficult to agree with Said. To express one's solidarity with Said's position leads one to the logical necessity of somehow disagreeing with it, or modifying it in the interests of the production of criticism, and in the interests of escaping its 'domination' of one's critical practices. This is close to the paradox encountered in all such forms of 'oppositional criticism', such as it is expressed, for instance, in the recent work of Parrinder, for whom criticism is essentially 'disagreement': one simply cannot 'agree' with this, if one wishes to remain critical, not to mention radical.[11] The logic of the 'oppositional' position demands its own rejection.

The second objection to this oppositional position is perhaps more consequential. For opposition, in whatever form, is simply not enough in the postmodern condition. Indeed, it is what might be called this 'mere opposition' which enables the capitalist system to revitalise itself and to keep itself going. Opposition is always already catered for in capitalist ideology. Baudrillard refers to this as the system's 'operational negativity'. He writes:

It would take too long to run through the whole range of operational negativity, of all those scenarios of deterrence which, like Watergate, try to regenerate a moribund principle by simulated scandal, phantasm, murder — a sort of hormonal treatment by negativity and crisis. It is always a question of proving the real by the imaginary, proving truth by scandal, proving the law by transgression, proving work by the strike, proving the system by crisis and capital by revolution . . . without counting:
 — proving theatre by anti-theatre
 — proving art by anti-art
 — proving pedagogy by anti-pedagogy
 — proving psychiatry by anti-psychiatry, etc., etc.
Everything is metamorphosed into its inverse in order to be perpetuated in its purged form. Every form of power, every situation speaks of itself by denial, in order to attempt to escape, by simulation of death, its real agony. Power can stage its own murder to rediscover a glimmer of existence and legitimacy.[12]

It is, in short, the very possibility of opposition which 'proves' or validates and legitimises the identity of capital. Capital needs Marxism, which helps regenerate it all the more strongly the more that Marxism itself becomes institutionalised.

Opposition, beginning as a challenge to the all-embracing or totalising 'identity' of the system of capital, turns out to be itself fully implicated in the production and maintenance of the very principle of identity which it proposes to question. The position advanced by Said, like that proposed by pragmatism, marks an

essential return to phenomenology. Each pragmatic act of criticism produces the identity of the subject of consciousness *vis-à-
vis* a particular historical situation. Opposition, at bottom, is
concerned with the establishment of individual identity, an identity which refuses collectivisation.

Postmarxism, it must be stressed, is no more favourably dis-
posed towards collectivisation than those oppositional forms of
Marxism. As Baudrillard remarks, *les masses font masse*: the
masses form an earth, which, as in an electrical earth, safely
discharges all disturbing power. The concept of the masses is
simply that which arrests criticism. The postmarxist position is
not one which claims to be more 'collectivist' than other forms of
Marxism, which it pronounces assimilated fully to the bourgeois
order of individualism. Rather, the postmarxist position is one
which challenges the very principles of identity and reality which
underpin that order themselves.

Rather than the consolidation of a principle of identity, postmarxism operates on an ethics of alterity. The principle of identity
shared by Marxist and bourgeois thought is essentially a comforting principle. In its operations, everything that is 'Other', everything that is alien or which resists undertstanding according to the
parameters of understanding formulated in the ideology of the
subject of consciousness, is reduced to an identity with the
subject. Everything Other becomes the Same; everything becomes
always already known and the world and its history become not
enacted but simply remembered. Levinas writes that in such a
situation:

everything has become indifferent. The unknown is immediately rendered
familiar and the new habitual. There is nothing new under the sun. The crisis
spoken of in Ecclesiastes is not due to sin but to *ennui*. Everything becomes
absorbed, engulfed and immured in the Same.[13]

Marxism's guiding principles of production, representation and
political economy leave it powerless to address those movements
or struggles which are not primarily concerned with the economics of the system of capital but with the very system itself and its
inscriptions of hierarchies and powers. Marxism thinks the feminist movement, say, in terms of the class struggle in which women
are the new proletariat; it thinks that other dispossessed groups

are motivated primarily by economic demands; and it fails entirely to account for, say, the Green political movement. Marxism collapses everything, including *all world history*, into a framework of political economy. When faced, for example, with feminism, this has two options. Either it can ignore the movement (as something which does not fit readily and easily into the established Marxist framework), or it can colonise it, reducing its difference from Marxism and rendering it simply part of an 'expanded Marxism'.[14]

This, clearly, is exactly the same manoeuvre as that deployed by Enlightenment rationality, which was — despite itself — broadly imperialist and racist in its theoretical underpinnings. It must be countered with a postmodern orientation towards alterity and heterogeneity, such as we have it in, for example, the ethics of Levinas or the psychoanalysis of Kristeva or Lacan, for whom the unconscious is the discourse of the Other.[15] In what Levinas calls the 'face-to-face', there is an ethical imperative which demands that the Other be regarded as fundamentally inassimilable, and as the very precondition of the possibility of the subject's own 'identity'. This 'principle of identity' is based entirely upon the prior ethical principle of alterity, and establishes a mutual interdependence among subjects. This, though close to Habermasian notions of 'communicative action', avoids that danger of a slippage into imperialism and totalitarianism which is run by the 'project of Modernity', as Habermas calls it.

The consequences of the shift to an ethics of alterity mark an enormous alteration in epistemology. The pursuit of knowledge is purged of its orientation to power or domination. Rather than making the world and history more 'comprehensible', this postmarxist position accepts the fundamental unknowability of the world and its history. History becomes not the site of a *totalising* (if latent) knowledge but rather the site of a struggle or of eventful action. It must be stressed that the attack here is on a totalising knowledge, a knowledge which makes an exclusive claim upon truth, based upon its theoretical efficiency or adequacy. Postmarxism accepts the necessary historicity of political and ethical practices, the historicity of truth itself.[16] In its respect for heterogeneity, it must reject all systems of Grand Theory, all systems which make a claim upon the ability to totalise knowledges and synthesise them in one consciousness or identity. Knowledge is nothing unless shared by the Other (or conditioned by alterity), and unless oriented towards difference rather than the construction of the identity of an individualisable consciousness or subject. The political point of this is to open the subject to the availability of her or his own historicity and mutability. The mere opposition advanced by Marxism is not enough for a radical criticism; it must be fully implicated in the much more radical pursuit of the unknown rather than the always-already-known-but-merely-forgotten; and it must be fully implicated in the ethics of alterity. Otherwise, one remains entirely within the totalising and dominating powers of theory, and fails to reach the emancipatory and radical potential of the postmodern moment 'after theory'.

9.2 SEDUCTION AND IRRESPONSIBILITY

In a letter to Samuel Cassin in 1984, Lyotard indicates that 'Dans *La Condition postmoderne* et dans les autres livres de cette époque . . . j'ai éxagéré l'importance à donner au genre narratif'.[17] But this stage in his thinking, a step towards the elaboration of the concept of *le différend*, allowed him to raise two issues of importance. The first — and the real object of his critique in *La Condition postmoderne* — is *totality*; the second is the power of narrative, essentially a power of *seduction*, in the term which is related more closely to the writings of Baudrillard.

When he questioned the '*grands récits*', Lyotard saw them as being implicated in an Idealist 'project', in the gradual realisation of an Idea (of freedom, socialism and so on). What worried him was their totalising 'monotheism', so to speak. Working with a Wittgensteinian notion of the social as constituted by 'language-games', Lyotard was at some pains to stress the absolute heterogeneity of those games or discourses. As he later developed this, in *Le Différend*, the tendency to terror and totalitarianism lay in the reduction of the heterogeneity of language-games to a fundamental identity. If, for example, one makes a pronouncement according to the rules of one language-game, it is unjust to have that formulation judged or even understood according to the tenets of another. So, to simplify the proposition, it is unjust to reduce the language-game of feminism, say, to that of Marxism. In that reduction of heterogeneity to homogeneity, there lies the root of totalising terror and the crushing of difference which is axiomatic to imperialism. (And while it would be true to say that Lyotard's arguments were actually more technical than this, concerning the impermissibility of deducing prescriptions from descriptions, say, nonetheless this (rather crude) version of his philosophy is the one which has gained ground.)

The figure of 'experience' itself, of personal or lived history, is susceptible to such imperialism and totalisation. As Lyotard argued in *L'assassinat de l'expérience par la peinture, Monory*:

L'expérience est une figure moderne. Il y faut un sujet d'abord, l'instance d'un Je, quelqu'un qui parle à la première personne. Il y faut une disposition temporelle type Augustin, *Confessions XI* (oeuvre moderne s'il en est), où la vue sur le passé, le présent et le futur est toujours prise du point de vue d'une conscience actuelle insaisissable. Avec ces deux axiomes, on peut déjà engendrer la forme essentielle de l'expérience: je ne suis déjà plus ce que je suis, et je ne le suis pas encore . . . Un troisième axiome donne à l'expérience toute son ampleur: le monde n'est pas une entité extérieure au sujet, il est le nom commun des objets dans lesquels le sujet s'aliène (se perd, meurt à soi) pour parvenir à soi, pour vivre. . . . Ainsi dessinée, la figure de l'expérience est chrétienne, on le voit, comme tout ce qui est moderne. Elle gouverne de loin l'idée de salût, donc de progrès, de révolution, il suffit de donner au Je des noms différents.[18]

Lyotard argued, during the late 1970s, for a 'pagan' position against the idealism of this 'christian experience' which constitutes modernity. He stressed that this was not at all an atheist position; rather, it was one which denied the monotheistic attitude in favour of the notion of a multiplicity of 'gods', a multiplicity of discourses which governed the modes of legitimation and the modes of thinking of social formations. It is this multiplicity which Marxism cannot accept, for Marxism is based upon a dialectic of appearance versus reality, figured in terms of superstructure versus base; and this base is a unifiable or identifiable entity: a universal history. It is, indeed, only in its unity that the base is susceptible to theoretical knowledge and uncomplicated understanding. To respect the heterogeneity of language-games means that one must accept the multiplicity of 'micro'-narratives which are deployed to make sense of the world and of history. It is the tendency to homogenise the heterogeneity of language-games under the rubric of a totalising system or theory, a '*grand récit*', which Lyotard identified as a major source of totalitarian thought. As Deleuze and Guattari also recognised, Grand Theory itself, in its most sophisticated forms (Marxism and psychoanalysis), is susceptible to precisely this tendency to totalisation and unjust homogenisation.

The postmarxist response to this situation is not the retreat into pragmatism or into a bland rejection of the successes of 'theoretical inquiry'[19] in the past. On the contrary, the response, as figured for instance in Baudrillard, is a further complication of the entire theoretical and epistemological terrain. In Baudrillard, a Lyotardian 'paganism' appears when Baudrillard rejects Marxism's domination by the form and metaphor of 'production'. For Baudrillard, thinking which is dominated by the question of production is itself part of the problem:

Failing to conceive of a mode of social wealth other than that founded on labor and production, Marxism no longer furnishes in the long run a real alternative to capitalism . . . It becomes impossible to think outside the form production or the form representation.[20]

Baudrillard's proposition, in the face of this, is that the form production can be dropped, to be replaced by what he terms *séduction*. In present epistemologies, it is difficult to think seduction without a corollary production; but it is this which is to be resisted. In the sexual domain, for example, seduction is always thought as the merest of foreplays to the real event, which is production (of bodily fluids, of children through labour, and so on). But for Baudrillard, seduction has nothing to do with this 'preparation for the real'.

The very principle of reality itself is what is in question in much of Baudrillard's sociology. In the present political and cultural debates, everyone makes a claim upon some kind of access to reality in its true or brute state. But this is not only fallacious; it is also dangerous. Baudrillard argues that an excess of reality, as it is available, for instance, in four-dimensional music in Japan, abolishes the distance which is required for the very experience of reality itself: 'le réel devient un phantasme vertigineux d'exactitude qui se perd dans l'infinitessimal'.[21] No seduction is possible in this situation (which is that of pornography), for seduction requires distance. It requires that inaccessibility of the Other in all its inassimilability. Seduction is not like a stripping naked or a revelation of truth; rather it is, as Virilio has it, an *esthétique de la disparition*, concerned with the play of appearance and disappearance, and not a dialectic of appearance and reality. Baudrillard refers to seduction as a play of veils:

Jamais de nudité donc, jamais de corps nu, et qui ne serait que nu — jamais de corps tout simplement. C'est ce que dit l'Indien quand il répond au Blanc qui lui demande pourquoi il vit nu: 'Chez moi, tout visage.' Le corps dans une culture non fétichiste (qui ne fétichise pas la nudité comme vérité objective) ne s'oppose pas comme pour nous au visage, seul riche d'expression, seul doué de regard: il est lui-même visage et vous regarde. Il n'est donc pas obscène, c'est-à-dire fait pour être vu nu. Il ne peut pas être vu nu, pas plus que pour nous le visage, car il est voile symbolique, il n'est que cela, et c'est ce jeu de voiles, où à proprement parler le corps est aboli 'en tant que tel' qui fait la séduction. C'est là ou elle se joue, et jamais dans l'arrachement du voile au nom de la transparition d'un désir ou d'une vérité.[22]

Seduction makes no claims upon a reality principle. What it does make a claim upon is an abiding 'rituality' through which social formations always organise themselves.

For Baudrillard, seduction and rituality are logically prior to production and sociality, which he sees as deviant versions of the mode of social organisation of a community. He considers feminism, for example, under the terms of its refusal of anatomy as destiny. According to such feminist thinking, sexuality is *produced*, not innate. But Baudrillard indicates the long history of the refusal of anatomy as destiny, and points out that what is at stake in that history is not the mere production of sexuality but a *seduction* of destiny itself, an attempt to seduce the gods:

Le déni de l'anatomie et du corps comme destin ne date pas d'hier. Il fut bien plus virulent dans toutes les sociétés antérieures à la nôtre. Ritualiser, cérémonialiser, affubler, masquer, mutiler, dessiner, torturer — pour séduire: séduire les dieux, séduire les ésprits, séduire les morts. Le corps est le premier grand support de cette gigantesque entreprise de la séduction.[23]

An important difference between Lyotard and Baudrillard is that the latter is not entirely averse to drawing '*grands récits*' of

history. Broadly, he outlines three phases, which might be use-
fully thought of as the pre-modern, the modern and the postmodern. These ages are dominated by certain figures or modes of
social organisation. They can be tabulated as follows, according to
their various social determinants, such as the force which organises them, the 'sociology' appropriate to them, their dominant
mode of social relation, their semiotic or manner of signifying
practices, and their politics:

		Pre-Modern	Modern	Postmodern
Force	:	La Règle	La Loi	La Norme
Sociology	:	Ritualité	Socialité	(Modèles)
Relation	:	Dualité	Polarité	Digitalité
Semiotic	:	Métamorphose	Métaphore	Métastase
Politics	:	Séduction	Production	'Irresponsibility'[24]

In the postmodern condition, it is useless to apply the terms of
modernity for any social analysis, for the current state of technology has rendered all the rules of modernity redundant. We no
longer live in a world organised by the polarity of appearance
versus reality, for instance; our world is the world of the simulacrum in which there are only appearances and disappearances, and
no claims can be made upon any fundamental ontological reality
at all. We have arrived at 'the end of the social', and current
culture is dominated by 'normativity' (as Attali likewise argued in
relation to music). The problem, as Baudrillard sees it, is that
contemporary political theory, especially Marxism, is working
within the framework of the modern, which is nothing more or
less than a kind of aberration from a more archaic scenario. Since
that more archaic situation is more fundamental, it would be
useful to address it in our present social analyses. Hence seduction will not be simply opposed to production; rather it will be
thought as that which seduces production, draws it in a force of
attraction and repulsion. It is this force, Baudrillard argues, that is
more basic and which should organise our socio-political thinking.

There is, clearly, a hint of mysticism here, or, as Baudrillard
might admit, a hint of *magic*. Magic is, at its most basic, concerned
precisely with appearances — appearances and disappearances.

'Where did the rabbit come from?' 'Where did the silk handker-
chief go to?' These are the typical questions proposed by the stage-
magician, whose magic is a simulacrum of those more important
powers of seduction of the gods and so on. But what these
questions indicate is that magic is fundamentally the short-
circuiting of narrative. Narrative operates by establishing and
articulating the historical or temporal movements from one state
of affairs to another; it is a temporalised metaphor. But in magic
we see the basic metamorphosis which underpins metaphor, for
the simple reason that magic by-passes the normal circuitous
routes of narrative and simply shifts instantly from one state to
another. In this, magic is opposed to science and to Enlightenment
rationality, both of which organise themselves according to the
determining instances of a particular version of legitimate narrative. Narrative is, one can suggest, answerable to the ideological
norms of rationality which govern the modern society; magic, on
the other hand, opens the door to an unanswerability, an irresponsibility.

Postmarxism shares in the call for a kind of critical irresponsibility, in a very specific sense of this term. In aesthetics, Lyotard
argues that it is the function of postmodern art to question the
very terms and condition of the rules which govern its possibility.
In short, painting must ask the question 'What is an image'; music
asks 'What is sound'; philosophy asks 'What is thought',[25] and so
on. The responsibility of the artist here is to the art itself and to its
framing rules, which are never known in advance. But the fact
that these rules are never known — the fact that it is these rules
which the artist or philosopher is in search of — means that the
question of 'responsibility' has taken an odd turn. What, then, is
this postmodern irresponsibility?

Responsibility, at least understood in terms of social or political
responsibility, implies an awareness of the Other, of a social
formation which surrounds the responsible subject. That subject
acts in a way which is 'answerable' to the prescriptions and norms
which govern the society; otherwise she or he will simply be
marginalised, ostracised or imprisoned, as being guilty of 'social
irresponsibility'. However, this makes it perfectly clear that this
understanding of responsibility is instrumental in the maintenance of a principle of identity which governs the social

formation. One is to be 'responsible' to an Other, certainly, but this Other is always only a displaced version of the Self or of the Same. It is only by acting in accord with a social norm, *known in advance*, that such responsibility becomes possible. In other words, this responsibility is profoundly narcissistic and conformist in the most extreme sense of the word, for it must always assume a fundamental normativity which makes the Other the Same as the Self, the Same as the Same.

Further, such responsibility is always nothing more or less than acting in accordance with a dominant ideology or dogma. It is, as it were, profoundly 'grand theoretical', in the sense that it is action which responds or answers to a systematised theory of what is normative, of what is legitimated in the social formation itself. But given that the social formation organises itself according to an identifiable system of norms, legitimation here is drawn from the normative language-game of the system itself. It thus becomes unjust, totalising and totalitarian, ignorant of the ethical demands of the *différend* or of the *face-to-face* so vital to an ethics of alterity in Lyotard or Levinas. It is at this point that a theory of critical irresponsibility can make a mark.

Postmarxism, as developed from the thought of Baudrillard and Lyotard,[26] proposes a mode of action which is as irresponsible as magic, or as unanswerable to the requirements of a social formation as art. If I think only according to the ideology of a particular language-game, then, postmarxism asserts, I am not thinking at all. One need only consider once more that mode of thinking called 'western mathematical logic' to make this clear. Given a 'scientific' framework, all that is fundamentally required is the distribution of the various counters in any computation; the rules of the scientific logic itself will do the rest. Similarly with the discourse of Marxism: simply identify the mode of production relevant to a particular event, and the system of Marxism itself will fill in all the blanks and produce an answer to our problem. This, clearly, is not thought at all, as the 'rogue' scientists such as Capra or Feyerabend have pointed out.[27] Postmodern philosophy operates differently from this. It begins in an orientation towards alterity and heterogeneity, acknowledging the Lyotardian *différend*, which would make it an unjust and totalitarian exercise to think one problem in the language-game of another. Further than this, the orientation towards alterity is a constant. This means that the postmarxist does not simply take the Other of Marxism, say, as her or his model for thinking; this would simply be the replacement of one ideological frame with another, the evasion of one mode of thinking with an evasion in the terms of another. Rather, post-marxism asserts that thought is only possible at the very interface between theoretical systems. In other words, it is not so much 'after theory' as 'inter-theoretical', or 'ana-theoretical', if I may coin a phrase. Here the sense of the term 'post-theoretical' becomes more apparent. 'Post-' here is to be understood not temporally but rather in Lyotard's terms as 'un procès en ana-':

le 'post-' de 'postmoderne' ne signifie pas un mouvement de *come back*, de *flash back*, de *feed back*, c'est-à-dire de répétition, mais un procès en 'ana-', un procès d'analyse, d'anamnèse, d'anagogie, et d'anamorphose, qui élabore un 'oubli initial'.[28]

In this postmodern and postmarxist orientation towards alterity and heterogeneity, it is not that one simply substitutes one formulated theory for another. On the contrary, the rules of the theory governing one's own work or thinking are precisely what the work or thinking is looking for. Postmarxism is like post-modernism in this: it makes thought once more possible by working at the interface of ideologies.

This means, however, that postmarxist or postmodern thought is not 'responsible' or answerable to any determining or governing theory. This does not mark a shift, let me stress once more, into pragmatism (which is itself in any case a theoretical position). Rather, it suggests that it is only in refusing the domination by any governing theory, by any position which makes a fundamental claim upon truth, totality or reality, that the possibility of thought remains. At the interface between theories, where one works without rules and judges 'without criteria', it becomes possible to effect an 'event': that is, it becomes possible to enter history, a history in which 'it happens', but where there is no prescribed identity or concept given in advance of the 'what' it is that happens. Postmarxism's interest in seduction is an interest in the attractions of alterity and heterogeneity, fundamentally with the goal of getting a critical history — an event — started. Its responsibility to intellectual practices lies in its interest in the magic of this seduction and, paradoxically, in the very critical irresponsibility which it asserts to theory as such. It is only in the refusal to be answerable to a governing theory that thought, historical thinking, and above all theoretical thought, becomes possible once more.

Notes

INTRODUCTION

1. Jurgen Habermas, 'Modernity — an Incomplete Project', in Hal Foster, ed., *Postmodern Culture*, Pluto Press, London 1985, p. 9.
2. Zygmunt Bauman, *Legislators and Interpreters*, Polity Press, Oxford 1987, p. 1.
3. Jean-François Lyotard, '*Appendice svelte à la question postmoderne*', in *Tombeau de l'intellectuel*, Galilee, Paris 1984, p. 81; quoted here from my own translation in Richard Kearney, ed., *Across the Frontiers*, Wolfhound Press Dublin, 1988, p. 265, *Cf.* Gianni Vattimo, *La fine della modernità*, Garzanti, Milano 1985, and Gianni Vattimo e Pier Aldo Rovatti, eds, *Il pensiero debole*, Feltrinelli, Milano 1983.
4. Lyotard, *Tombeau de l'intellectuel*, 15, *Cf.* here Richard Rorty, 'Postmodernist Bourgeois Liberalism', *Journal of Philosophy*, 80 (1983), pp. 583–9, where Rorty asserts, though from an entirely different politics, that intellectuals have no special social responsibilities. *Cf. also* a typical comment from an artist who broadly works in the manner described by Lyotard: Pierre Boulez: 'the composer's primary consideration must be the actual technique of his musical language', 'Putting the Phantoms to Flight', in *Orientations: Collected Writings*, ed., Jean-Jacques Nattiez, trans. Martin Cooper, Faber and Faber 1986, p. 66; Boulez has often polemically suggested his disregard for the demands of an audience: see, e.g., his *Penser la musique aujourd'hui*, Gonthier, Paris 1963, passim.
5. Louis Althusser, *Essays on Ideology*, Verso, London 1984, p. 44.
6. Ibid. p. 69.
7. Michael Ryan, *Marxism and Deconstruction*, Johns Hopkins University Press 1982, p. 6.
8. Frederic Jameson, 'Postmodernism and Consumer Society', in Foster, ed., *Postmodern Culture*, p. 115; *cf.* his arguments concerning Joyce's relations to and with modernism and imperialism worked through in his pamphlet,

Modernism and Imperialism, Field Day Pamphlet 14, in the series 'Nationalism, Colonialism and Literature', Field Day, Derry 1988, and see also my critique of this in *The New Nation*, 4 (1989).

9. Habermas, in *Postmodern Culture*, p. 12; *cf.* the arguments below in 'Theory, Enlightenment and Violence'. The historical logic here is profoundly Optimistic: history is considered as being the site of a progressive elimination of past errors, and the effect of this thinking is to identify the past *as* error with the (banal) corollary that the present, the here, now, is identified with truth (even if this truth is but the pragmatic 'what is best in the way of belief'). See Michel Serres, *Eclaircissements*, Flammarion, Paris 1992, p. 75ff, on this somewhat banal and Whiggish notion of time.

10. Jean-François Lyotard, *The Postmodern Condition*, trans. Geoff Bennington and Brian Massumi, Manchester University Press 1984, p. 81, offers a definition of Postmodernism in these terms. Lyotard, *Le postmoderne expliqué aux enfants*, Galilee, Paris 1986, p. 126, describes this understanding of 'post-'.

11. See Michel Foucault, *The Archaeology of Knowledge*, trans. A.M. Sheridan Smith, Tavistock London, 1974, p. 47. For 'New Historicism', see, for instances, Stephen Greenblatt, *Renaissance Self-Fashioning*, University of Chicago Press 1980 and *Shakespearean Negotiations* (University of California Press 1988; *cf.* the special number of *English Literary Renaissance* 16 (1986) dedicated to the New Historicism; and see my critique of this kind of work in 'Criticism, History, Foucault', *Journal of the History of Ideas* (forthcoming).

12. See, e.g., Gilles Deleuze, *Le bergsonisme*, Presses universitaires de France, Paris 1966, *Cinema:1*, minuit, Paris 1983, *Cinema:2*, minuit, Paris 1985; Paul Virilio, *Vitesse et politique*, Galilee, Paris 1977, *L'horizon négatif*, Galilee, Paris 1984; Pierre Klossowski, *Un si funeste désir*, Galilee, Paris 1963.

13. Jean Baudrillard, *In the Shadow of the Silent Majorities* trans. Paul Foss, Paul Patton and John Johnston, Semiotext(e), New York 1983, *passim*.

14. Fredric Jameson, *The Political Unconscious*, Methuen, London 1981, p. 9.

15. Julia Kristeva, 'A new Type of Intellectual; the Dissident' in Toril Moi, ed., *The Kristeva Reader*, Blackwell, Oxford, 1986, pp. 292–300; Edward Said, 'Secular Criticism' in his *The World, The Text and The Critic* Faber and Faber 1984, p. 1–30, and 'Opponents, Audiences, Constituencies and Community', in Foster, ed., *Postmodern Culture*, 135–159; Lyotard, *Tombeau, passim*.

16. Habermas, in *Postmodern Culture*, p. 5.

17. See Josef Koudelka's photographs taken during the Prague Spring, some of which are reproduced in his *Exiles*, Aperture 1988, and *cf.* 'Photography as Postmodern Cartography' below.

18. It should be made clear that at no point in this work do I wish to question the positive gains in emancipation made by Marxist revolutions or advances made by Marxist theory in situations such as Cuba or Nicaragua and so on. My *differend* with Marxism here is worked through at the level of the philosophy of Marxism, which I would argue must be retained as *one strategy among others*, and to which — following the suggestiveness of Vattimo — I am precisely *uncommitted*. For a fuller explication of the reasons for such 'disengagement', as I might call it, *see* my critique of Terry Eagleton, *Nationalism; Irony and Commitment*, Field Day Pamphlet 13, in the series 'Nationalism, Colonialism and Literature', Field Day, Derry 1988, in *The New Nation 4* (1989), as well as the practice and theory of the present study.

19. See Vincent Descombes, *Le même et l'autre*, minuit, Paris 1979, and Peter Dews, *Logics of Disintegration*, Verso 1987 for a fuller description and delineation of this turn from Hegel to Kant in recent French philosophy.

CHAPTER 1 POSTMODERNISM

1. Linda Hutcheon, *A Poetics of Postmodernism*, Routledge, London 1988.

2. This movement, from production to seduction, is suggested by the work of Jean Baudrillard, especially his study *De la séduction*, (Denoel, Paris 1979).

3. The single most relevant study here is Allon White and Peter Stallybrass, *The Poetics and Politics of Transgression*, Methuen, London 1986.

4. At some level, then, postmodernism might have strengthened itself in order to address the question of feminism. Luce Irigaray, *Speculum* (minuit, Paris 1974), attacked the prioritisation of the visual in 'modern' thinking since Descartes, a prioritisation whose effect, she argued, was the psychoanalytic degradation of woman. But while she proposes that tactility might now come into its own, as against specularity, my own argument here stresses aurality, partly consequent upon the increased attention to temporality and historicity in the postmodern, partly consequent upon the figure of the labyrinth which recurs in the postmodern mind. The attack on *speculation*, in the work of various thinkers examined in this study, can be construed as an attack upon the pretensions of theory itself, especially upon its aspirations to reveal certain 'self-evident' realities purportedly occluded by ideologies and so on. Baudrillard's work, in recent years especially, has been instrumental in questioning our sociological notions of 'reality' as some kind of grounding or foundational principle of thought. See especially Baudrillard, *L'Echange symbolique et la mort* (Gallimard, Paris 1976), *Amérique* (Bernard Grasset, Paris 1986), and *L'Autre par lui-même*, (Galilee, Paris 1987).

5. Jean-François Lyotard, 'What is Postmodernism?', in *The Postmodern Condition*, trans. Geoff Bennington and Brian Massumi, Manchester University Press 1984, p. 79.

6. See, of course, T.S. Eliot, 'Tradition and the Individual Talent', in *Selected Essays*, (Faber and Faber, London (1932) repr. 1980).

7. For the terms of this debate, see Jürgen Habermas, 'Modernity — an Unfinished Project' and accompanying essays in Hal Foster, ed., *Postmodern Culture*, (Pluto Press, London 1985); Habermas, *The Theory of Communicative Action*, in 2 vols. (trans. Thomas McCarthy, Polity Press, London 1984); Fredric Jameson, 'Postmodernism; or, the Cultural Logic of Late Capitalism', (*New Left Review*, 146 (1984), pp. 56–92) and the most recent updating of this text in Jameson, *Postmodernism*, (Verso, London 1992)); Jean-François Lyotard, *The Postmodern Condition, Tombeau de l'intellectuel*, (Galilee, Paris 1984) and *Le Postmoderne expliqué aux enfants*, (Galilee, Paris 1986); 'p.m.', *Bolo'Bolo*, (Semiotext(e), New York 1985). See also, for a wider range of materials emanating from these debates, Thomas Docherty, ed., *Postmodernism: A Reader*, (Harvester-Wheatsheaf, Hemel Hempstead 1993). The reference to Baudelaire and the Symbolist aesthetic is to Baudelaire's poem, 'Correspondances' in *Les Fleurs du mal*.

8. Christopher Bruce, programme notes to *Cruel Garden*; Kenneth Frampton, 'Critical Regionalism' in Foster, *Postmodern Culture*; Paul Durcan, *The Berlin Wall Cafe*, Blackstaff, Belfast 1985.

9. Bruce, programme notes to *Sergeant Early's Dream*.

10. See Leslie Fiedler, 'Archetype and Signature: A study of the relationship between biography and poetry', (*Sewanee Review*, 60 (1952), pp. 253–273); cf. also the Derrida/Searle debate on the matter of signatures and nominations. Other choreographers seem to fit on a sliding scale between a Brucean postmodern and Clarkean modernist reaction: Siobhan Davies, for example, comes closer to Bruce, while Robert North or Tom Jobe seem closer to Clark. A fuller discrimination in these terms would demand an extensive debate confined to matters in the history of dance and choreography at least since Macmillan, and that exceeds the scope of the present argument.

11. Rosalind Krauss, 'Sculpture in the Expanded Field', in Foster, *Postmodern Culture*.

12. Susan Compton, 'Anthony Caro and Sixties Abstraction', in Susan Compton, ed, *British Art in the Twentieth Century*, Prestel, London 1987, p. 356.

13. Richard Long, quoted in Richard Cork, 'The Seventies and After', in Compton, *British Art*, pp. 394–95.

14. See Richard Pearce, 'Enter the Frame' in Raymond Federman, ed., *Surfiction: Fiction Now . . . and Tomorrow*, Swallow Press, Chicago 1975.

15. Tom Wolfe, *The Painted Word*, Bantam Books, New York 1975.

16. Lyotard, *The Postmodern Condition*, p. 78

17. On the interference of the discursive with the figural as I am discussing it here, see Lyotard, *Discours, figure*, (Klincksieck, Paris 1971). On parody, see Linda Hutcheon, *A Theory of Parody*, (Methuen, London 1985). One typical recent example of the interference of discursive with figural wouold be Mark Turnage's composition, *Three Screaming Popes*, after Bacon's painting.

18. A typical example of such misunderstanding, deriving to an extent from Jameson, is Terry Eagleton, 'Capitalism, Modernism, and Postmodernism', in his *Against the Grain*, (Verso, London 1986).

19. A fuller exploration of this film in terms of the 'postmodern imagination' can be found in Richard Kearney, *The Wake of Imagination*, (Hutchinson, London 1988, pp. 322–32). See also my forthcoming study, *Alterities*, (Oxford University Press 1996), for a more sustained consideration of this entire cinematic issue.

20. See, for example, Ihab Hassan, *The Literature of Silence*, Knopf, New York 1967, and John Cage, *Silence*, Wesleyan University Press, Connecticut 1961.

21. Julia Kristeva, 'The Novel as Polylogue' in her *Desire in Language*, ed. Leon S. Roudiez, trans. Thomas Gora, Alice Jardine, Leon S. Roudiez; Basil Blackwell, Oxford 1981). See especially Figure 2 in this piece (ibid., pp. 176–7), where the text begins to assume a figural shape (as in painting) while yet remaining discursive.

CHAPTER 2 THEORY, ENLIGHTENMENT, VIOLENCE

1. Paul Ricoeur, *De l'interpretation: Essai sur Freud*, Seuil, Paris 1965, pp. 35–6.

2. Richard Rorty, 'Habermas and Lyotard on Postmodernity', *Praxis International*, 4 (1984), p. 40.

3. Stanley Fish, *Is There a Text in This Class?* Harvard University Press 1980. See also Jonathan Culler, *On Deconstruction*, (Routledge & Kegan Paul, London 1983, pp. 66–7), where he discusses the theoretical problems involved in Fish doing Fishian readings as a Fishian reader. Fish has, of course, moved on from this position to a more fully-fledged 'New Pragmatism' in which he tacitly accepts Culler's commentary. For a context of this shift, see the essays from *Critical Inquiry* collected together by W.J.T. Mitchell, ed., in *Against Theory*, University of Chicago Press, 1985).

4. See Jacques Derrida, 'White Mythology' in *Margins*, (trans. Alan Bass; Harvester, Brighton 1982) on the violence of light; and cf. Derrida, *D'un ton apocalyptique adopté naguère en philosophie*, (Galilee, Paris 1983), and Gerald L. Bruns, *Inventions*, (Yale University Press, 1982, p. 5).

5. Bruns, *Inventions*. I use the term 'chrono-political' here in the manner of Paul Virilio in his *Vitesse et politique*, (Galilee, Paris 1977); *L'Horizon négatif* (Galilee, Paris 1984), and his interviews with Sylvere Lotringer, *Pure War*, (trans. Mark Polizotti; Semiotext(e), New York 1983).

6. Karl Marx, 'Theses on Feuerbach' in Friedrich Engels, ed., *Ludwig Feuerbach and the End of Classical German Philosophy*, Foreign Languages Press, Peking 1976, p. 65.

7. See Kenneth Burke, *Language as Symbolic Action*, (University of California Press 1968); and cf. Ricoeur, *De l'interprétation*, pp. 26–7 on symbolicity as the locus of hermeneutic as such.

8. Harold Bloom, *Agon*, Oxford University Press 1982, p. 248; Wallace Stevens, *Collected Poems*, Faber, London 1984, pp. 193–4.

9. See Julia Kristeva, *Pouvoirs de l'horreur*, (Seuil, Paris, 1980), especially ch. 1 on abjection.

10. All quotations here are from Ovid, *Metamorphoses*, (trans. Mary Innes; Penguin, London 1955).

11. For a fuller explanation of the theoretical link between narrative and nomination, see my *John Donne, Undone* (Methuen, London 1986). Basically, the observation stems from the fact that, for instance, an oral culture which can have no conception of a 'list' (since that depends on spatial and graphological arrangement) must discover mnemonic devices for linking together a series of proper names. Narrative is one obvious way of linking; hence, one might make the inverse suggestion that every act of narrative can be reduced, finally and fundamentally, to an act of nomination, name-giving, name-calling or identifying. I owe the seed of this observation to Geoffrey Hartman, in conversation at The School of Criticism and Theory, Northwestern University 1983; but, for a fuller (and slightly different) explication of this in terms of the differences between oral and literate cultures, see Walter J. Ong, *Orality and Literacy*, (Methuen, London 1982, p. 99).

12. Pierre Macherey, *Pour une théorie de la production littéraire*, (François Maspero, Paris 1980), pp. 45–6.

13. Ricoeur, *De l'interprétation*, pp. 174–5.

14. Friedrich D.E. Schleiermacher, *Hermeneutics*, as cited in Kurt Mueller-Vollmer, ed., *The Hermeneutics Reader*, (Basil Blackwell, Oxford 1986, p. 94). See Paul Ricoeur, *Hermeneutics and the Human Sciences*, (trans. John B. Thompson, Cambridge University Press 1981) for an explication of this point in detail.

15. Sigmund Freud, *The Interpretation of Dreams*, trans. James Strachey, Penguin 1976, p. 422.

16. Ricoeur, (*De l'interprétation*, p. 36), sees this as imbued with violence or with a kind of iconoclasm. Cf. also W.J.T. Mitchell, *Iconology*, (University of Chicago Press 1986, p. 45), and his more recent *Picture Theory*, (University of Chicago Press 1994).

17. Freud, *Dreams*, p. 45.
18. See Carl E. Schorske, *Fin-de-siècle Vienna*, (Cambridge University Press 1981); and cf. Freud's own comments in the Preface to the Second Edition of *The Interpretation of Dreams*.
19. See my study *On Modern Authority*, (Harvester, Brighton 1987) for a full discussion of this issue of authority, not only in respect of Freud but also in relation to the constructed history of modern writing.
20. Freud, *Dreams*, pp. 494ff., 254ff., 386ff.
21. This makes the operations of the text approximate to those obtaining in a Raymond Roussel novel: see Roussel, *Comment j'ai ecrit certains de mes livres*, (Jean-Jacques Pauvert, Paris 1963).
22. Freud, *Dreams*, p. 496. Strictly speaking, the precise analyst/patient relation described here is that between Alfred Robitsek and one of his patients, for Freud is citing wholesale — and, importantly, endorsing — the interpretation of a dream advanced in Robitsek's 1912 paper, 'The Question of Symbolism in the Dreams of Normal Persons'. This further complicates the issue regarding 'Whose text is this anyway?' Freud, like T.S. Eliot, 'steals' rather than 'borrows' or 'imitates' (to use the terms advanced by Eliot in his essay on Philip Massinger, in *Selected Essays*, (Faber and Faber, London 1932; repr. 1980, p. 206); Robitsek's paper, which enjoys Freud's endorsement and which Freud uses to corroborate his own grander arguments, becomes as fully a part of *The Interpretation of Dreams* by Freud as, say, the lines which Eliot steals from Dante or Marvell become a part of *The Waste Land*. As I pointed out already, however, the issue of an authorisation of meaning for the words in which this dream is reported is endlessly complex. It is not simply the dreamer's; nor is it Robitsek's; nor Freud's alone; nor, of course, even that of the present author (who owes part of this observation to Valentine Cunningham in any case). Rather, the issue of authorisation or legitimation of meaning over any text, it now becomes apparent, depends upon the historical enactments of the text (i.e., how readers 'link' with it in their engagements), the ways in which it is used or understood at any given point in history by any given culture or community of interpreters. But such a community, as Fish, Holland, Jauss and many others have discovered, is itself virtually impossible to identify. As a final point here, despite the strict sense in which this issue may be thought to relate Alfred Robitsek and his female patient, the simple fact that Freud endorses the text as one which suits the evolving project of writing *The Interpretation of Dreams* (allowing thus its full incorporation) enables the more general argument concerning Freud's authoritative relation (not his personal relation) with his — predominantly female — patients.
23. Freud, *Dreams*, p. 386; cf. ibid., p. 254.
24. Ibid., p. 257.
25. Ibid., p. 388.

26. See Schorske, *Vienna*, p. 181, for Freud's jokey letter to Fleiss on the 'public enthusiasm' for his *Interpretation of Dreams*. In this letter, part of the joke is that Freud gets his flowers back, so to speak: 'The public enthusiasm is immense. Congratulations and *bouquets keep pouring in*, as if the role of sexuality had been suddenly recognized by his Majesty, the interpretation of dreams confirmed by the Council of Ministers' (my italics).

27. Freud, *Dreams*, p. 388.

28. Ricoeur, *De l'interpretation*, p. 41.

29. See David Trotter, *The Poetry of Abraham Cowley*, (Macmillan, London 1979, p. 8), on civil war and the re-drawing of boundaries within a *stasis*.

30. Most immediately, this name is usually that of the artist, and it is supposed to guarantee the validity of our understanding of the work of art; but this is akin to that mode of criticism which reveals or discovers or names a work of art according to a style or an epoch, a moment in a historical narrative, such as the Marxian or Freudian metanarratives. This is a critical position which I argue in this study to be invalid.

31. Paul Virilio and Sylvere Lotringer, *Pure War*, trans. Mark Polizotti, Semiotext(e), New York 1983, pp. 61, 64–5. Note, in passing here, the link between speed and nuclear war: the political 'space' we inhabit today is a temporal one, that of the last couple of minutes necessary to begin and end a war. Note also the link of speed to aspects of modernism, especially through Marinetti and the Futurists. For more on this, see 'Photography as Postmodern Cartography' below.

32. On 'legitimation' here, see my *On Modern Authority*, especially the theoretical introduction to that book.

33. Rorty, 'Habermas and Lyotard', p. 40.

34. Jürgen Habermas, *Legitimation Crisis*, trans. Thomas McCarthy, Heinemann, London 1976, pp. 107–8.

35. Frederick Crews, 'In the big house of theory', *New York Review of Books*, 33 (29 May 1986), p. 38.

36. Lyotard, *The Postmodern Condition*, trans. Geoff Bennington and Brian Massumi, Manchester University Press 1984, p. xxiv.

37. See Gilles Deleuze and Felix Guattari, *Anti-Oedipus*, (trans. Robert Hurley, Mark Seem, Helen R. Lane, Athlone Press, London 1984), and *A Thousand Plateaus*, (trans. Brian Massumi, Univertsity of Minnesota Press 1987), especially the latter, for such Deleuzian 'nomadism'. See also Lyotard, *Rudiments paiens*, (Christian Bourgois et 10/18, Paris 1977), and *Instructions paiennes*, (Galilee, Paris 1977), where Lyotard thinks through the valorisation of 'local' knowledge in terms of the *pagus*, that space inhabited by the 'pagan'. Such knowledge, like that advanced by Deleuze and Guattari, takes on the cast of a knowledge which refuses complicity with the 'official' epistemologies of the State, and begins to assume a shape

as a knowledge opposed to a monotheology or a universal history which would have pretensions to at least the possibility of a single global knowledge.

38. Lyotard, *Rudiments*, pp. 50–1.

39. Hannah Arendt, *On Revolution*, (1963) repr. Penguin, London 1984, pp. 18–19.

40. Lyotard et Rorty, 'Discussion', *Critique*, 41 (*mai* 1985), pp. 581–4.

41. Alexander Pope, 'Essay on Man', in *Poems*, ed. John Butt, Methuen, London 1963, p. 515.

42. Rorty, 'Habermas and Lyotard', p. 35.

43. Rorty, '*Le cosmopolitisme sans emancipation: en reponse a Jean-François Lyotard*', *Critique*, 41 (*mai* 1985), p. 570.

44. Rorty, 'The Contingency of Language', *London Review of Books*, 8 (17 April 1986), p. 3.

45. Ibid., p. 4.

46. For the sense of 'appropriation' in this context, see Paul Ricoeur, 'Appropriation' in *Hermeneutics and the Human Sciences*.

47. Ricoeur, *De l'interpretation*, p. 41.

48. Ibid., p. 53; cf. ibid., p. 52. See also Sissela Bok, *Secrets* (Oxford University Press 1984), pp. 286 n6 for the etymological links relating separation, secrecy and criticism; cf. Barbara Johnson, *The Critical Difference*, (Johns Hopkins University Press 1980), p. ix and my *John Donne, Undone*, (Methuen, London 1986), pp. 2–8.

49. Rorty, 'Postmodernist Bourgeois Liberalism', *Journal of Philosophy* 80 (1983), pp. 583–9. I quote here from a version of the paper circulated in The School of Criticism and Theory at Northwestern University, 1983.

50. Lyotard, *The Postmodern Condition*, p. 36

51. See Lyotard and Rorty, 'Discussion', pp. 581–4, for a debate on the relations between rhetoric and violence impinging on this point. It is worth remarking here a point developed in fuller terms as the present study progresses: for Lyotard, it is the historicity of the making of political and aesthetic judgements which is important; such acts of judgement thus acquire the status of an 'event' which escapes methodological formulation or totalising and grounded theorisation. They belong to Lyotard's reading of the Kantian category of 'reflective', rather than 'determining' judgements. On the status of the event in Lyotard, see Geoffrey Bennington, *Lyotard: Writing the Event*, (Manchester University Press, 1988) 'Introduction', and cf. a more engaged introduction to the topic in David Carroll, *Paraesthetics*, (Methuen, London 1988), ch. 1, 2 and 7).

52. See, for typical instances, Ricoeur, *De l'interpretation*, (pp. 206–7); Arendt, *On Revolution*, (pp. 20, 38–9, 208–9); Jacques Derrida, *L'Ecriture et la difference*, (Seuil, Paris 1967), p. 11; Derrida, *Of Grammatology*, (trans. Gayatri Chakravorty Spivak, Johns Hopkins University Press 1976),

pp. 108–9; Derrida, *Margins*, (pp. 211, 256–7); Jeffrey Mehlman, *Revolution and Repetition*, (University of California Press 1977), p. 107; Harold Bloom, 'The Breaking of Form', in Bloom et al., *Deconstruction and Criticism*, (Routledge and Kegan Paul, London 1976), p. 6. On the important question of the relation of violence and its ethical position with regard to Marxism, see Steven Lukes, 'Can a Marxist Believe in Human Rights?', *Praxis International*, 1 (1982), pp. 334–45; and cf. Arendt, *On Revolution*, (p. 62ff).

53. Derrida, *Margins*, p. 213; cf. ibid., pp. 268–9.

54. Hans Blumenberg, *The Legitimacy of the Modern Age*, (trans. Robert M. Wallace, MIT Press, Cambridge, Mass., 1983), pp. 232, 404.

55. Arendt, *On Revolution*, p. 79.

56. Bruns, *Inventions*, p. 34.

57. Ibid., p. 9.

58. Arendt, *On Revolution*, p. 18.

59. Ricoeur, *De l'interpretation*, p. 36.

60. Terry Eagleton, 'Capitalism, Modernism and Postmodernism', in *Against the Grain*, (Verso, London 1986); Gillian Rose, *Dialectic of Nihilism*, (Basil Blackwell, Oxford, 1884), p. 1 and *passim*.

61. Blumenberg, *Legitimacy*, p. 442.

62. Marx, in Engels, *Ludwig Feuerbach*, p. 61.

63. See Walter Benjamin, *Illuminations*, (ed. Hannah Arendt, trans. Harry Zohn; Fontana, Glasgow, 1973), p. 257); and Marx, *The Eighteenth Brumaire of Louis Bonaparte*, (Foreign Languages Press, Peking, 1978), p. 13, where he wrote: 'The social revolution of the 19th century cannot draw its poetry from the past, but only from the future. . . . In order to arrive at its own content, the revolution of the 19th century must let the dead bury their dead. Then the words went beyond the content; now the content goes beyond the words'. This is precisely the problem for a cultural *practice*: how does the content go beyond its words? The answer proposed here is simply that it goes beyond the words to the extent that it is *gestural*, referential — but to a referent whose ontological essence is not yet.

64. Andreas Huyssen, *After the Great Divide*, Macmillan, London 1986, p. vii.

Chapter 3 Photography as Postmodern Cartography

1. Walter Benjamin, 'The Work of Art in the Age of Mechanical Reproduction', in *Illuminations*, ed. Hannah Arendt (trans. Harry Zohn; Fontana, Glasgow, 1973); Alvin Langdon Coburn, 'The Relation of Time to Art', *Camera Work*, 36 (1911), pp. 72–73, repr. in Nathan Lyons, ed., *Photographers on Photography*, (Prentice-Hall, Englewood Cliffs, NJ, 1966), p. 52. For a similar characterisation of postmodernity, of course, see Jean-

François Lyotard, *The Postmodern Condition*, (trans. Geoff Bennington and Brian Massumi; Manchester University Press, 1984), and *Le Postmoderne expliqué aux enfants*, (Galilee, Paris 1986).

2. Jean-François Lyotard and Thierry Chaput, *Les Immateriaux*, (Centre Georges Pompidou, Paris, 1985); Gilles Deleuze and Felix Guattari, *A Thousand Plateaus*, (trans. Brian Massumi; University of Minnesota Press 1987), especially 'Rhizome' (also published in Deleuze and Guattari, *On the Line*, (trans. John Johnston; Semiotext(e), New York, 1983). Deleuze and Guattari argue here that the photograph is not 'rhizomatic'; the pages below are a counter-argument to this.

3. For the Kodak advertising slogan, see, for example, Gisele Freund, *Photography and Society*, (David R. Godine, Boston, 1980, pp. 86–87). For America (or a mythic 'America') as a locus of theory and criticism, see my arguments in the following pages, and cf. Terence Hawkes, 'Telmah', in *Shakespeare and the Question of Theory*, (ed. Patricia Parker and Geoffrey Hartman, Methuen, London 1985, pp. 330–1), and Jonathan Arac, Wlad Godzich and Wallace Martin, eds, *The Yale Critics: Deconstruction in America*, (University of Minnesota Press 1983).

4. The most obvious reference here is to the work of Jean Tinguely and those many other artists working since early Dada who have made a virtue of destroying their various constructions. But a similar tendency is apparent in some recent literary criticism. Consider, for example, Stanley Fish's *Self-Consuming Artifacts*, (University of California Press 1972), which seems to mimic the workings of those very texts it reads and describes. The appendix to the book, a book which has difficulty concluding or making sense of its ending, suggests that 'In short, the theory, both as an account of meaning and as a way of teaching, is full of holes; and there is one great big hole right in the middle of it, which is filled, if it is filled at all, by what happens inside the user-student. The method, then, remains faithful to its principles; it has no point of termination; it is a process; it talks about experience and is an experience; its focus is effects and its result is an effect' (ibid., p. 246). Other relevant examples might be Terry Eagleton, *Literary Theory*, (Basil Blackwell, Oxford 1983), where Eagleton argues, at the end of the book, that since he has previously maintained the case that 'Literature' does not exist, it must thus logically follow that 'Literary Theory' also does not exist; or cf. Roland Barthes, *Camera Lucida*, (trans. Richard Howard; Fontana, London 1984), whose self-destruction is detailed below.

5. Barthes, *Camera Lucida*, pp. 85, 91.

6. T.S. Eliot, 'Four Quartets', in *Complete Poems and Plays*, (Faber and Faber, London 1969), p. 173.

7. Barthes, *Camera Lucida*, p. 65.

8. Joseph Conrad, *The Secret Agent*, (1907) repr. Dent, London 1974, p. 66.

9. Ibid., p. 81.

10. See F.T. Marinetti, *Selected Writings*, ed. R.W. Flint (trans. R.W. Flint and Arthur A. Coppotelli; Secker and Warburg, London 1972), p. 136; and cf. Caroline Tisdall and Angelo Bozzolla, *Futurism*, (Thames and Hudson, London 1977), p. 146ff.

11. Michel Foucault, *Discipline and Punish*, (trans. Alan Sheridan; Penguin 1977).

12. Conrad, *Secret Agent*, p. 76.

13. Freund, *Photography and Society*, p. 71.

14. Ibid., p. 72.

15. See Aaron Scharf, *Art and Photography* (1968) repr. Penguin, London 1983, pp. 170–1.

16. Barthes, *Camera Lucida*, p. 6.

17. Ibid., pp. 9, 31–2.

18. Ibid., pp. 93–4 (and cf. note 4 above).

19. Ibid., p. 9. Cf. Jacques Derrida, *Spectres de Marx*, (Galilee, Paris, 1993), for a re-reading of Marxist political theory as a story of *'revenants'*, of returns and thus of nostalgia and mourning.

20. J. Hillis Miller, 'The Critic as Host', in Harold Bloom et al., *Deconstruction and Criticism*, (Routledge and Kegan Paul, London 1979); and cf. many issues of *Spectator* papers concerned with the themes of ghosts, witches and the supernatural in Joseph Addison, Richard Steele et al., *The Spectator*, in 4 vols, ed. C. Gregory Smith, Dent, London (1907) repr. 1961.

21. Addison, *Spectator*, vol 1, p. 5.

22. Ibid., pp. 5, 16.

23. Ibid., p. 5. See also Patrick Parrinder, *The Failure of Theory*, (Harvester, Brighton 1987, p. 14), for a definition of theory broadly corresponding to Addison's understanding here.

24. Addison, *Spectator*, vol 1, p. 32.

25. Ibid., p. 39.

26. Scharf, *Art and Photography*, p. 170.

27. Cited in Tisdall and Bozzolla, *Futurism*, p. 138.

28. Virginia Woolf, *To the Lighthouse* (1927) repr. Dent, London 1978, p. 182.

29. Ibid., p. 242; and cf. ibid., p. 98. (Note also the fact that this central line is one which designates a tree, and compare the comments of Deleuze and Guattari below on 'arborescent' and rooted thinking.)

30. Ibid., p. 113.

31. Virginia Woolf, *Letters 3: 1923–1928*, ed. Nigel Nicolson, Hogarth Press, London 1977, p. 4.

32. Ibid., pp. 270–1.

33. Virginia Woolf, *A Writer's Diary*, ed. Leonard Woolf (1953) repr. Panther Books, London 1979, p. 109.

34. Virginia Woolf, 'Introduction' to *Victorian Photographs of Famous Men and Fair Women by Julia Margaret Cameron*, expanded and revised edn, ed. Tristram Powell, Hogarth Press 1973, p. 18.

35. Woolf, *Writer's Diary*, p. 105.

36. Benjamin, *Illuminations*, p. 226.

37. Paul Virilio, *Vitesse et politique*, (Galilee, Paris 1977), p. 16. Virilio also goes on to indicate that this is particularly true of Japan; it may thus be worth considering here Japan's pre-eminence in terms of the industrial production of cameras. Japan's excellence in this area in the contemporary world places the culture in a position analogous to that of Holland in the early seventeenth century, a time when the Dutch excelled in the production of lenses for machines such as the telescope. Coincidentally, Dutch painting in this time also excelled in the area of 'interiority', of the painting of spatial interiors or 'rooms'; yet typically such paintings also indicated some source of light or 'exterior' pressure upon the space of the painting, such as the lateral window or doorway or, as in Vermeer's *Geographer*, not only such a window through which a light slants (a lens, therefore), but also a map and a globe implying the interiorisation of a whole external space. This idea, of the internalisation or 'apprehension' of exteriority, is an idea which informs most notions of the function of the photograph (in terms, at least, of its supposed ability to 'capture' the reality of a moment and a space). For a fuller exploration of some of the argument here, especially as it impinges upon the seventeenth-century understanding of the scopophiliac lens, see my *John Donne, Undone*, Methuen, London 1986, p. 53ff.

38. This is akin to the Heideggerian *Dasein*; cf. my arguments on this in *Reading (Absent) Character*, Oxford University Press 1983.

39. Alvin Langdon Coburn, quoted in Richard Cork, *Vorticism and Abstract Art in the First Machine Age*, vol. 2, Gordon Fraser, London 1976, p. 499.

40. Woolf, *Letters 3*, p. 280.

41. Woolf, *To the Lighthouse*, pp. 197–8.

42. Quentin Bell, *Virginia Woolf 1: 1882–1912* (1972) repr. Paladin, London 1976), p. 14.

43. Woolf, *To the Lighthouse*, pp. 198–9.

44. Roger Fry, *Vision and Design*, ed. J.B. Bullen, Oxford University Press, 1981, p. 64; and cf. Scharf, *Art and Photography*, passim.

45. See Jacques Derrida 'White Mythology', in *Margins*, (trans. Alan Bass; Harvester, Brighton 1982); and cf. my own extrapolations from this in the preceding chapter of the present study.

46. Fry, *Vision and Design*, p. 70; cf. Wyndham Lewis, *Paleface*, in E.W.F. Tomlin, ed., *Lewis: An Anthology of his Prose*, (Methuen, London 1969) on the negritude of culture.

47. D.H. Lawrence, *Women in Love* (1921) repr. Penguin, London 1969, p. 73.
48. Ibid., pp. 85–6.
49. Ibid., pp. 82–83.
50. Ibid., pp. 69, 71.
51. Ibid., p. 68.
52. See Guy Debord, *La Société du spectacle*, (Champ Libre, Paris 1967); Jean Baudrillard, *L'Echange symbolique et la mort*, (Gallimard, Paris 1976), *Les Stratégies fatales*, (Grasset, Paris 1983), *Amérique*, (Grasset, Paris 1986); *L'Autre par lui-même*, (Galilee, Paris 1987).
53. Lawrence, *Women in Love*, pp. 82, 86–7.
54. Freund, *Photography and Society*, pp. 12–13.
55. Horace, *Ars Poetica* in *Classical Literary Criticism*, ed. and trans. T.S. Dorsch, (Penguin, 1965), p. 84; Addison, *Spectator*, vol. 1, p. 3.
56. Addison, *Spectator*, vol. 1, p. 3.
57. Joseph Conrad, *Heart of Darkness*, in Conrad, *Three Short Novels*, (Bantam Books, New York, (1960) repr. 1976), p. 2.
58. Ibid., p. 4.
59. Ibid., p. 4.
60. See Henry Miller, *Tropic of Cancer* (1934) repr. Panther, London 1971, p. 10: 'This is not a book. This is libel, slander, defamation of character. This is not a book, in the ordinary sense of the word. No, this is a prolonged insult, a gob of spit in the face of Art, a kick in the pants to God, Man, Destiny, Time, Love, Beauty ... what you will'. Cf. also Jacques Derrida, *Of Grammatology* (trans. Gayatri Chakravorty Spivak; Johns Hopkins University Press, Baltimore, 1976), ch. 1, 'The End of the Book and the Beginning of Writing'.
61. Lawrence, *Women in Love*, pp. 77, 78.
62. On 'blessing' and 'cursing' see, for example, Geoffrey H. Hartman, *Saving the Text*, (Johns Hopkins University Press, Baltimore, 1981), and cf. Kenneth Burke, *Philosophy of Literary Form*, (University of California Press 1973).
63. Lawrence, *Women in Love*, p. 78.
64. Ibid., pp. 80, 81.
65. Coburn, in Lyons, *Photographers on Photography*, p. 53.
66. Freund, *Photography and Society*, pp. 32–33.
67. Gilles Deleuze and Felix Guattari, *A Thousand Plateaus*, (trans. Brian Massumi; University of Minnesota Press 1987), p. 15; the translation quoted here, however, is that by John Johnson from Deleuze and Guattari, *On the Line*, (Semiotext(e), New York 1983, p. 33).
68. *Deleuze and Guattari, A Thousand Plateaus*, pp. 9–10, 7; *On the Line*, pp. 18, 12–13.

69. Sergei Eisenstein, *Film Form*; the relevant passages are cited from Gerald Mast and Marshall Cohen, eds, *Film Theory and Criticism*, (2nd edn; Oxford University Press 1970), pp. 85, 104.
70. Deleuze and Guattari, *A Thousand Plateaus*, p. 8; *On the Line*, p. 15.
71. Deleuze and Guattari, *A Thousand Plateaus*, p. 18; *On the Line*, p. 40.
72. Deleuze and Guattari, *A Thousand Plateaus*, p. 19; *On the Line*, p. 43.
73. Terence Hawkes, 'Telmah', in Patricia Parker and Geoffrey Hartman, eds, *Shakespeare and the Question of Theory*, (Methuen, London 1985), pp. 330–1.
74. Various contemporary thinkers have attended to such a construction — or deconstruction — of the myth of 'America'. See, for examples, Jean Baudrillard, *Amerique*; Paul Virilio, *L'Espace critique*, (Christian Bourgois, Paris 1984); Jean-François Lyotard, *Le Mur du pacifique*, (Galilee, Paris 1979); Umberto Eco, *Travels in Hyperreality*, (trans. William Weaver; Pan Books, London 1987); Sol Yurick, *Metatron*, (Semiotext(e), New York, 1985); Deleuze and Guattari, 'Rhizome' in *A Thousand Plateaus*; and many others.

Chapter 4 Representing Postmodernism

1. For postmodern art described in terms such as this, see Linda Hutcheon, *A Poetics of Postmodernism*, (Methuen, London 1988); for the political issues involved here, see, e.g., Jonathan Arac, ed., *Postmodernism and Politics*, (Manchester University Press 1986) and Catherine Gallagher, 'The Politics of Culture and the Debate over Representation', *Representations*, 5 (Winter 1984), pp. 115–147.
2. Arac, 'Introduction' in *Postmodernism and Politics*, p. xxi.
3. Ibid., p. xxiv.
4. Jean-François Lyotard, *The Postmodern Condition*, trans. Geoff Bennington and Brian Massumi; Manchester University Press 1984, p. 81.
5. Gerard Genette, *Figures of Literary Discourse*, trans. Alan Sheridan; Basil Blackwell, Oxford, 1982, pp. 132–3.
6. Paul de Man, 'The Rhetoric of Temporality', in *Blindness and Insight*, 2nd edn.; Methuen, London 1983, p. 211.
7. Charles Baudelaire, '*De l'essence du rire*', in *Oeuvres completes*, (Seuil, Paris 1968), p. 245.
8. Baudelaire, *Oeuvres*, p. 251. When de Man quotes this passage, he cuts it off before the phrase '*le cas est rare*', and thereby implies a situation in which the rare case can be proposed as normative.
9. Baudelaire, *Oeuvres*, p. 254.
10. de Man, *Blindness*, pp. 220–222
11. Ibid., p. 222.
12. Baudelaire, *Oeuvres*, p. 248.

13. Plato, *Republic*, 395d trans. Desmond Lee, revised edn; Penguin, London 1974, pp. 153–4.

14. See Hutcheon, *Poetics of Postmodernism*, chs 2 and 8, and her *A Theory of Parody*, (Methuen, London 1985). Cf. Fredric Jameson, 'Postmodernism; or, the Cultural Logic of Late Capitalism', *New Left Review* (1984), pp. 53–92. A recent text which focussed on this debate, but led to no rethinking of its terms, is D.M. Thomas, *The White Hotel*, (Penguin, London 1981). For the debate on plagiarism regarding this text, see letters in The *Times Literary Supplement* in March and April 1982. 'Enthusiasm' in these pages is to be understood with reference to its sense of being 'filled with the gods', senses which are of particular relevance to both twentieth- and eighteenth-century modernisms; in this regard, see Jean-François Lyotard, *L'Enthousiasme: la critique kantienne de l'histoire*, (Galilee, Paris 1986).

15. Samuel Beckett, *How It Is*, (John Calder, 1961).

16. Beckett, ibid; and cf. Jacques Derrida, *La Carte postale*, (Flammarion, Paris 1980), '*Envois*', for an interesting commentary on the relations between Plato and Socrates in this regard.

17. de Man, *Blindness*, p. 211.

18. Genette, *Figures*, pp. 130–1.

19. Ibid., p. 132.

20. This — highly polemical — term, to describe the US and its political allies, is used most provocatively by philosophers such as Rorty. The provocation lies in the fact that it is stated as an axiomatic truth, forestalling any critical questioning of the political reality — or otherwise — of democracy and freedom in the USA and in western Europe. It is this, among other things, which the present study hopes to question.

21. Karl Marx, *The Eighteenth Brumaire of Louis Bonaparte*, Foreign Languages Press, Peking 1978, p. 9.

22. Michel de Certeau, *Heterologies*, trans. Brian Massumi; Manchester University Press 1986, pp. 3–4.

23. See Jacques Derrida, *Writing and Difference*, (trans. Alan Bass; Routledge and Kegan Paul, London 1978), ch. 8 'The Theatre of Cruelty and the Closure of Representation'. But on this issue of a project being undone through repetition, see also Barbara Johnson, 'The Frame of Reference' in her *The Critical Difference*, (Johns Hopkins University Press 1985) where, in considering Derrida's reading of Lacan's reading of Poe's 'The Purloined Letter', she shows how Derrida merely reiterates precisely the failings which he finds in Lacan, thus undoing his own project through a repetition of error.

24. Walter Benjamin, *Illuminations*, ed. Hannah Arendt, trans. Harry Zohn, Fontana, Glasgow, 1973, p. 226.

25. Ibid., p. 223.

26. Ibid., p. 231.

27. Ibid., p. 231.

28. Ibid., p. 249.
29. This is a limitation — though not necessarily an inherent one — in much Marxist theory. While many Marxists will endorse Jameson's rallying cry, 'Always historicise', the one limit is the historicisation of the Marxist's own representation of history. If Marxist criticism did resort to such a fuller self-historicisation, it would inevitably be caught up in an endless chain of self-referential self-questioning, making any straightforward proposition, purportedly devoid of provisionality, an impossibility. Such a critique, in both theory and practice, begins to assume the condition of the 'New Pragmatism' as I described it in ch. 2 above, and enters into self-contradiction and political inefficacy. To counter this, it is wiser to attend fully to the project of the historicising of all acts of representation and of representations themselves; but this leads, as my study shows, to a postmarxist theory and critical practice.
30. Benjamin, *Illuminations*, p. 239.
31. Ibid., pp. 233, 234.
32. Jean Baudrillard, *Simulations*, trans. Paul Foss and Paul Patton; Semiotext(e), New York, 1983, p. 25.
33. Ibid., p. 27.
34. Ibid., p. 37.
35. Ibid., p. 38.
36. Ibid., p. 38.
37. Ibid., p. 40.

CHAPTER 5 POSTMODERN (DIS)SIMULATION

1. Robert Lowell, 'Eye and Tooth', in *For the Union Dead*, Faber and Faber London (1965) repr. 1985, pp. 18–19.
2. Karl Marx, *Capital*, vol. 1, trans. Ben Fowkes; Penguin, London 1976), pp. 178–9.
3. Erich Auerbach, *Mimesis*, trans Willard R. Trask; Princeton University Press 1968, p. 552.
4. Edward Said, *The World, the Text, the Critic*, Faber and Faber, London 1984, pp. 5–9.
5. For further corroboration of the point concerning the invention of 'human nature' as an escape from history, see my study *On Modern Authority*, (Harvester, Brighton 1987, esp. chs. 7 and 8). Foucault, of course, offers a different mode of argument concerning the invention of 'Man', 'an invention of recent date', in his *The Order of Things*, (Tavistock, London 1970, p. 387 and *passim*).
6. Virginia Woolf, 'Modern Fiction', in *The Common Reader*, Hogarth Press, London 1929, p. 189.
7. Paul de Man, *The Rhetoric of Romanticism*, Columbia University Press 1984, p. viii; cf. Richard Rorty, 'The World Well Lost', in *Consequences of*

Pragmatism, (Harvester, Brighton 1982), and see also Frank B. Farrell, *Subjectivity, Realism and Postmodernism: The Recovery of the World in Recent Philosophy*, (Cambridge University Press 1994).

8. Ian Hamilton, *Robert Lowell: A Biography*, Faber and Faber, London 1983, p. 309.

9. Robert Lowell, in the *Kenyon Collegian*, 15 December 1974, as cited in Hamilton, *Robert Lowell*, p. 57.

10. Paul de Man, *Allegories of Reading*, Yale University Press 1979, p. 280.

11. Ibid., p. 280.

12. Paul de Man, *Blindness and Insight*, 2nd edn.; Methuen, London 1983, p. 182–3; cf. Frank Lentricchia, *After the New Criticism*, ((1980) repr. Methuen, London 1983), p. 283. 'Lyric and Modernity', from which the cited passage is lifted, was originally delivered to the English Institute in 1969; Harold Bloom's *Anxiety of Influence* was published in 1973. The 'forecasting' by de Man of Bloom's theory was performed four years before Bloom published, and not three as Lentricchia asserts.

13. George Herbert, 'The H. Scriptures (ii)', in *The Temple*, in *The English Poems of George Herbert*, ed. C.A. Patrides, Dent, London 1974, p. 77.

14. For a concise attack on the *ideology* of common sense and how it afflicts criticism, see Catherine Belsey, *Critical Practice*, (Methuen, London 1980, pp. 1–36). For more detailed considerations of 'common sense', especially in relation to the Kantian *sensus communis* and related philosophical issues, see, e.g., Paul Hamilton, *Coleridge's Poetics*, (Blackwell, Oxford 1983, p. 27ff), where there is an argument bearing an uncanny resemblance to Lyotard's *Discours, figure*, (Klincksieck, Paris 1971), though deriving from entirely different origins. See also Lyotard, 'Sensus Communis' *Le Cahier du College, International de Philosophie*, 5 (1987), pp. 67–87 and Gilles Deleuze, *Kant's Critical Philosophy*, (trans. Hugh Tomlinson and Barbara Habberjam; University of Minnesota Press 1984), pp. 21–4.

15. Lowell, 'Dropping South: Brazil', *For the Union Dead*, p. 62. The poem appeared as one of 'Five Poems for John Crowe Ransom' in *Kenyon Review*, (26 (Winter 1964), pp.–25–8). The image of spiders 'crying, but without tears', appears in 'Fall 1961'; Lowell claimed in a letter to Randall Jarrell that it was suggested to him by his daughter, Harriet, who used the image herself to describe the sound of Webern's music: see Hamilton, *Robert Lowell*, pp. 295–6.

16. Lowell, 'For the Union Dead', *For the Union Dead*, p. 72.

17. Edmund Wilson, *Patriotic Gore*, (1962) repr. Oxford University Press New York, 1966, p. xi. For the Leiris materials, see Michel Leiris, *L'Age d'homme*, (Gallimard, Paris 1946, p. 10ff). See also Picasso's paintings and sculptures of this period, as well as Mark Rothko's *Syrian Bull*, a painting which begins to indicate Rothko's transition into abstraction. In literature, see Ernest Hemingway, *Death in the Afternoon* ((1932) repr. Grafton

Books, London 1977) and *Fiesta*, ((1927) repr. Heinemann, London 1977). For Lowell's letter signalling his agreement with Wilson, see Hamilton, *Robert Lowell*, pp. 301–2.

18. Lowell, 'Four Speeches from Racine's "Phèdre" ', *Partisan Review* (Jan–Feb, 1961), pp. 36–47; the passage cited is from p. 39. My reference is to this partial translation quite simply to indicate the seeming importance of the bull and of the Minotaur myth for Lowell in these early stages of the translation.

19. Lowell, 'Alfred Corning Clark', *For the Union Dead*, pp. 20–1.

20. Lowell, 'The Drinker', *For the Union Dead*, pp. 36–7.

21. Lowell, 'Buenos Aires', *For the Union Dead*, pp. 60–1.

22. Ovid, *Metamorphoses*, trans. Mary Innes, Penguin, London (1955) repr. 1986, p. 73.

23. In an interview for the Granada television documentary, *It was twenty years ago today*, (broadcast on 2 June 1987), Abbie Hoffman repeated this claim about the levitation of the Pentagon. At one level, he was making it clear that the suggestion was, of course, metaphorical; but he also claimed that 'We did it', for it led to the publication of 'the photograph we wanted'. Interestingly, it became clear in this programme that there remains precisely the same kind of east/west cultural axis in the USA as I am tracing here. In the documentary, Ponderosa Pine remarked on the Pentagon-levitation exercise that it was at this time that he realised the difference between the west coast and the east coast: on the east, he and everyone else knew that the idea was a publicity stunt or media-event; but he also realised that those from California actually meant what they were saying, literally, and that one might deduce therefore that while the east was concerned about the media, the west was into lifestyle. The crucial difference mapping east and west in these terms is, of course, a rhetorical one: they read metaphor differently from each other.

24. See Paul Virilio, *Vitesse et politique*, (Galilee, Paris 1977), p. 136, and Paul Virilio and Sylvere Lotringer, *Pure War*, (Semiotext(e), New York 1983), passim.

25. Lowell, 'Caligula', *For the Union Dead*, pp. 49–51.

26. Virilio, *Vitesse*, passim; and Virilio, *L'Horizon négatif*, (Galilee, Paris 1984, pp. 267ff, 281ff.

27. Virilio, *Vitesse*, p. 136.

28. Ibid., p. 136.

29. Lowell, *For the Union Dead*, passim.

30. Ibid., p. 11.

31. Ibid., pp. 11, 70.

32. Ibid., p. 71.

33. Virilio, *Vitesse*, passim.

34. de Man, *Blindness*, p. 211 (italics mine).

CHAPTER 6 LISTENING: POISONS IN THE EAR

1. See Luce Irigaray, *Speculum* (minuit, Paris 1974); and *Ce Sexe qui n'en est pas un* (minuit, Paris 1977).
2. Jürgen Habermas, 'Modernity — an Incomplete Project', in Hal Foster, ed., *Postmodern Culture*, Pluto Press, London 1985.
3. See, e.g., Jean Baudrillard, *De la séduction*, (Denoel, Paris 1978), p. 44ff.; *Les Stratégies fatales*, (Grasset, Paris 1983), pp. 61, 70ff.; on iconoclasm, see W.J.T. Mitchell, *Iconology*, (University of Chicago Press 1986), passim.
4. Jacques Attali, *Noise*, trans. Brian Massumi, Manchester University Press 1985, esp. p. 133ff.
5. Jean-François Lyotard, *Discours, figure*, Klincksieck, Paris 1971, p. 13.
6. Ibid., p. 14.
7. Ibid., pp. 14–15.
8. Ibid., p. 281; a crucial poet for Lyotard's argument throughout *Discours, figure* is, as this passage might suggest, Mallarmé; but one might also consider writers such as Michel Butor or Roy Fisher or Ian Hamilton Finlay in this regard as exemplary and explicit validation of Lyotard's thinking.
9. Attali, *Noise*, p. 3.
10. Henrik Ibsen, *Ghosts*, in *Four Major Plays*, trans. James McFarlane and Jens Arup, Oxford University Press 1981, p. 91.
11. Stéphane Mallarmé, 'L'Après-midi d'un faune', in *Oeuvres completes* 1: *Poesies*, ed. Carl P. Barbier et Charles G. Millan, Flammarion, Paris 1983, p. 264.
12. Virginia Woolf, *Diaries*, 2: 1920–1924, ed. Anne Olivier Bell assisted by Andrew McNeillie, Hogarth Press, London 1978, p. 178, entry for 11 June 1922.
13. Peter Ackroyd, *T.S. Eliot* (1984) repr. Abacus, London 1985, p. 116, cf. p. 117ff.
14. T.S. Eliot, *The Waste Land: A Facsimile and Transcript of the Original Drafts including the Annotations of Ezra Pound*, ed. Valerie Eliot, Faber and Faber, London 1971, p. 1.
15. Ezra Pound, *Selected Letters 1907–1941*, ed. D.D. Paige, (1950) repr. Faber and Faber, London 1983, p. 170, letter of 24 December 1921.
16. Ovid, *Metamorphoses*, trans. Mary Innes, Penguin, London 1955, p. 149.
17. See Eliot, *Facsimile*, passim.
18. See Attali, *Noise*, passim, on the relation of music to sacrifice, and on the political economy articulated in classical romantic harmony.
19. Maud Ellmann, 'Eliot's Abjection', paper delivered at the conference on 'Desire and Love: the Work of Julia Kristeva', Warwick University, 24 May 1987; cf. her *Poetics of Impersonality*, (Harvester, Brighton 1987).
20. T.S. Eliot, 'Seneca in Elizabethan Translation', in *Selected Essays* (1932) repr. 1980), pp. 70, 80ff.

21. Ibid., p. 82.
22. Thomas Kyd, *The Spanish Tragedy*, ed. J.R. Mulryne, Ernest Benn, 1970, p. 38 (Act 2, scene ii, ll. 42–51).
23. Ibid, p. 93 (Act 3, scene xiii, ll. 161–75).
24. John Keats, 'Ode to a Nightingale', in *Selected Poetry and Letters*, ed. Richard Harter Fogle, Rinehart Press, San Francisco 1969, p. 246 (italics mine).
25. T.S. Eliot, 'Four Quartets' in *Complete Poems and Plays*, Faber and Faber, London 1969, p. 171.
26. Shakespeare, *Hamlet*, Act 3, scene iv, ll. 89–92 and 95–7.
27. Ibid., Act 1, scene iii, l. 68.
28. This is most apparent, of course, in Gertrude's difficulty in hearing the Ghost.
29. Shakespeare, *Hamlet*, Act 4, scene v, ll. 7–10.
30. Ibid., Act 4, scene vii, ll. 166–75.
31. Pound, *Letters*, p. 170.
32. Ovid, *Metamorphoses*, p. 227.
33. Ibid., p. 230.
34. Ibid., p. 230.
35. Shakespeare, *Hamlet*, Act 4, scene v.
36. Kyd, *Spanish Tragedy*, p. 121, (Act 4, scene iv, ll. 185–8).
37. Geoffrey H. Hartman, *Criticism in the Wilderness*, Yale University Press 1980, pp. 55–6; cf. Harold Bloom, *Anxiety of Influence* (Oxford University Press 1973) and *A Map of Misreading* (Oxford University Press 1975).
38. Hartman, *Criticism*, pp. 55–6.
39. Eliot, *Selected Essays*, p. 14.
40. Ibid., pp. 19–20.
41. Ibid., p. 17.
42. Ibid., p. 14.
43. T.S. Eliot, 'Introduction' to *The Use of Poetry and the Use of Criticism*, Faber and Faber, London (1933) repr. 1980, p. 25.
44. Ibid., p. 18.
45. Ibid., pp. 18–19.
46. Eliot, *Selected Essays*, p. 14.
47. T.S. Eliot, *To Criticize the Critic*, Faber and Faber, London 1978, p. 39.
48. Elizabeth Bishop, 'In the Waiting Room', in *Complete Poems, 1927–1979*, (1983) repr. Hogarth Press, London 1984, p. 161.
49. Walter Benjamin, *Illuminations*, ed. Hannah Arendt, trans. Harry Zohn, Fontana, Glasgow 1973, p. 243.
50. See Vincent Descombes, *Modern French Philosophy*, (trans. L. Scott-Fox and J.M. Harding; Cambridge University Press 1980); Luc Ferry et Alain Renault, *La Pensée '68*, (Gallimard, Paris 1985); Hugh Silverman, ed., *Philosophy and Non-Philosophy since Merleau-Ponty*, (Routledge, London 1988) for some mappings of the terrain and its seismic shifts since 1968.

51. Descombes, *Modern French Philosophy*, p. 13.
52. Ibid., p. 38.
53. Christine Buci-Glucksmann, *La Raison baroque*, Galilee, Paris 1984, p. 124.
54. Ibid., pp. 114–15.
55. Ibid., p. 117.
56. Ibid., p. 119.
57. This 'poison' can be — and has been, of course — read ambiguously, thanks to the logic of deconstruction. See Jacques Derrida, 'Plato's Pharmacy' in *Dissemination*, (trans. Barbara Johnson; University of Chicago Press 1981).

CHAPTER 7 DETERRITORIALISATION: ENDING CULTURE

1. Jacques Derrida, 'Tympan', in *Margins*, trans. Alan Bass, Harvester, Brighton 1982, p. xvii.
2. Jean Baudrillard, *Simulations*, trans. Paul Foss, Paul Patton and Philip Beitchman, Semiotext(e), New York 1983, pp. 26ff., 36ff.
3. Karl Marx, *The Eighteenth Brumaire of Louis Bonaparte*, Foreign Languages Press, Peking 1973, pp. 9–10.
4. Hans Blumenberg, *The Legitimacy of the Modern Age*, trans. Robert M. Wallace; MIT Press, Cambridge, Mass. 1983, p. 596.
5. See Gilles Deleuze, *Différence et Répétition*, (PUF, Paris 1969); cf. Jeffrey Mehlman, *Revolution and Repetition*, (University of California Press 1977).
6. Seamus Deane, *Celtic Revivals*, Faber and Faber, London 1985, pp. 175, 177.
7. The references are to Seamus Deane, *History Lessons*, (Gallery Books, Dublin 1983) and Seamus Heaney, *Field Work*, (Faber and Faber 1979). The implication of this proposition is that Deane's work, in being more *historical* than Heaney's, is akin to that discordant music of the nightingale written of in my preceding chapter. Heaney's poetry, I argue, when placed alongside that of Deane, shows a tendency to collapse the historical into the traditional, to shift history into heritage: a move which makes his verse more acceptable or audible to a dominantly anti-historical ideology. It is interesting, however, to note Heaney's clear geo-political awareness deployed to greater effect in his *The Government of the Tongue*, (Faber and Faber, London 1988), essays written to commemorate T.S. Eliot, the great believer in 'tradition'.
8. Vincent Descombes, *Modern French Philosophy*, trans. L. Scott-Fox and J.M. Harding; Cambridge University Press 1980), p. 111
9. W.B. Yeats, *Collected Poems* (Macmillan, London 1979), p. 101.

10. John Keats, *Selected Poetry and Letters*, ed. Richard Harter Fogle, Rinehart Press, San Francisco 1969, p. 250.

11. Yeats, *Collected Poems*, p. 218.

12. *The Times*, Tuesday, 14 January 1879, p. 9; cf. *The Times* leaders and articles on related issues mentioned on 4 January 1879, p. 11; 6 January 1879, (p. 8, letters); 8 January 1879, p. 8 on the Irish Land Question; 10 January 1879, p. 8 on Mortality in Dublin; 11 January 1879 (p. 8 on the Irish Burial Question). In the ideology of this moment, there is a more or less explicit identification between these Irish issues and the events in Asia Minor (not restricted, of course, to Schliemann's dig). *The Times* of 14 January 1879 sums up many of the pressing concerns of the previous days' issues when the leader column suggests that 'the present condition of Asia Minor is manifestly due to four causes in the main — to apathy, to instability, to injustice, and to religious inequality'; but these are very clearly also pertinent 'causes' for the Irish questions being debated in the previous leader columns. When the correspondent writes that 'our world has begun to die in Asia Minor', it sounds a fairly strident note about 'our' world closer to England.

13. 'When Xerxes invaded Greece, his troops marched along a well-made road, with stations at convenient intervals, from Susa to Sardis, and thence to the northern coast. A map of this royal road, exhibited by ARISTAGORAS of Miletus to CLIOMENES, King of Sparta, in order to tempt the latter to an Asiatic invasion, was probably the first map ever seen in Europe' (*The Times*, 14 January 1879, p. 9)· cf. ch. 3 above.

14. Brian Friel, *Translations*, Faber and Faber 1981, passim.

15. Seamus Heaney, 'Digging', in *Death of a Naturalist*, Faber and Faber, London 1966, repr. in *Selected Poems 1965–1975*, Faber and Faber, London 1980, p. 10.

16. See William Wordsworth, 'The Prelude' in *Poetical Works*, (ed. Thomas Hutchinson, revised by Ernest de Selincourt (1904) repr. Oxford University Press 1969, p. 498, (Bk 1, ll. 303ff.). Heaney quotes these lines — from the 1805 edition (which changes the 'we were transplanted' to 'I was transplanted' — as a preface to 'Singing School' in *North*, (Faber and Faber, London 1975, p. 62). The other author quoted as a preface is Yeats.

17. Seamus Heaney, *The Haw Lantern*, Faber and Faber, London 1987, p. 30.

CHAPTER 8 'LIST, LIST, O LIST . . .'

1. John Berger et al., *Ways of Seeing*, BBC and Penguin, London 1972; cf. more recent work in art-history, such as Norman Bryson, *Word and Image*, (Cambridge University Press 1981); *Vision and Painting*, (Macmillan, London 1983); T.J. Clark, *The Absolute Bourgeois*, (Thames and Hudson, London 1973); *Images of the People*, (Thames and Hudson, London 1973);

The Painting of Modern Life, (Thames and Hudson, London 1985), as well as the work of critics such as Griselda Pollock, Stephen Bann, Michael Fried, W.J.T. Mitchell and many others. Cf. also recent work in aesthetics such as Lyotard, *L'Assassinat de l'experience par la peinture: Monory*, (Le Castor Astral, Paris 1984).

2. For a theorisation of architecture as lived space, see Christian Norberg-Schulz, *Existence, Space and Architecture*, (Studio Vista, London 1971).

3. Jean Baudrillard, *Amérique*, Grasset, Paris 1986, pp. 66, 113–14.

4. An early example of this 'historical' architecture would be the Brant House (discussed in my opening chapter on 'Postmodernism' above), designed by Venturi, Rauch and Scott-Brown. A similar effect might be discerned in the by now 'conventional' example of postmodern architecture, John Portman's Bonaventure Hotel in Los Angeles. The particular effect of 'historicity' of which I write here is described, *a propos* this building, by Richard Kearney in his *The Wake of Imagination*, (Hutchinson, London 1988), p. 352. It is important, of course, that a theorist such as Charles Jencks does not accept this 'conventional' example as a postmodern building at all, labelling it rather as a 'traditional' one. Perhaps the transition in question here can best be described as a transition from a geo- to a chrono-architecture. In this regard, it is useful to recall Richard Neutra's comments on architecture. This architect of the International Style building such as 'The Health House' in California (1927) argued that 'Before destruction by civilization, Nature, its objects, its constellations of stars or landscapes, its natural sites, were regarded as animated. Like human faces they had a physiognomy which conveyed a recognizable and expressive message. They were thus evaluated. The promontorial rock past which the natives rowed was occupied by a spirit. A tree or a spring housed a nymph, and a certain individually characterized valley, or isle off shore, was the homestead of a God or the playground of a devil' (Neutra, quoted in Rupert Spade, *Richard Neutra*, with photographs by Yukio Futagana (Thames and Hudson, London 1971).)

Jencks's 'transition', then, might be thought in terms appropriate to the argument of the present study as a transition between the notion of architecture (and indeed other arts) as a 'charmed space' and the notion of art as 'charmed time'. In this regard, such a charming of time might also be further profitably related to Derridean *différance*, with its crucial *deferral* of finalities.

5. Michel Serres, *Esthétique sur Carpaccio*, (Hermann, Paris 1975), as quoted in Jacques Attali, *Noise*, (trans. Brian Massumi; Manchester University Press 1985, p. 9). The longer passage is from ibid., p. 7.

6. Attali, *Noise*, p. 3.

7. Ibid., p. 26.

8. Ibid., p. 7.

9. See Theodor Adorno, *Introduction to the Sociology of Music*, (trans. E.B. Ashton; Seabury, New York 1976), and *Philosophy of Modern Music*, (trans. Mitchell and Blomster, Seabury, New York 1973).
10. Attali, *Noise*, p. 19.
11. Ibid., p. 20.
12. Ibid., p. 83; cf. Baudrillard on this 'loss of reality' figured more politically as a loss of the *principle* of reality.
13. Attali, *Noise*, pp. 89–90.
14. Paul Griffiths, *Modern Music*, (1978) repr. Thames and Hudson, London 1986, pp. 178–9.
15. See Mircea Eliade, *Le Mythe de l'eternel retour*, (Gallimard, Paris 1949).
16. The reference is to Robert Hughes, *The Shock of the New*, (BBC, London 1980).
17. On this issue of 'soft imperialism', see Jean-François Lyotard et Richard Rorty, 'Discussion', (*Critique*, 41 (*mai* 1985), pp. 581–4); on the 'tort', see Lyotard, *Le Differend*, (minuit, Paris 1983); and, for a discussion of these matters in legal and political terms, see Costas Douzinas and Ronnie Warrington, *Justice Miscarried*, (Edinburgh University Press, Edinburgh 1994, *passim*).
18. Miller Levy, programme note to exhibition in Centre Beaubourg, Paris, 1987.
19. On the shift from metaphors of production to those of seduction, and a correpsonding interest in affairs which are usually relegated to the realms of the 'magical' or, more commonly, to the 'irrational', see Jean Baudrillard, *The Mirror of Production*, (Telos Press, St Louis, 1975) and *De la séduction*, (Denoel, Paris 1979).
20. Attali, *Noise*, p. 32.

CHAPTER 9 POSTMARXISM

1. Jean-François Lyotard and Thierry Chaput, *Les Immatériaux*, Centre Georges Pompidou, Paris 1984.
2. Cf. Michel Foucalt's claim that, after Deleuze, thought has become possible once more or that 'Perhaps one day, this century will be known as Deleuzian', in *Language, Counter-Memory, Practice*, (ed. and trans. Donald F. Bouchard and Sherry Simon, Blackwell, Oxford 1977), p. 165.
3. See, of course, Michel Foucault, *Folie et déraison*, (Plon, Paris 1961), as well as subsequent revised editions of this work, where Foucault traces the incidence of madness in the so-called age of reason.
4. Jean-François Lyotard, *The Postmodern Condition*, (trans. Geoff Bennington and Brian Massumi, Manchester University Press 1984); Gilles Deleuze and Felix Guattari, *Anti-Oedipus*, (trans. Robert Hurley, Mark Seem, Helen R. Lane, Athlone Press, London 1984); *A Thousand Plateaus*, (trans. Brian Massumi; University of Minnesota Press 1987). It should be

stated that Lyotard, more recently, has pointed out that his insistence on the question of narrative and metanarrative in the concerns of *The Postmodern Condition* was slightly overstated, perhaps: see his 'Apostille aux récits' in *Le Postmoderne expliqué aux enfants*, (Galilee, Paris 1986).

5. Lyotard, *Postmodern Condition*, p. 72.
6. Lyotard, 'Le différend' in *Tombeau de l'intellectuel et autres papiers*, Galilee, Paris 1984; cf. Lyotard, *Le Différend* (minuit, Paris 1983).
7. Jean Baurillard, *The Mirror of Production*, trans. Mark Poster, Telos Press, St Louis 1975, pp. 32–3.
8. Ibid., p. 135.
9. Edward Said, *The World, the Text, the Critic*, Faber and Faber, London 1984, p. 28.
10. Ibid., p. 29.
11. See Patrick Parrinder, *The Failure of Theory*, Harvester Press, Brighton 1987.
12. Jean Baudrillard, *Simulations*, trans. Paul Foss, Paul Patton and Philip Beitchman, Semiotext(e), New York, 1983, pp. 36–7.
13. Emmanuel Levinas, 'Idéologie et Idéalisme' in *De Dieu qui vient à l'idée*, Vrin, Paris 1982, as quoted in Richard Kearney, *The Wake of Imagination*, Hutchinson, London 1988, p. 365.
14. This latter strategy is that adopted by Fredric Jameson, *The Political Unconscious*, (Methuen, London 1981, p. 100). While Jameson explicitly acknowledges the strategy, many other critics have, less overtly, deployed a similar tactic in their own practice, making token feminist gestures. For a fuller exploration of what is at stake in this issue regarding the colonisation of feminism by male Marxists, see Alice Jardine and Paul Smith, eds, *Men in Feminism*, (Methuen, London 1987). Elaine Showalter's piece in that collection, written in response to Terry Eagleton, makes the point most clearly that the other strategy — that of the willed ignorance of feminism — is also at work. For a fuller discussion of the theoretical basis for this kind of strategy, in which alterity is always reduced to homogeneity, see my *Alterities*, (Oxford University Press 1996).
15. See, e.g., Jacques Lacan, 'Situation de la psychanalyse en 1956', in *Ecrits*, (Gallimard, Paris 1966), pp. 468–9.
16. Truth, here, is being understood as a function of propositions. It is thus a matter of rhetoric as much as a matter of logic; and, as de Man has argued in 'The Rhetoric of Temporality' (and as I have myself argued in preceding pages of the present study), there is a necessary and inevitable *historicity* imbricated throughout such a rhetoric and logic. In short, there is a certain discrepancy between truth, thus understood, and phenomenology; and it was to this that Lyotard addressed himself when he argued that:

> There is thus no absolute truth, the postulate common both to dogmatism and scepticism; truth is defined in its becoming, as the revision,

correction and surpassing of itself — a dialectical operation which always takes place within the living present (*lebendige Gegenwart*). (Lyotard, *La Phénoménologie*, PUF, Paris 1953, pp. 40–1); as quoted in Vincent Descombes, *Modern French Philosophy*, (trans L. Scott-Fox and J.M. Harding, Cambridge University Press 1980), p. 64.

Descombes himself goes on here to indicate concisely what is at issue in this 'debate' or differend between phenomenology and historicity:

> The phenomenological concept of time, as Husserl was reputed to have developed it in his later philosophy, was considered the key to the question of history ... But it was precisely from this inclusion of the *absent* within the *present* (the *yesterday* and the *tomorrow* within the *today*) that Derrida was to launch his offensive against phenomenology.

In this regard, the subsequent attack on Marxism, and especially on Marxist history, is made on the grounds that it is simply not historical enough. Descombes, in discussing Kojève's 'dual ontology', explains part of the distinction between 'natural being' and 'historical being'. 'To be', in 'natural being', means '*to remain the same*, to preserve identity'; in 'historical being', 'to be' is 'defined by negativity. The being of the protagonist consists in *not remaining the same*, in will to difference' (Descombes, *Modern French Philosophy*, pp. 34–5). Baudrillard's attack on Marxism can thus be explicated in terms of this activation of negativity/historicity. He writes:

> The proposition that a concept is not merely an interpretive hypothesis but a translation of universal movement depends upon pure metaphysics. Marxist concepts do not escape this lapse. Thus, to be logical, the concept of history must itself be regarded as historical, turn back upon itself, and only illuminate the context that produced it by abolishing itself. Instead, in Marxism history is transhistoricized: it redoubles on itself and thus is universalized. To be rigorous the dialectic must dialectically surpass and annul itself. (Baudrillard, *Mirror*, p. 47)

For concerted attacks on 'totality' and on 'universal history', see Lyotard, especially *Tombeau*, passim, and *The Postmodern Condition*, pp. 81–2.

Finally, on the issue of truth (much exercising the mind of Christopher Norris in all his recent books), see, for a different — though still postmarxist view — the work of Alain Badiou and the final chapter of my *Alterities*.

17. Lyotard, *Tombeau*, p. 40.
18. Lyotard, *L'Assassinat de l'expérience par la peinture: Monory*, Le Castor Astral, Paris 1984, p. 7. Cf. Lyotard's 'peregrinations' on his own early monkishness in *Pérégrinations*, (Columbia University Press 1988), ch. 1.

19. The term is used here in the sense given by Hans Blumenberg in *The Legitimacy of the Modern Age*, (trans. Robert M. Wallace, MIT Press, Cambridge, Mass., 1983).
20. Baudrillard, *Mirror*, p. 29.
21. Jean Baudrillard, *De la séduction*, Denoel, Paris 1979, p. 47; cf. Baudrillard, *L'Autre pau lui-même*, (Galilee, Paris 1987), ch. 1 and *Les Stratégies fatales*, (Grasset, Paris 1983), pp. 70–98.
22. Paul Virilio, *L'Horizon négatif*, Galilee, Paris 1984, p. 99ff.; Baudrillard, *De la séduction*, p. 51.
23. Baudrillard, *De la séduction*, p. 123.
24. Ibid., p. 209.
25. Lyotard, *Tombeau*, p. 15; for Baudrillard on magic, see *De la séduction*, pp. 102–22.
26. It is clear here that I have concentrated, for reasons of economy, on these two thinkers; but I might have added to and complicated the argument by alluding to the work of Deleuze, Vattimo, Virilio, Gorz, Badiou and many others. That would, needless to say, have given a series of different inflections to the resulting characterisation of postmarxism from that advanced. This, however, is part of the point of my characterisation of postmarxism: postmarxism is tied to a certain provisionality — actually historicity — with respect to its truth-bearing propositions; it is also pluralistic, and not merely in the sense that it can bear a number of simultaneous differends, but also in the sense that those differends themselves become constitutive of histories.
27. See, e.g., Fritjof Capra, *The Tao of Physics* ((1975) repr. Fontana, London 1976); Paul Feyerabend, *Against Method* ((1975; repr. Verso, London 1978), and *Science in a Free Society*, (Verso, London 1978). Broadly, the kind of 'irresponsibility' of which I write here can be thought in terms of a demand for the rejection of what Kant called 'determining' judgement — at least in matters of aesthetics and politics — and its replacement by what he called 'reflective' judgement; these, of course, are the terms in which Lyotard frequently argues the case. The opening to 'reflection' is an opening to that which is not always already known, an opening to the unforeseen and unpredicted — and hence an opening to a history whose programme has not been determined in advance by the categories of thought through which we understand it. The result would be the eruption of history as the 'event', an 'it happens' whose sense is not determinable in advance. On the other hand, 'responsibility' — the contract with determining judgement — makes the future always simply a different version of the past, in which the past is seen, paradoxically, as 'responsive' or responsible to the future; or, in which the past not only conditions the future, but is conditioned by it. As Lyotard argues in *The Inhuman*, (trans. Geoffrey Bennington and Rachel Bowlby; Polity Press, Cambridge, 1991), pp. 65–6, this is a conception of time which is profoundly capitalist: its aim is to

allow the subject always to be in a position to insert any event into a narrative which makes a single univocal sense, thus emptying out its historical substance. For more on this, see my *Alterities*, especially the introduction.

28. Lyotard, *Le postmoderne*, p. 126.

Index